TEACHING COMPUTING IN SECONDARY SCHOOL

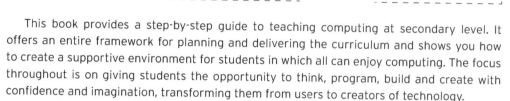

The website for this title's eResources c
9781138238060. All features in this book ɑ
can be found here, along with additional res

This book provides a step-by-step guide to teaching computing at secondary level. It offers an entire framework for planning and delivering the curriculum and shows you how to create a supportive environment for students in which all can enjoy computing. The focus throughout is on giving students the opportunity to think, program, build and create with confidence and imagination, transforming them from users to creators of technology.

In each chapter, detailed research and teaching theory is combined with resources to aid the practitioner, including case studies, planning templates and schemes of work that can be easily adapted. The book is split into three key parts: planning, delivery, and leadership and management, and covers topics such as:

- Curriculum and assessment design
- Lesson planning
- The cognitive science behind learning
- Computing pedagogy and instructional principles
- Mastery learning in computing
- How to develop students' computational thinking
- Supporting students with special educational needs and disabilities
- Encouraging more girls to study computing
- Actions, habits and routines of effective computing teachers
- Behaviour management and developing a strong classroom culture
- How to support and lead members of your team.

Teaching Computing in Secondary Schools is essential reading for trainee and practising teachers, and will prove to be an invaluable resource in helping teaching professionals ensure that students acquire a wide range of computing skills which will support them in whatever career they choose.

William Lau is currently in charge of Key Stage 4 computing at Central Foundation Boys' School in London. Lau has taught computing from Key Stages 1 through 5 in three London state schools and in an International school in Seychelles. He has delivered CPD at various UK schools and universities, specialising in curriculum design, assessment design and computing pedagogy. He has mentored trainee teachers at King's College London and the University of Roehampton. Lau is a CAS Master Teacher and a Google Certified Innovator. In July 2017 he received an international Award for Teaching Excellence in computer science from the Infosys Foundation in the US, The Association for Computing Machinery and the Computer Science Teachers Association. He was head of computing at the Greenwich Free School until August 2017.

"Schools in the US and UK are wisely striving to bring the study of computing into the mainstream and make it accessible to all students. But as valuable as it is, it remains a complex subject, challenging to teach and fraught with logistical and pedagogical challenges that demand consideration. This book should be on the must-read list for any school or teacher that wants to add or refine a high-quality Computing curriculum. It's informed by careful study and application of learning science and drills down in the details of curriculum design and instructional methods. I highly recommend it."

– Doug Lemov, Managing Director of Uncommon Schools,
and author of Teach Like a Champion

"I will be recommending this book to all the secondary school computer science teachers I know. The book is filled with insights from both scholarly research and the author's years of experience as a computing teacher. I predict that it will become part of the toolkit for all new computing teachers." Best wishes for the book!

– Mark Guzdial, Professor in the College of Computing
at Georgia Institute of Technology

"William Lau has created a wonderful resource for secondary school teachers to bring computing into the classroom. Lau's beautifully written book provides a cross curricular approach, where computing is seen as a tool for problem-solving, self-expression and asking fertile questions about the world."

– Linda Liukas, author of Hello Ruby *and Founder of* Rails Girls

"A sensible, practical and thorough book for secondary computing teachers at any level of experience."
– Jane Waite, CAS London Project Manager at the CAS Regional Centre
for London, PhD Student at Queen Mary University of London

"William's insight into computing is amazing! The book thoroughly explores the foundation of computing and provides very useful advice. I highly recommend this book if you want to take your teaching and innovation in your lessons to the next level."

– Mark Martin, Urban Teacher Ed-Tech Expert | Start-Up Mentor

"Following his demonstration of exemplar studentship here at Warwick University, William has pursued a deep interest in the teaching of Computing in Key Stages 1–5. Through intensive study and practice, he has developed a deep understanding of teaching and learning especially as it applies to this challenging subject. He communicates his enthusiasm energetically, both in his own teaching and throughout the book. The book interleaves pedagogy, Computing content, theoretical principles and good practices according to a well thought out, integrated and explicit architecture. It promises to be a valuable resource for teachers of this exciting and current subject."

– Dr Andrew Martin, Principal Teaching Fellow at the
Warwick Business School (University of Warwick)

"This book is a one-stop shop for both teachers and leaders of computing in secondary schools (although much of it will be of use to primary colleagues too). The author, drawing on copious research as well as his own experience, provides extensive guidance. A must for every computing teacher's bookshelf."

– Terry Freedman, education technology consultant, writer, speaker and
trainer, and publisher of the ICT & Computing in
Education website www.ictineducation.org

"William's book merges both theoretical and practical topics in an engaging way that is useful for both the trainee teacher and the seasoned veteran."

– Peter Kemp, Senior Lecturer for PGCE Secondary
Computing at the University of Roehampton

TEACHING COMPUTING IN SECONDARY SCHOOLS

A Practical Handbook

William Lau

Routledge
Taylor & Francis Group

LONDON AND NEW YORK

First published 2018
by Routledge
2 Park Square, Milton Park, Abingdon, Oxon OX14 4RN

and by Routledge
711 Third Avenue, New York, NY 10017

Routledge is an imprint of the Taylor & Francis Group, an informa business

British Library Cataloguing in Publication Data
A catalogue record for this book is available from the British Library

Library of Congress Cataloging in Publication Data
A catalog record for this book has been requested

ISBN: 978-1-138-23805-3 (hbk)
ISBN: 978-1-138-23806-0 (pbk)
ISBN: 978-1-315-29821-4 (ebk)

Typeset in Interstate
by Deanta Global Publishing Services, Chennai, India

Visit the eResources: www.routledge.com/9781138238060

Printed and bound by CPI Group (UK) Ltd, Croydon, CR0 4YY

For Suki, Zi, Mum, Dad and Anita

CONTENTS

FIGURES

TABLES

FOREWORD

Computing has been a mandatory part of the national curriculum in England at Key Stage 1 through 4 since 2014 and many teachers have found themselves on a steep learning curve in getting to grips with teaching its various aspects effectively, particularly some of the new computer science elements which were not in the previous ICT curriculum. Whilst many, many resources exist to help teach computing, often these are isolated offerings and teachers are left bewildered about how to put them all together to make a coherent curriculum. In addition, the national curriculum published in 2014 does not flesh out any detail beyond an outline of the overall aims. In this book, William Lau has put together a guide for teachers who need some inspiration, ideas and practical advice on teaching computing effectively. He is very well qualified to do so, having built up computing in his department, and developed his own resources, many of which he shares with other teachers. William is also a PGCE mentor and CAS master teacher and in these capacities he is also able to pass on what he has learned and to support others.

Rooted directly in practical experience, this guide will give considerable support to a new computing teacher, or an experienced teacher delivering computing for the first time, as they try to structure and sequence topics in the curriculum. Drawing on a range of exemplars from the work at Greenwich Free School, the book outlines an adoptable approach to the teaching of computing based on education research and personal experience. It focuses on the teaching of computing from age 11-16, and looks at computing in relation to the three areas of planning, delivery and leadership.

The first part includes example planning documents from William's own teaching experience that can be adapted and used. In addition, the book provides a rationale for the approaches used based on cognitive psychology and education research. It provides information about planning over a five-year period; this is exactly the sort of information that teachers have been asking for. The key ingredients of William's approach, including Fertile Questions, are explained and exemplified. It also looks in detail at medium-term and lesson planning in detail, again with key pointers about what to include in lessons.

Part 2 is about delivery and includes a wealth of material, drawing on research into instructional practice. Chapters 4 and 5 contain advice and examples that would be useful to all teachers as well as computing teachers. In Chapter 6, more specific unpicking of the pedagogical content knowledge of computing – that knowledge that experienced teachers gain as they gain familiarity with the best ways to teach topics in their subject area – is carried out;

this is a valuable chapter incorporating good advice to help teachers tackle particular topics on the curriculum. My own research is in this area, and there is still much more yet to find out about how students learn computing concepts, and how we can support them effectively.

Part 3 focuses on leadership and management in computing, and will help those aspiring to be a head of department and to support and develop other staff. William gives us a very personal perspective on what has worked for him in his school leadership roles, and how to develop effective patterns of work. These chapters may be useful to many non-computing teachers too, as many of William's insights will apply across the curriculum.

I hope you will enjoy reading, and more importantly, using this book in your teaching, whether you are looking for assistance with planning, or help with delivery. I believe that this is a book that you will keep coming back to as you refine and develop your teaching over time.

Dr Sue Sentance
King's College London

ACKNOWLEDGEMENTS

There are many people that have directly or indirectly contributed towards this book, firstly I would like to thank Oliver Knight. My teaching practice and this book have been greatly influenced by his expertise and guidance. As an author, Oliver was able to provide a wealth of first-hand advice regarding the writing and drafting process. In many ways this book is inspired by his writing and you will see many of his concepts and works referenced in this book. As a head teacher, Oliver provided me with generous curriculum time, CPD opportunities and autonomy. Like many of my colleagues at Greenwich Free School, I feel lucky to have such a supportive, trusting and experienced head teacher.

The computing-specific pedagogy that I cover in this book is predominantly based on my learning experiences as a member of the Computing At School (CAS) community. I've attended many high quality CPD events via CAS and many of the teachers in this rich network have spared their time and resources generously. Those who have influenced my practice directly include: Dan Aldred, Ilia Avroutine, David Batty, Miles Berry, Trevor Bragg, Simon Brown, Mark Clarkson, Andy Colley, Dan Copeman, Mark Dorling, James Franklin, Dan Fraser, Terry Freedman, Mark Guzdial, Elizabeth Hidson, Anthea Hoverd, Chris Joy, Peter Kemp, Martyn Lassey, Simon Johnson, Mark Martin, Stephen O'Callaghan, Alan O'Donohoe, Simon Peyton Jones, Carrie Anne Philbin, Meg Ray, Chris Roffey, Sue Sentance, Sarah Shakibi, Lloyd Stevens, Darren Travi, Jane Waite, Sam Wickins, Tom Wilkinson and Pat Yongpradit. From this list, Elizabeth Hidson and Peter Kemp deserve a special mention as they have mentored me since my very first days of teaching. In Part 1 of this book, I discuss the concept of a computing expert and what it means to be an expert. If I were to make a list of expert computing teachers, Elizabeth and Peter would be at the top of that list. When I am struggling for answers and solutions in my teaching and leadership, I know that I can rely on their support and wisdom.

There are also many individuals who work in the technology sector who have coached and supported me. I would like to thank three people in particular for their continued support over the years. First, thank you to Merijn Broeren at PDT Partners for helping me transition from ICT to computing and supporting me in developing my programming skills. Secondly, I want to thank Andy Swann at Sony PlayStation London for volunteering at our Code Club and supporting our students with their programming, 3D modeling and game design. Andy inspired many of our students to pursue Computer Science at GCSE level; he is humble in his achievements, generous with his time and, most of all, a dear friend. The third person I would like to thank is Carl Stratton. I had the pleasure of living with Carl during my early teaching career and Carl provided regular feedback on my graphic design and web design work as well as the work of my students. Some evenings, we would sit down for hours as he critically dissected my students' work and offered each student specific actionable feedback. Whilst Carl may be unaware of how influential these ad-hoc sessions were, his guidance had a significant impact on my teaching and students' academic achievements. I am indebted to these three individuals and would highly recommend that teachers connect with industry professionals. Our academic discipline is constantly changing, more so than any other subject, and it is very difficult to stay current with the latest tools, best practice and trends whilst teaching full time.

Whilst there are some elements of computing pedagogy that are unique to our subject, so much of the best practice that I've picked up over the years has come from expert teachers, researchers and instructors outside of the computing classroom. I would like to thank the following leaders from education for shaping my pedagogy: Mike Baxter, Gus Beamish, Danny Brown, David Didau, Jess Dumbreck, Corinne Flett, Sarah Jones, Martin Kennedy, Joe Kirby, Oliver Knight, Doug Lemov, Rebecca Ngakane, Giles Niklaus, Jo Parkes and Dylan Wiliam. Our dialogues about teaching and learning have been fascinating and whilst I may have once had the pleasure of being one of your colleagues, I'll forever remain one of your students.

I would also like to thank the computing teachers that I've had the privilege of working alongside on a daily basis: Jeff Bates, Jack Caine, Paranita Gokhale, Elizabeth Hidson, Blessy Joseph, Maria Parkes, Alex Parry, Niraj Sanghvi and Waheeda Shaikh. I extend this thanks to my esteemed colleagues from Central Foundation Boys' School, Greenwich Free School, Vijay International School Praslin and St Marylebone CE School. I am lucky to have worked with such dedicated teachers, performing at the highest level in a highly stressful profession, often with little recognition for their efforts. I recognise your commitment to improving the lives of the young people you come into contact with every day.

There were many people involved in the production of this book. Firstly thank you to Annamarie Kino at Routledge for commissioning the book. Thanks to Clare Ashworth and Alice Gray at Routledge for their thoroughness in editing the manuscript and responding to all my queries so promptly. Thanks to all those that offered feedback throughout the drafting process: Oliver Knight, Elizabeth Hidson, Terry Freedman, Mark Dorling, Sue Sentance, Jane Waite, Simon Peyton Jones and Simon Humphreys. Thanks also to Seth Townley at Routledge and Lisa Keating and her team at Deanta Global for their support in the management of the production process. Their expertise and attention to detail ensured that the whole process was stress-free for me as a first-time author.

Finally, I would like to thank my wife, Suki Chan. This book would not have been possible without her patience and support. Writing this book has been a rewarding experience and I was granted this privilege by Suki's willingness to sacrifice her own time. As my wife, dear friend and the mother of our child, I could ask for nothing more.

Introduction

Computing as a subject can be defined as a combination of three separate strands: computer science, information technology (IT) and digital literacy (DL). Traditionally, in UK secondary schools there was more of an emphasis on IT and Digital Literacy, specifically office productivity software (Peyton Jones, 2011). In 2011, the Department for Education (DFE) began a review of the national curriculum and in September 2014, a new computing curriculum was launched by the DFE to replace the existing ICT curriculum. The new computing curriculum was informed and influenced by several key parties: the Computing At School (CAS) group, Google's executive chairman Eric Schmidt and The Royal Society. These new programs of study have a much stronger emphasis on computer science as a rigorous subject discipline which should be studied by all students at primary and secondary levels.

Whilst the new curriculum was being drafted in 2012, the CAS group and the DFE quickly identified that there was a skills shortage amongst the teachers who were currently delivering the ICT curriculum (Peyton Jones, 2015). I was one of these 15,000 teachers working in one of the 6,000 secondary schools across the UK. Like the large majority of these teachers, I was not delivering a qualification in computer science at any of the Key Stages that I taught. However, I was part of a small minority who had a background in computer science, having studied the subject at university. Even with this solid grounding, I knew that I would have to make fundamental changes to my current practice, particularly with regard to pedagogical content knowledge. My motivation for writing this book is to serve as a guide for both experienced ICT teachers and for new computing teachers entering the profession. I believe that the challenges that computing teachers face in the UK are not unique; and as other countries such as the US, Canada, South Korea, India, The Netherlands, New Zealand, Australia, Finland, Ireland and Greece begin their curriculum reforms in computing, there is an exciting opportunity to create a powerful network of computing teachers who can all learn from each other.

At the time of writing, most subjects in the national curriculum have books offering advice on how to plan and deliver the subject, yet no such book exists for computing. Indeed, very little has been written about computing pedagogy at the secondary school level. Having taught all three strands of the computing curriculum across Key Stages 1-5 in inner-city London schools and internationally over the past ten years, I feel well placed to provide a guide on the teaching of computing. In writing this book, I also draw on the collective experiences and resources of countless practitioners that I have met on my journey. Many of these practitioners are members of the CAS network and I am indebted to them for helping me develop. I hope that this book will serve as a useful handbook for both teachers and heads of department, and at the same time I hope that it will encourage others to reflect on their practices and share their experiences of teaching computing.

The national curriculum in computing is split into four programs of study, one for each Key Stage in Key Stages 1-4. This book will focus on the programs of study at Key Stages 3 and 4 in the secondary curriculum; these Key Stages are the Key Stages where the majority of secondary school teachers will be required to teach. I will make reference to Key Stages 1, 2 and 5 where this additional context is useful; however, these Key Stages will not be covered in detail as they are somewhat beyond the scope of this book.

The book's content will be split into three parts:

1 Planning
2 Delivery
3 Leadership and management.

Each section will reflect on mistakes made by myself and other practitioners and also offer solutions and best practice. As we know, the best teachers plan for likely misconceptions in advance, so we begin this journey into teaching computing by looking at five fallacies that many new teachers need to be aware of.

The website for this title's eResources can be found at www.routledge.com/ 9781138238060. All features in this book accompanied by the e-resources logo ( ) can be found here, along with additional resources and activities.

Five fallacies in computing education

Fallacy 1: Students born in the 21st century are digital natives. This is an often-held belief by parents, senior leadership and even teachers of computing. However, it is a dangerous belief to hold because of how far away this statement is from reality. Imagine if we believed the same of literacy or numeracy: that students born in the 21st century are born literate and numerate. Most adults would admit that this statement was absurd. Yet, often we hear from parents and teachers that we can't teach our children much because they're already ahead of us and already know more than us. This is simply not true. Knowing how to turn on an iPad and posting a photo to a social media website is not the same as being digitally literate, and this common task certainly does not fulfil the basic requirements of the computing national curriculum. The term 'digital native' is a dangerous one because all our students need the guidance and support that experience brings (Kirschner & De Bruyckere, 2017). All adult readers of this book will have more computing experience than the majority of our students in a secondary school setting, particularly when it comes to choosing the correct tool to solve a problem and using technology appropriately. It is our duty to share this knowledge and guide our learners to achieve success in computing.

Fallacy 2: Computing is all about code and programming. The media frequently use the terms 'computing', 'computer science', 'coding' and 'programming' interchangeably and most headlines about the curriculum reforms in the UK have used these words synonymously. This distorts the reality that programming is a skill which all computer science students will need to learn but it is not the only skill which is required in computing. Programming pedagogy is an important part of a teacher's toolkit and as such there is a detailed chapter dedicated to this. However, equally important are other key software applications and the theoretical subject knowledge which the computing curriculum is built on. This book aims to offer a broad and balanced coverage of all the skills, concepts and knowledge required to cover the secondary computing curriculum.

Fallacy 3: A busy and quiet classroom where all students are working hard is a good indication that everyone is learning. There are many false proxies for learning and the only genuine way to tell if a student has learnt anything is to check to see if their thinking, skills or attitudes have changed (Nuthall, 2007) and if these changes are retained over time. The only way to do this is through assessment. This is one of the most complicated and controversial areas of teaching but fortunately it is also where there is a lot of research. The reason why it is difficult to know whether students are genuinely learning is because it is very difficult to see what students are thinking. Indeed, often it is difficult for students to understand our thinking unless we narrate our thinking out loud (Collins *et al.*, 1991) (Guzdial, 2015). In the following chapter, we will explore different activities which encourage deep thinking and learning, and in Part 2 of the book we will look at how we can assess student's understanding and learning.

Fallacy 4: Mistakes are bad and the best lessons are the ones that look effortless. It is really important that we teach our students to embrace their mistakes and failures; it is the best way for them to learn (Clarkson, 2012). We learn very little from our successes, because we are generally less reflective when things are going well (Boulding, 1971). We should let our students know that mistakes are not only inevitable, but necessary for good learning. Mistakes also show that students are taking risks and pushing themselves outside of their comfort zone. Both of these are necessary for rich learning and purposeful practice (Syed, 2015). The same can be said for teachers: It is not our great lessons, but rather our mediocre lessons that often make us reflect and think about what went wrong and what we should change next time. When we play it safe and all the students complete all the work effortlessly and the lesson goes smoothly, it is possible that students were merely coasting and had not learnt that much. It is possible that the students in the 'effortless' lesson may have not thought about much, but were just busy 'doing', that is, completing the activity which they already had the skills and knowledge to complete.

Fallacy 5: Computing is only for students with high prior attainment. Computing is the same as any other subject in that hard work and persistence will result in improvements in knowledge, skills and learning. It is not true that students with special educational needs and disabilities (SEND) cannot access the computing curriculum. Having taught over 1,500 students from diverse backgrounds with a wide range of prior attainment and learning needs, I have found that computing is actually a subject where any pupil can succeed and demonstrate progress from their starting point. It is those students and teachers that spend time thinking about computing and solving problems using a range of software applications that outperform their peers, not necessarily those with high prior attainment.

What is computing?

The national curriculum that was introduced in 2014 is heavily weighted towards the computer science strand; this is evident in Table 0.1 on page 5. Indeed, the abolition of numerous ICT GCSE qualifications and the introduction of GCSE computer science by all major exam boards is a clear indication of the move away from IT and a new emphasis on computer science in the English national curriculum. The book's content will reflect these changes and acknowledges that the computer science strand is the strand which new teachers of computing will need the most support and guidance with. However, Kemp advises that there is a significant overlap between the strands and that the labels and divisions are merely placeholders indicating a principal emphasis (Kemp, 2014). The Venn diagram below (Table 0.1) illustrates how some of the content overlaps and why the teaching of discrete strands is neither necessary nor advised.

In order to clarify my rationale for decisions in planning, delivery and management, I have found that the process of formulating a vision for computing has been incredibly useful. In the following pages, I put forward my philosophy for computing education in the form of a vision statement.

An overview of the national curriculum for computing

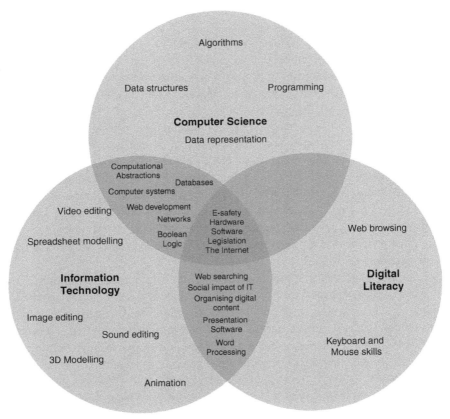

Figure 0.1 An overview of the computing national curriculum programs of study.

Table 3.1 An overview of the computing national curriculum programmes of study.[1]

Computing Strand	Key Stage 1	Key Stage 2	Key Stage 3	Key Stage 4	Key Stage 5
Computer Science (CS) The rigorous academic discipline, encompassing principles such as programming languages, data structures, algorithms, systems architecture, design, problem solving, etc. In addition to principles and a stable set of concepts, computer science incorporates rigorous techniques, methods and ways of thinking including "computational thinking"	• Understand what algorithms are, how they are implemented as programs on digital devices, and that programs execute by following precise and unambiguous instructions • Create and debug simple programs • Use logical reasoning to predict the behaviour of simple programs	• Design, write and debug programs that accomplish specific goals, including controlling or simulating physical systems; solve problems by decomposing them into smaller parts • Use sequence, selection, and repetition in programs; work with variables and various forms of input and output • Use logical reasoning to explain how some simple algorithms work and to detect and correct errors in algorithms and programs • Understand computer networks, including the internet; how they can provide multiple services, such as the World Wide Web, and the opportunities they offer for communication and collaboration	• Design, use and evaluate computational abstractions that model the state and behaviour of real-world problems and physical systems • Understand several key algorithms that reflect computational thinking [for example, algorithms for sorting and searching]; use logical reasoning to compare the utility of alternative algorithms for the same problem • Use two or more programming languages, at least one of which is textual, to solve a variety of computational problems; make appropriate use of data structures [for example, lists, tables or arrays]; design and develop modular programs that use procedures or functions • Understand simple Boolean logic [for example, AND, OR and NOT] and some of its uses in circuits and programming; understand how numbers can be represented in binary, and be able to carry out simple operations on binary numbers [for example, binary addition, and conversion between binary and decimal] • Understand the hardware and software components that make up computer systems, and how they communicate with one another and with other systems • Understand how instructions are stored and executed within a computer system; understand how data of various types (including text, sounds and pictures) can be represented and manipulated digitally, in the form of binary digits	• Develop students' capability, creativity and knowledge in computer science, digital media and information technology • Develop and apply students' analytic, problem-solving, design, and computational thinking skills	• Identify a problem or investigation of sufficient complexity • Create a programmed solution to a complex problem or investigation • Problems may include a complex data model in a database, a complex scientific, mathematical, robotic, control or business model • Complexity may also be achieved through the creation of a user-defined object-oriented programming model • Programmed solutions would typically include complex data structures such as hash tables, lists, stacks, queues, graphs, trees, multi-dimensional arrays and dictionaries • Understand key Computing principles of contemporary systems architecture. This includes the characteristics of contemporary processors, computer organisation and architecture, software and software development, programming, communication and networks, data types, data structures, data representation, databases, legal, moral, cultural and ethical issues • Understand how algorithms can be compared based on their efficiency and complexity using Big O Notation • Understand a wide range of searching, sorting, graph traversal and optimisation algorithms • Apply computational thinking to solve a range of complex problems by thinking procedurally, logically and concurrently

Continued

Table 0.1 Continued

Information Technology (IT) The use of computers, in industry, commerce, the arts and elsewhere, including aspects of IT systems architecture, human factors, project management, etc.	• Use technology purposefully to create, organise, store, manipulate and retrieve digital content • Recognise common uses of information technology beyond school	• Use search technologies effectively, appreciate how results are selected and ranked, and be discerning in evaluating digital content • Select, use and combine a variety of software (including internet services) on a range of digital devices to design and create a range of programs, systems and content that accomplish given goals, including collecting, analysing, evaluating and presenting data and information	• Undertake creative projects that involve selecting, using, and combining multiple applications, preferably across a range of devices, to achieve challenging goals, including collecting and analysing data and meeting the needs of known users • Create, re-use, revise and re-purpose digital artefacts for a given audience, with attention to trustworthiness, design and usability	• Understand a range of IT systems and the implications of their use. • Design, create, test and evaluate a relational database system to manage information • Understand how businesses use social media to promote their products and services • Understand how data modelling can be used to solve problems by designing and implementing a data model to meet client requirements • Investigate website development principles to design and develop a website using scripting languages such as HTML, CSS and JavaScript
Digital Literacy (DL) The general ability to use computers. This is a set of skills rather than a subject in its own right	• Use technology safely and respectfully, keeping personal information private; identify where to go for help and support when they have concerns about content or contact on the internet or other online technologies	• Use technology safely, respectfully and responsibly; recognise acceptable/unacceptable behaviour; identify a range of ways to report concerns about content and contact	• Understand a range of ways to use technology safely, respectfully, responsibly and securely, including protecting their online identity and privacy; recognise inappropriate content, contact and conduct and know how to report concerns	• Understand how changes in technology affect safety, including new ways to protect their online privacy and identity, and how to report a range of concerns

(The Royal Society, 2012; Department for Education, 2013; Kemp, 2014; Webb *et al.*, 2016; OCR, 2016; AQA, 2016; Pearson, 2017).

ᴵ The national curriculum for Computing covers Key Stages 1-4. Key Stage 5 has been included to provide the reader with a clear road-map.

Vision for computing

From nanotechnology to synthetic biology, from wearable computers to self-driving cars; computing will continue to shape the future that we live in.

As we look back at the past decade, we can safely say that computers have transformed the world. Historical commentators have referred to this age as the Information Age, the Second Machine Age or the Digital Revolution (Brynjolfsson & McAfee, 2014). In much the same way that electrical engineering revolutionised the 20th century and steam engines impacted the 19th century, the computer can be seen as one of the most significant change agents of our era. Robertson argues that history has never seen a revolution on the scale of the one that is being triggered by computer technology (Robertson, 1998). For many of our students it is difficult to imagine the world without computers; these devices are synonymous with technology and form a part of their everyday lives.

Numeracy and literacy are fundamental to any educational system and nobody would argue against the teaching of reading, writing and arithmetic through English and Maths. Given the importance of computers in our increasingly digital world, I would argue that a comprehensive computing education should be a fundamental requirement of a secondary school experience.

Computing teaches us how to solve problems by breaking them down into manageable components. In developing our own original solutions, computing requires us to be both logical and creative. Computing enables us to develop a skillset and mindset which will be useful in practically every other discipline.

As a teacher and student of computing, I believe that being a digital native and a mere user of technology is not enough. Technology is changing at such a rapid pace that in order to thrive and succeed in the Information Age, we need to understand how computers work. As computing teachers, one of our primary aims should be to transform users of technology into creators of technology by giving all our students the opportunity to think, create, persevere and grow.

To achieve this aim, we must strive to:

- Create an environment in which all pupils enjoy computing and feel they can do well in computing.
- Create well-rounded users and creators of computer technology with a focus on independent problem-solving skills.
- Engage pupils and expose them to a wide range of computing skills which will empower them in whatever career path they choose.

Too often, students come into our classrooms with a preconceived notion of whether they are good at computing or not. These beliefs are what Carol Dweck would refer to as a "fixed mindset"; the belief that ability is innate and static (Dweck, 2006). As a result, some students have gotten into the habit of giving up easily or not attempting difficult tasks due to a fear of failure. Inspired by the work of Carol Dweck, I believe that the growth mindset is fundamental to teaching and learning computing. We need to help our students realise that they can achieve great things if they persevere and are resilient when faced with challenges and setbacks. There is a risk of students believing that as digital natives, they have little to learn and that everything they want to do with a computer has already been created or will be invented by someone else. There is also a fear that programming and computer science are difficult and too technical. However, by eliminating these misconceptions, our students will be able to push themselves and learn to enjoy the learning process despite the many challenges that they will encounter.

Finally, computing lessons should not just be about 'doing'; the focus should always be on what the pupils are thinking about. Lessons should aim to teach pupils the real-world relevance of computing; this relevance comes ultimately from a Fertile Question which feeds into every lesson question.

References

Boulding, K., 1971. The diminishing returns of science. *New Scientist and Science Journal*, 25 March, 49(744), pp. 682–85.

Brynjolfsson, E. & McAfee, A., 2014. *The Second Machine Age - Work, Progress, and Prosperity in a Time of Brilliant Technologies*. 1st ed. New York: W. W. Norton.

Clarkson, M., 2012. *GCSE Computing the Unofficial Teacher's Guide*. [Online] Available at: http://www.ocr.org.uk/Images/139051-the-unofficial-teacher-s-guide-for-gcse-computing.pdf [Accessed 30 August 2015].

Collins, A., Holum, A. & Seely Brown, J., 1991. Cognitive apprenticeship: making thinking visible. *American Educator: The Professional Journal of the American Federation of Teachers*, 15(Winter), pp. 38–46.

Dweck, C. S., 2006. *Mindset*. 1st ed. New York: Random House.

Guzdial, M., 2015. *Media Computation Teachers*. [Online] Available at: http://coweb.cc.gatech.edu/mediaComp-teach [Accessed 21 September 2015].

Kemp, P., 2014. *Computing in the National Curriculum - A Guide for Secondary Teachers*. 1st ed. s.l.:computing at School.

Kirschner, P. A. & De Bruyckere, P., 2017. The myths of the digital native and the multitasker. *Teaching and Teacher Education*, 67, pp. 135–142.

Nuthall, G., 2007. *The Hidden Lives of Learners*. Wellington: NZCER Press.

Peyton Jones, S., 2011. *Computing at School, International Comparisons*, Cambridge: Microsoft Research.

Peyton Jones, S., 2015. *The Dream of a Lifetime, Shaping How Our Children Learn Computing*, Cambridge: Microsoft Research and Computing at School.

Robertson, D. S., 1998. *The New Renaissance: Computers and the Next Level of Civilization*. New York: Oxford University Press.

Syed, M., 2015. *Black Box Thinking: The Surprising Truth About Success*. London: John Murray Publishers.

Part 1
Planning

1 Designing a secondary curriculum map

Before we can discuss the teaching of computing, we must first plan the material which we want to deliver. In most cases, this will involve designing a five-year curriculum map which outlines all the topics, skills, concepts and knowledge which a student will need to succeed in our subject. This may seem like a daunting task at first; however, having re-written an entire curriculum map based on the new national curriculum of 2013, I can assure the reader that this undertaking can be broken down into a series of procedural processes. This chapter will guide the reader through creating their own curriculum map, and the accompanying eResources contain a comprehensive five-year curriculum which can be used or adapted.

It is important to start the planning process with a firm grasp of the end point i.e. what does a student need to know or be able to do in my subject by the time they leave school? We can then plan backwards from this point. Perkins suggests that we need to understand what "playing the whole game" looks like in our subject (Perkins, 2009). Knight and Benson go on to suggest that it is useful to think about what it means to be an expert in our subject. (Knight & Benson, 2014). It is the clarity of this end goal – moving beyond creating a little living library on our subject to creating a student who through an apprenticeship has developed an understanding of how an expert within the domain, thinks, acts and communicates – that helps ensure our curriculum prepares pupils for expertise and not just the recital of content.

Being a computer scientist – what does this mean?

Computer scientists study, create and maintain computer systems to solve real-world problems. In order to do this, they must master a certain way of thinking and have an understanding of hardware and software. The emphasis of the previous ICT curriculum was on using software, for example office and multimedia applications. However, to be a computer scientist one is expected to not only know how to use software but also how to build one's own hardware and software solutions.

To become an expert in computer science, our students will need to master a particular way of thinking and problem solving. This way of addressing problems is aptly called computational thinking and consists of the following key skills:

- Decomposition – the ability to break down a problem into smaller solvable parts.
- Logical reasoning – organising and analysing data logically, leading to the systematic application of rules to solve a problem.
- Abstraction – reducing complexity by hiding irrelevant details and focussing on the most important elements.

- Pattern matching – finding similarities between different problems.
- Generalisation – adapting a solution that solved one problem to solve another problem, that is, making one solution work for multiple problems.
- Algorithm design – planning a set of steps which detail how to solve a specific problem, represented in a form that can be effectively carried out by an information-processing agent.
- Prediction – hypothesising what will happen at each stage of an algorithm as it is computed and predicting how a human (or any living organism) will subsequently behave and react as they interact with the system.
- Testing and debugging – checking that programs work and are free from logic, syntax and runtime errors by using typical, erroneous and extreme data. Debugging is the process of fixing problems that arise out of testing.
- Evaluation and optimisation – through iterative development, continuously assessing a solution and improving it to ensure that the most effective and efficient combination of steps and resources have been used.

(Wing, 2006; CSTA, 2011; Zagami, 2013; Bagge, 2014; Code.org, 2014; Selby & Wollard, 2014; White, 2016; Papert, 1980)

It is important to note that computational thinking is distinct from other ways of thinking and solving problems and so our curriculum needs to be designed to develop these particular ways of approaching and solving problems. Wing stresses the importance of computational thinking. As a follow-up, Wing goes on to state that the expert computer scientist therefore is someone who chooses the right abstractions and the right tool(s) to automate and mechanise a task (Wing, 2008). Whilst the computer scientist uses logical reasoning, the computer scientist is not merely thinking like a machine; the thought process is creative and considered. In solving problems and designing systems, the computer scientist also has to be aware of human behaviour and the hardware which their programs will run on. Whilst we refer to this way of thinking as computational thinking', it can only be achieved by a human and this ability to work at different levels of abstraction is the true sign of an expert in computer science.

It is worth contrasting the expert skills in computer science, with those in IT. Many of these skills are covered to an extent by the remaining Level 2 and 3 vocational qualifications in IT, for example BTEC diplomas, technical awards and IT qualifications (ITQs). Whether you choose to deliver these vocational IT qualifications at Key Stages 4 and 5 or not, it would be prudent to think about these skills when you are planning your Key Stage 3 curriculum. Developing a solid IT skillset at Key Stage 3 will certainly benefit students across their other subjects at Key Stage 4 and will also be essential for most careers. The following list of expert IT skills is not exhaustive and would require that the person had already developed digital literacy skills as previously outlined in Table 0.1:

- Select, combine and use office and multimedia applications appropriately.
- Select and use hardware and software appropriately.
- Use digital tools to communicate and collaborate effectively.
- Understand and use cloud computing effectively: software as a service, platform as a service and infrastructure as a service.

- Present data and information for a given audience and purpose.
- Perform web-based research and the evaluation of sources.
- Manage complex projects with time, cost and resource constraints.
- Understand and consider the social impact of IT.
- Comply with and be able to advise on the following legislation: computing, intellectual property, copyright and licensing.
- Setup, maintain and manage computer systems.
- Evaluate solutions critically.

(Department for Education, 2013; The Learning Machine [TLM], 2016)

It is evident from this list that the skillset of an IT expert is quite broad. Most IT experts will specialise in a particular area after having developed their expert practice through a combination of professional certifications, qualifications and employer-based training. Our remit as computing teachers is to ensure that students are exposed to these IT skills and to ensure that students are equipped with the IT skills that they need for the future world of work. The programme of study for Key Stage 4 explicitly states that "All pupils must have the opportunity to study aspects of information technology and computer science at sufficient depth to allow them to progress to higher levels of study or to a professional career" (Department for Education, 2013).

For the purposes of this book, we will be referring to both the computer science expert and the IT expert. As we refer back to "playing the whole game" or the big picture, we will be referring to the skills in both strands, that is, the computing expert.

Shaun Lloyd created a useful subject audit for computing under a Creative Commons Attribution-ShareAlike 3.0 Unported CC BY-SA 3.0 Licence (Lloyd, 2015). Mark Dorling and Abigail Woodman also developed a computing skills and knowledge audit tool for the CAS QuickStart Computing continuing professional development (CPD) toolkit for secondary teachers (Dorling & Woodman, 2015). These have been modified to include IT and DL strands in Figure 1.1 on the following pages:

All teachers should be encouraged to complete a subject knowledge audit on an annual basis to identify three targets for development. In Coe *et al.*'s. influential report What Makes Great Teaching, they identified six characteristics of great teaching. The first characteristic which had strong evidence of a positive impact on student outcomes was teacher (pedagogical) content knowledge (Coe *et al.*, 2014). Rob Coe and his colleagues found that,

> The most effective teachers have deep knowledge of the subjects they teach, and when teachers' knowledge falls below a certain level it is a significant impediment to students' learning. As well as a strong understanding of the material being taught, teachers must also understand the ways students think about the content, be able to evaluate the thinking behind students' own methods, and identify students' common misconceptions.
>
> *(Coe et al., 2014)*

To help our students become experts, we as teachers should audit our subject knowledge and then commit ourselves to continuously developing our knowledge as we embark on our own journeys to become expert teachers.

Subject knowledge audit for computing

Teacher Name:_____   Date:_____

Key:
Red: I cannot do this yet
Amber: I know the main ideas and topics, but I would need to do some further reading and studying to be ready to teach this
Green: I am confident I can teach this to my students and other teachers
*Indicates KS5 content.

Subject Audit – Algorithms	Red	Amber	Green
Break down complex problems into smaller parts (decomposition)			
Identify patterns and similarities with how previous problems have been solved			
Identify computational abstractions in order to discount unnecessary information			
Explain how the choice of an algorithm should be influenced by the data			
Be able to explain and use several key algorithms (e.g. sorting, searching, shortest path*)			
Explain how algorithms can be improved, validated, tested and corrected			
Explain that a single problem could be solved by more than one algorithm			
Explain and show how different algorithms can have different performance characteristics for the same task			
Explain the efficiency and complexity of algorithms using Big O notation*			
Successfully apply algorithms in solving GCSE and A level type problems			
How would you rate your knowledge of algorithms overall?			

Subject Audit – Programming	Red	Amber	Green
Program competently in a least two programming languages, at least one of which must be 'textual'			
Explain and use programming concepts such as selection, repetition, procedures, constants, variables, relational operators, logical operators and functions			
Explain and use trace tables to track the values of variables as they change whilst a program is run			
Explain and use arrays or lists			
Explain and use truth tables and Boolean valued variables			
Explain and use tables and dictionaries			
Explain and use two dimensional arrays			
Explain and use three dimensional arrays (records, lists, tuples)*			
Explain and use complex data structures such as trees, hash tables, graphs, stacks and queues*			
Explain and use nested constructs/loops			
Explain and create modular programs using procedures (sub-routines)			
Explain the concept of procedures that call procedures			

Figure 1.1 Subject knowledge audit for computing. This is a derivative work based on documents published on the CAS community website (Lloyd, 2015; Dorling & Woodman, 2015; Kemp, 2014; Sentance et al., 2017).

	Red	Amber	Green
Explain and create modular programs using functions and parameter passing			
Explain how parameters may be passed by value or by reference*			
Explain and use different data types appropriately: integer, real, Boolean, char, string			
Explain how to test programs using valid, erroneous and boundary data			
Identify and explain logic, syntax and runtime errors			
Explain and use a range of validation errors			
Explain how low level languages work and be able to give simple examples, e.g. using Little Man Computer			
Explain that a program can be written to satisfy requirements and that they should be corrected if they do not meet these			
Explain and use object-oriented programming (classes, objects, methods, attributes, inheritance, encapsulation and polymorphism)*			
Explain and use regular expressions*			
Explain and use Backus-Naur Form and Syntax Diagrams*			
Successfully apply programming in solving Computing/Computer Science GCSE and A level type problems			
How would you rate your knowledge of programming overall?			

Subject Audit – Data	Red	Amber	Green
Explain the difference between data and information			
Explain how sound and pictures can be represented and manipulated in binary			
Explain how numbers and text can be manipulated using different character sets such as ASCII and UNICODE			
Explain how to perform simple operations on binary numbers, e.g. addition, subtraction and conversion between binary and decimal			
Explain how to perform bitwise operators and bit shifts*			
Explain the need for and use of hexadecimal, two's complement*, signed integers*, and string manipulation*			
Explain the need for data compression, and be able to describe simple compression methods			
Explain the need for analogue to digital conversions and how this works			
Explain the limitations of using binary representations, e.g. rounding errors, sampling frequency and fractional numbers			
Explain how structured data can be represented in tables in a relational database, and simple database queries			
Explain how to normalise data to 3NF*			
Explain and use SQL to create, delete, insert, update and search across multiple tables			
Explain the concepts of transaction processing, ACID (Atomicity, Consistency, Isolation, Durability), record locking, and redundancy*			
Explain and use Boolean algebra including de Morgan's Laws and Karnaugh maps*			

Figure 1.1 Continued

	Red	Amber	Green
Explain the logic associated with D type flip flops, half and full adders*			
Explain and use Reverse Polish Notation*			
How would you rate your knowledge of data overall?			

Subject Audit – Computers and Social Informatics	Red	Amber	Green
Explain the use of logic gates and circuits			
Explain how hardware and software components make up a computer system and how they communicate with one another and with other systems			
Explain Von Neumann architecture (CPU, Memory, Input/Output)			
Explain the differences and uses for various storage technologies including magnetic, solid state/flash, optical and hybrid			
Explain how instructions are stored and executed within a computer system including the CPU instruction cycle, ALU, CU and registers			
Explain the factors affecting the performance of the CPU: clock speed, cache and number of cores			
Explain the concept of instruction pipelining and concurrency*			
Explain the various models of computer architecture including Von Neumann, Harvard, multicore, parallel systems and contemporary processor architecture*			
Explain the differences between CISC and RISC processors*			
Explain the use of registers including the Program Counter, Accumulator, MAR, MDR, CIR			
Explain how different buses are used and how they relate to assembly language programs*			
Explain and use low level instruction sets and assembly code			
Explain the differences between main memory, virtual memory and secondary storage			
Explain the different modes of addressing memory (immediate, direct, indirect and indexed)*			
Explain what compilers and interpreters are and do and give some examples of when they are used			
Explain the main functions of operating systems			
Explain the different between open source, proprietary, bespoke and off the shelf software			
Explain the differences between the following software development cycles: Waterfall, agile, extreme programming, spiral model and rapid application development and protyping*			
Explain the concepts of linkers, loaders and libraries*			
Explain the various stages of compilation (lexical analysis, syntax analysis, code generation and optimisation)*			
Explain the difference between various models of computation such as Finite State Machines and Turing Machines*			
How would you rate your knowledge of computers & social informatics overall?			

Figure 1.1 Continued

Subject Audit – Communication and the Internet	Red	Amber	Green
Explain the concepts of client/server models			
Explain MAC addresses, IP addresses and domain names			
Explain how different protocols and layers are used on LANs and WANs			
Explain packet and circuit switching			
Explain the use of frames on LANs			
Explain the benefits and disadvantages of different network topologies			
Explain various cyber security methods including encryption, firewalls, VPNs			
Explain various cyber threats and malware			
Explain the components and the differences between the Internet and the WWW			
Explain routing, redundancy, error correction, compression and hashing*			
Explain the different network hardware required to set up a LAN and WAN			
Explain and use HTML, CSS and Javascript to create multi-page websites			
How would you rate your knowledge of communications and the internet overall?			

Subject Audit – Administrative IT	Red	Amber	Green
Use word processing software competently to create documents with appropriate formatting and layout			
Use spreadsheet software competently to create spreadsheets which utilise a range of formulae, functions, formatting and analytical tools including conditional formulae, lookups, scenarios and charts			
Use presentation software competently to create structured presentations using appropriate multimedia, consistent formatting and layout			
Use competently a range of office applications in combination to produce documents which may include charts, diagrams or mail-merged elements			
How would you rate your knowledge of administrative IT overall?			

Subject Audit – Creative IT	Red	Amber	Green
Use competently a range of office, image editing and multimedia applications to create digital artefacts for a given audience and purpose on a range of devices			
Explain how to select, use and combine multiple applications			
Explain how to collect and analyse data to meet the needs of users			
Explain how to re-use, revise and re-purpose digital artefacts with attention to intellectual property, trustworthiness, design and usability			
How would you rate your knowledge of creative IT overall?			

Figure 1.1 Continued

Subject Audit – Digital Literacy	Red	Amber	Green
Explain a range of ways to use technology safely, respectfully, responsibly and securely			
Explain various computing-related legislation including the Data Protection Act, Computer Misuse Act, Copyright Designs and Patents Act, Creative Commons Licensing, Health and Safety at Work Act, Freedom of Information Act, Investigatory Powers Act			
Explain how to protect online identity and privacy			
Explain how to recognise inappropriate content, contact and conduct and how to report concerns			
Explain how to recognise bias, misleading or potentially "fake news" and websites			
How would you rate your knowledge of Digital Literacy overall?			

Figure 1.1 Continued

Now that we have established what an expert is and what playing the whole game looks like, we can start to plan backwards from our end point. Although you may not teach undergraduate-level or even A-level computer science at present, it is still worth researching what a junior version of a computer scientist or IT consultant does; that is, what is required at undergraduate level. This is useful because our oldest students are just one step removed from the real-world computer scientists, IT consultants, network engineers, web developers, games designers, visual effects supervisors and so on. Our students will want to know how their curriculum relates to real-world skills and we can also use this knowledge to help plan units of work which are exciting and relevant.

It is important that whilst we are designing our curriculum, we do not fall into the trap of simply teaching skills and knowledge through software and content. The software will have changed by the time your Year 7 students leave secondary school and new hardware will also be introduced. We must therefore remember that being a computing expert is not about the mastery of particular range of software but the mastery of particular ways of thinking. Whilst we may use a certain programming language and suite of applications, these are a vehicle and means for teaching and developing students' computational thinking. Even if the software and hardware changes over time, the ways of thinking and approaching problems should always remain useful and transferrable.

Another trap is designing a discrete curriculum for each Key Stage. If your end point is (say) Year 11 GCSE computer science, it is here that you should begin designing a five-year curriculum map which maps back to Year 7. If you know what exam(s) your students will be taking in Year 11, it makes sense to treat the GCSE as a five-year qualification. This is not capitulating to exam pressures and merely teaching towards the test; it is a way of structuring your curriculum over an extended period of time, thereby allowing more creative freedom and a much richer enquiry-based curriculum. Given the GCSE curriculum changes in 2016, specifically the reduction in coursework and controlled assessments, and the volume of skills, concepts and knowledge required in the formal written exams, it is unrealistic to start teaching GCSE content in Year 10.

Planning your curriculum over a five-year map also allows you to interleave elements from the IT and digital literacy strands of the curriculum. In many schools, students will get to choose between either computer science or an IT qualification (e.g. a Certificate in Digital Applications [CiDA], the Oxford Cambridge and RCA Examinations [OCR]/Cambridge Nationals, the Business and Technology Education Council's (BTEC's) Level 2 Diplomas, Technical Awards, TLM Level 2 ITQs). As the students may not know which qualification they will choose until the end of Year 9, it is necessary to ensure your computing curriculum is broad and balanced from the outset.

Applying cognitive psychology to curriculum design

The rationale behind the five-year curriculum map has also been influenced by cognitive psychology. In many schools that I have taught at, schemes of work have been organised into distinct units. Spreadsheet modelling, programming, data representation and computer architecture were all separate units. For many years, I did not question this. It makes sense to teach one topic at a time and to have summative tests at the end of each main unit. This is after all how most of us were taught in school. However, whilst this approach is intuitive, cognitive psychology tells us that we can improve learning by following certain teaching practices. It is worth prefacing this chapter with the warning that many of these practices are counter-intuitive; Coe *et al.* note in their report commissioned by The Sutton Trust, "One paradoxical finding is that some approaches that may appear to make learning harder in the short term, and less satisfying for learners, actually result in better long-term retention" (Coe *et al.*, 2014).

In order to understand what learning is, we must first look at memory. The importance of memory can be found in the definition of learning as the processes which lead to information – that is, skills and knowledge – being committed to long-term memory.

An information processing model

Computer memory versus human memory

As a computer scientist, the concept of volatility in computer memory is a useful analogy for the process of forgetting in human memory. Volatile memory such as RAM is akin to working memory and non-volatile secondary storage is akin to long-term memory. Where data is not saved from RAM to secondary storage, data is lost. This is similar to the process of forgetting in working memory. Whilst the concepts of forgetting in humans and data loss in computers are similar, the processes of storage in long-term memory

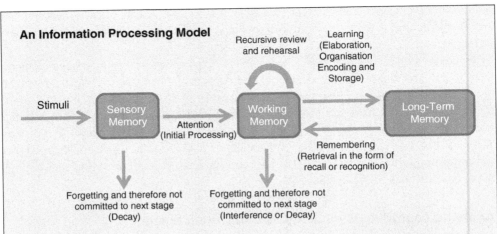

An Information Processing Model

Figure 1.2 An information processing model (adapted from Atkinson & Shiffrin, 1968; and Baddeley & Hitch, 1974).

and secondary storage are quite different. Committing to long-term memory requires recursive review and rehearsal; this process can be difficult at times, unlike the relatively straightforward process of saving data in a computer system. It is worth noting that these difficult learning activities which result in durable and flexible learning are actually deemed "desirable difficulties" (Bjork & Bjork, 2011). These will be explored in more detail in Chapter 4.

A further similarity can be found in the capacity of working memory, which like RAM is relatively small compared to secondary storage and long-term memory. Miller's research paper entitled "The magical number seven, plus or minus two" found that most humans can store between five and nine "chunks" in working memory (Miller, 1956).

Another similarity can be found in the retrieval speed from RAM compared to secondary storage; retrieval from RAM is much quicker than retrieval from secondary storage. This is akin to the quick and seemingly easy retrieval from working memory compared to the more difficult retrieval from long-term memory which seems to take longer. It is here where the similarities between computer memory and human memory end.

Whilst computer memory is generally reliable and retrieval from secondary storage is precise, David Didau and Nick Rose comment on the fascinating nature of human memory:

> "Our memories are reconstructive rather than recordings, associative rather than predictable, cue dependent rather than reliable."
>
> (Didau & Rose, 2016)

The following section explores the many nuances of human memory; where computer memory is logical and relatively reliable, human memory is much more complex and riddled with counter-intuitive properties!

The diagram in Figure 1.2 indicates that for effective learning to take place, the teaching activities must enable stimuli to pass from sensory memory to long-term memory via working memory.[1] It is here that cognitive psychology feeds directly into curriculum design. There are three theories which underpin successful curriculum design:

1   Distributed practice
2   Practice testing
3   Interleaved practice.

The first concept which leads to improved student memory and learning is distributed practice which is also known as 'spacing'. Research by Cepeda *et al.* found that spacing studying and conscious reviewing over several weeks and months, rather than massed cramming into single sessions greatly improves long-term retention (Cepeda *et al.*, 2006). In terms of the number of repetitions, Nuthall found that each student needed to encounter on at least three different occasions the complete set of the information she or he needed before they understood a given concept (Nuthall, 2007). Seeking to investigate if the amount of time between each repeated review affects learning and memory, Bahrik and Phelps found that increasing the interval between each repetition resulted in better retention over time; a 30-day spacing gap was found to be more beneficial than a one-day delay (Bahrick & Phelps, 1987). Further support for spacing studying and practice over time can be found in Ebbinghaus's experiments into transience; the exponential forgetting of information from memory over time. Ebbinghaus found that

> with any considerable number of repetitions a suitable distribution of them over a space of time is decidedly more advantageous than the massing of them at a single time … as the number of repetitions is … further increased, the … series fades out only after ever longer intervals … The series are gradually forgotten, but–as is sufficiently well known– the series which have been learned twice fade away much more slowly than those which have been learned but once. If the relearning is performed a second, a third or a greater number of times, the series are more deeply engraved and fade out less easily and finally, as one would anticipate, they become possessions of the soul.
>
> (Ebbinghaus, 1885)

In summary, the exponential forgetting curve becomes shallower as the number of spaced learning episodes increase and as the time between each review episode increases (Figure1.3). Whilst it is likely that students who are tested after the first interval may have forgotten some of the information they were first taught, this is to be expected and teachers should not be discouraged as subsequent repetitions will result in longer retention.

> Forgetting is likely to be a necessary consequence of reviewing information after long spacing gaps, re-exposing students to this information on a regular basis will keep it accessible in memory and render it less vulnerable to forgetting over time.
>
> (Carpenter *et al.*, 2012)

The five-year map should therefore allow opportunity to revisit content within each academic year and also within the five-year period. This spiral curriculum model where key concepts,

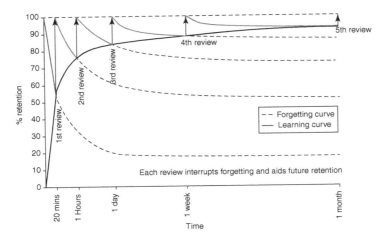

Figure 1.3 Ebbinghaus's forgetting curve (adapted from Learn That Foundation, 2005).

principles and issues are revisited each year is based on the work of Jerome Bruner (Bruner, 1960). Content should ideally be reviewed at least three times before a student's terminal exam. This can clearly be seen in Figure 1.4, where topics such as the central processing unit (CPU), data representation and networks are explicitly covered three times over the five-year period. Even though it appears that not all the topics are covered at least three times over the five-year map, these repetitive reviews are likely to occur in the form of practice testing (frequent low-stakes tests, homework and exit tickets) which will be covered in the following pages.

The importance of practice testing is emphasised by a review of ten learning techniques, spanning hundreds of years of research performed by Dunlosky *et al.* Their review found only two of the ten techniques to have a high utility for teaching and learning. The first was distributed practice and the second was practice testing (Dunlosky *et al.*, 2013). Practice testing differs from traditional end-of-unit summative tests in that they are low stakes or no stakes and are generally student led. However, Argarwal *et al.* go on to recommend that teachers can support students by frequently using low-stakes or no-stakes quizzes in the classroom (Deans for Impact, 2015). These frequent low-stakes quizzes can take the form of gap-fill, multiple-choice or short-answer questions. Studies by Bangert-Downs *et al.* also found that shorter, more frequent summative tests were not only more beneficial in terms of learning but also created a more positive classroom atmosphere compared to a smaller number of longer tests (Bangert-Downs *et al.*, 1991).

Roediger & Karpicke found that whilst repeated studying would appear to produce better performance in the short term, repeated testing produces better recall in the long term (Bjork & Bjork, 2011). Argawal *et al.* also confirm this somewhat counter-intuitive finding – that investing curriculum time on testing leads to better learning and retention than merely having more teacher-led lessons and classroom activities (Willingham, 2013). In the same blog post, Willingham references the work of Kornell *et al.* who found that testing remains more beneficial than additional studying, even if students get the answers wrong in their tests as long as they are provided with corrective feedback. In planning a curriculum, it is therefore important to try not to cover too many topics in each year and instead try to space this over five years with sufficient time within the year for frequent low-stakes testing in addition to the typical end-of-unit summative testing.

The final consideration when planning your curriculum is Interleaved practice: This involves the mixing of different types of problems and different kinds of material within a study session. Bjork adds that in addition to spacing studying over time, interleaving topics and tasks is also better than teaching topic blocks (Bjork, 2014). Blocking practice was also found to give students the illusion of learning, with greater rates of improvement and higher confidence (Bjork & Bjork, 2011). However, somewhat unexpectedly, Bjork encounters numerous studies whereby after a period of ten days or more, the students who were taught using interleaved practice performed better than those who had practiced under blocked practice. Bjork and Bjork conclude that "whilst blocked practice appears optimal for learning, interleaved practice offers superior long-term retention and transfer of skills". This trap is highlighted by research repeatedly and this illusion of performance is mainly as a result of confusing retrieval strength with storage strength.

Whilst the exam specifications and text books may have very clear units, there is a lot of scope for the overlap and interleaving of content and skills. For example, encryption can be taught through programming; the representation of images can be taught by manipulating cells in spreadsheets; Hypertext Markup Language (HTML) and Cascading Style Sheets (CSS) colour codes can be taught alongside hexadecimal number representation. The beauty of a five-year map is that all the topics can be presented side by side and links can be made between the topics.

Topics in computing do not exist in isolation, and therefore where possible we should expose students to the bigger picture by interleaving content and creating as many links as possible between the various concepts in computing. In making a case of interleaving, O. Roger Anderson a Senior Research Scientist at Columbia University states,

> By definition, knowledge is the meaningful recall of information, assembled in some organized way. The larger the number of interrelationships among the units of information organized in memory, the more likely the individual will have multiple ways of accessing and applying the information in a meaningful way. Hence, the more likely he or she will be able to think about it constructively and creatively.

(Anderson, 2011)

An example five-year curriculum map

We begin with the hypothesis that any subject can be taught effectively in some intellectually honest form to any child at any stage of development (Bruner, 1960)

When I produced the five-year map in Figure 1.4, I divided the curriculum into units, alternating between theory and practical units. In this case, the school offered both an IT and computer science qualification and it therefore made sense to identify the similarities in the practical and theoretical units and ensure that a broad range was covered in Key Stage 3 in preparation for Key Stage 4. The units with crossover were:

- Networks
- Computer systems
- Software
- Input and output devices
- Memory
- Storage
- Assistive technology

GFS COMPUTING		Year 7	Year 8	Year 9	Year 10	Year 11
		COMPUTER SYSTEMS: How can we design the fastest computer system in the world?	COMPUTING HARDWARE: How can we design the fastest computer system in the world?	INTERMEDIATE SPREADSHEET MODELLING: Can we accurately model the world using computer software?	ALGORITHMS/ PROGRAMMING: How can we think more like a computer?	PROGRAMMING THEORY: How can we produce robust programs which are effective and efficient?
	Computer Science	INTRO TO PROGRAMMING: Can a computer be more intelligent than the human who programmed it?	EFFICIENT PROGRAMMING: What is more important, hardware or software?	CYBER SECURITY: Why is our data so valuable to hackers?	SYSTEMS ARCHITECTURE: Is there anything more important than a CPU inside a Computer?	PROGRAMMING PRACTICE TASK
		E-SAFETY/GRAPHIC DESIGN: Are we ever safe online?	INTRO TO SPREADSHEETS: Can we accurately model the world using computer software?	EFFICIENT PROGRAMMING PART II: How can we solve problems with efficient programs?	WIRED AND WIRELESS NETWORKS: How can we guarantee that a data packet will reach its destination?	NON-EXAMINATION ASSESSMENT (NEA): (COMP 3 Programming Project) Jan-May HT
Overall theme for strands	IT	INTRO TO PROGRAMMING PART II: How can we solve problems with programs?	NETWORKS: Will the Internet slow down as it grows bigger and gets older?	ETHICAL, LEGAL, CULTURAL AND ENVIRONMENTAL CONCERNS: Have computers made the world better or worse?	SYSTEMS SOFTWARE: Which software is most important at an intelligence agency such as MI5 or the CIA?	DATA REPRESENTATION/ REVISION: Is there anything we cannot represent using 0's and 1's?
	Digital Literacy	THEORY REVISION	BUILDING A WEBPAGE: Will the Internet slow down as it grows bigger and gets older?	GRAPHICS: How can we manipulate images in 2D and 3D?	SQL: How can we query a large data set using a programming language?	REVISION: Examination preparation

Figure 1.4 A five-year curriculum map for computing.*

*This curriculum map shows GCSE computer science in years 10 and 11. For a curriculum map for IT qualifications, please see the eResources.

Term 1

Topic: Computer Systems

Fertile Question: How can we design the fastest computer system in the world?

Content:
Admin:

– Usernames/Passwords/Email/Google Classroom

Intro to
– Input
– Output
– Memory: RAM/ROM
– CPU
– Secondary Storage
– Von Neumann Architecture

Theory assessment: Analyse a computer system

Topic: Computing Hardware

Fertile Question: How can we design the fastest computer system in the world?

Content:
– Computer Systems (Von Neumann) Architecture)
– CPU Instruction Cycle
– Clock Speed, Cores, Cache
– Logic Gates
– Logic Circuits

Theory assessment: CPU and Logic questions from OCR GCSE Computing Unit 2.1.2

Topic: Intermediate Spreadsheet Modelling:

Fertile Question: Can we accurately model the world using computer software?

Content:
– Recap: Formula, IF, Functions
– 3D Referencing
– Conditional Formatting
– Goal Seek
– VLOOKUP
– Graphic Design tasks with sources table

Practical assessment: Greenwich DVDs Spreadsheet

Topic: Algorithms/Programming Techniques

Fertile Question: How can we think more like a computer?

Content:
– Computational Thinking
– Searching Algorithms
– Sorting Algorithms
– Pseudo Code and Flowcharts
– Sequence, Selection and Iteration using programming challenges (OCR/GSA)
– String Manipulation recap
– Arrays recap and 2D arrays
– Functions and Procedures recap
– Combining data types

Theory assessment: Algorithms and Programming techniques questions from OCR GCSE Computer Science Unit 2.1 and 2.2

Topic: Programming Techniques 2/ Producing Robust programs/Translators and Facilities of Languages

Fertile Question: How can we produce robust programs which are effective and efficient?

Content:
– Defensive design
– Maintainability
– Testing
– Identifying Syntax and Logic Errors
– Selecting and using suitable test data
– Practical: Exponentiation, MOD, DIV
– Different Languages incl Low Level recap
– Translators
– Assembler, Compiler and Interpreter
– Tools and Facilities of an IDE

Theory assessment: Programming questions from OCR GCSE Computer Science Unit 2.1, 2.2, 2.3, 2.4 and 2.5

Figure 1.4 Continued

Term 2				
Topic: Intro to Programming Part I **Fertile Question:** Can a computer be more intelligent than the human who programmed it? **Content:** Lyrics and Chatbot – Algorithms – Sequence – Selection – Computational Thinking – Quiz – Christmas Quiz Lists **Practical assessment:** Creating a chatbot about GFS	**Topic:** Efficient Programming **Fertile Question:** What type of problems are quicker to solve by writing a program and what type of problems are slower to solve? **Content:** – Parking meter software – Sequence/Selection/ Iteration – Modules (time, random, turtle) – Procedures – Capital Cities Quiz – String Manipulation – Buffer: Functions **Practical assessment:** Creating a program which simulates an ATM (Cash machine)	**Topic:** Cyber Security **Fertile Question:** Why is our data so valuable to hackers? **Content:** – Malware – Bloatware – Viruses and Trojans – Spam, Phishing, RATS – Skimming – Cyber Security Presentation – Ethical, Legal, Cultural and Environmental Concerns – Sources Table **Theory and practical assessment:** Cyber security presentation	**Topic:** Systems Architecture **Fertile Question:** Is there anything more important than a CPU inside a Computer? **Content:** Systems Architecture – CPU Recap: Instruction cycle, performance – Von Neumann architecture revisited – CPU components and their function using LMC – Embedded systems – Memory Recap: RAM, ROM, Virtual memory, Flash memory – Storage Recap: Magnetic, Optical, Solid State, Justifying choices incl cost **Theory assessment:** Algorithms and Programming technique questions from OCR GCSE Computer Science Units 1.1, 1.2 and 1.3 and a case study from unit 1.8	**Topic:** Programming practice task **Fertile Question: N/A** **Content:** Pupils will prepare for and complete a practice NEA element of the specification. This includes: – Programming techniques – Design – Development – Testing, Evaluation and Conclusion **Practical assessment:** Assessing the Design strand of the practice task

Figure 1.4 Continued

GFS COMPUTING	Year 7	Year 8	Year 9	Year 10	Year 11
Term 3	**Topic:** E-Safety/ Multimedia Design **Fertile Question:** To what extent is the online world more dangerous than the offline world? **Content:** – Usernames/ Passwords/Email/ Google Classroom – E-Safety videos – Sexting – Multimedia Presentation welcoming guests and new students to GFS. Must also include e-safety, digital citizenship or digital identity. – Sources Table **Practical assessment:** Evaluation of E-safety posters	**Topic:** Intro to spreadsheets **Fertile Question:** Can we accurately model the world using computer software? **Content:** – Basic Formula – Functions – Graphs and Charts – If statements – Graphic Design tasks with sources table **Practical assessment:** Aircraft booking system	**Topic:** Efficient Programming Part II **Fertile Question:** How can we write programs that never fail or crash? **Content:** – Cyber Security Quiz/ Maths Quiz/Piggy Bank – Algorithms -> Flowcharts and Pseudocode – Exception handling – String manipulation – Procedures – Functions **Practical assessment:** Pizza Program	**Topic:** Wired and Wireless Networks and Topologies **Fertile Question:** How can we guarantee that your passwords, personal information and snapchat photos are not hacked when travelling across a network? **Content:** Networks recap – LAN vs WAN – Hardware: WAPS, Routers, Switches, NICS, Transmission Media – Factors affecting performance – Roles of computers in client server, p2p – The Internet-DNS, Hosting, Cloud – Virtual networks – Star and Mesh – Wifi-freq, channels and encryption – IP/MAC Addressubg and Protocols – Network layers – Packet switching System Security recap – Forms of attack – Threats posed to networks – Identifying and preventing vulnerabilities **Theory assessment:** Network questions from OCR GCSE Computer Science Unit 1.4 and 1.5 and a case study from unit 1.8	**Topic:** COMP 3 Programming Project **Fertile Question: N/A 25-30 hrs** **Deadline: Fri 4th May 2018** **Content:** Pupils will prepare for and complete the NEA element of the specification. This includes: – Programming techniques – Design – Development – Testing Evaluation and Conclusion **Practical assessment:** Internally assessed externally moderated by OCR

Figure 1.4 Continued

Topic: Intro to Programming Part II	Topic: Networks	Topic: Ethical, Legal, Cultural and Environmental Concerns in Computing	Topic: Systems Software and Ethical, Legal, Cultural and Environmental Concerns	
Fertile Question: What types of problems are quicker to solve by writing a program and what types of problems are slower to solve?	**Fertile Question:** Will the Internet slow down as it grows bigger and gets older?	**Fertile Question:** Have computers made the world better or worse?	**Fertile Question:** Which software is most important at an intelligence agency such as MI5?	**25-30 hrs** **Non-Examination Assessment (NEA)** **(20%)**
Content: – Fruit machine – Sequence – Selection – Iteration – Modules – Data Structures (Lists and Dictionaries)	**Content:** – LAN vs WAN – LAN Hardware – Factors affecting performance – Star and Mesh Topologies – Wifi: Frequency, Channels, Encryption – The Internet: DNS, Hosting, The Cloud	**Content:** Case studies/Court room scenarios: – iPhone vs FBI (Privacy) – Intel (Green) vs Google (Server farms) – Wikileaks – Apple vs Microsoft and the Xerox Debate – Samsung vs Apple – Technology Addiction and Childhood development – Landfill and Waste – Job creation vs Automation – Users with specific needs – Sampling in music – Facebook and how it uses your data – Comparing different technology in context – Stakeholders (direct and indirect) and how they are affected – Analysis of solutions and its effects	**Content:** Systems Software – Purpose and functionality of systems software – Operating Systems – Utility System Software – Open Source vs Proprietary Legislation (Courtroom scenarios) – Data protection Act – Computer Misuse Act – Copyright, Design and Patents Act – Creative Commons Licensing – Freedom of Information Act – Comparing different technology in context – Stakeholders (direct and indirect) and how they are affected – Analysis of solutions and its effects	**Deadline Fri 4th May 2018** **Practical assessment:** Internally assessed externally moderated by OCR
Practical assessment: Creating a quiz	**Theory assessment:** Network questions from OCR GCSE Computer Science Unit 1.4 and 1.5	**Theory assessment:** Questions from OCR GCSE Computer Science Unit 1.8	**Theory assessment:** Software questions from OCR GCSE Computer Science Unit 1.7 and a case study from unit 1.8	

Term 4

Figure 14 Continued

GFS COMPUTING	Year 7	Year 8	Year 9	Year 10	Year 11
	Topic: Memory/Data Representation	**Topic:** Building a Webpage	**Topic:** Graphics/ Multimedia	**Topic:** SQL	**Topic:** Data Representation, System Security and Theory Revision
	Fertile Question: How can computers store and process everything in 1's and 0's	**Fertile Question:** Will the Internet slow down as it grows bigger and gets older?	**Fertile Question:** How do media companies use Computers to construct their products?	**Fertile Question:** How can we query a large data set using a programming language?	**Fertile Question:** Is there anything we cannot represent using 0's and 1's?
	Content: – Binary representation of number – Binary representation of characters – Binary representation of images – Units – Hexadecimal	**Content:** – My favourite book/film webpage – HTML Tags – Images – Embedding content – CSS	**Content:** – Logo Branding – Photo editing – Magazine Graphic Design (Front cover, Advert and DPS)	**Content:** – Creating a table – Querying a table – Advanced queries using logical operators	**Content:** Data Representation – Recap: Units, Numbers – Character – Images – Sound – Compression System security – Forms of attack – Threats posed to networks – Identifying and preventing vulnerability
		Practical assessment: Creating a website about a prominent computer scientist	**Practical assessment:** Create a school magazine cover	**Practical and Theory assessment:** Playlist Creator from https:// www.khanacademy.org/ computing/computer-programming/sql/ and Programming technique questions from OCR GCSE Computer Science 2.2, 1.6 (SQL injection) and a case study from 1.8	Pupils will revise topics in preparation for their examinations. This includes: – re-teach of specific areas – practice of examination technique – past-paper analysis
	Theory assessment: Mock exam on Computer Systems				**Theory assessment:** Walking Talking Mock **Fri 11th May 2018**
Term 5					

Figure 1.4 Continued

Term 6				
Topic: Theory Revision **Fertile Question:** How does theoretical knowledge help us become better computer scientists? **Content:** Pupils will revise topics in preparation for their examinations. This includes: – re-teach of specific areas – practice of examination technique – past-paper analysis **Theory assessment:** Computer Systems, Data Representation, Programming	**Topic:** Theory Revision **Fertile Question:** How does theoretical knowledge help us become better computer scientists? **Content:** Pupils will revise topics in preparation for their examinations. This includes: – re-teach of specific areas – practice of examination technique – past-paper analysis Topics: – Flowchart algorithms – Input/Output/Storage/SEND – Adding Binary/Ascii – CPU/Networks/Logic Gates **Theory assessment:** Computer Systems, Data representation, Logic gates, Networks Programming	**Topic:** Theory Revision **Fertile Question:** How does theoretical knowledge help us become better computer scientists? **Content:** Pupils will revise topics in preparation for their examinations. This includes: – re-teach of specific areas – practice of examination technique – past-paper analysis **Theory assessment:** Computer Systems, Data representation, Logic gates, Networks Programming, Cyber Security, Spreadsheets, Ethical, Legal, Cultural and Environmental Concerns	**Topic:** Theory Revision **Fertile Question:** How does theoretical knowledge help us become better computer scientists? **Content:** Pupils will revise topics in preparation for their examinations. This includes: – re-teach of specific areas – practice of examination technique – past-paper analysis **Theory assessment:** Theory questions from questions from OCR GCSE Computer Science Units 1, 2.1, 2.2, 2.4, 2.6	**External Examinations Fri 1st June 2018**

Figure 1.4 Continued

- System security
- Ethical, legal, cultural and environmental concerns in computing
- Web design.

Whilst text-based programming is not assessed in most IT Level 2 qualifications, given the growing popularity of computer science and the shrinking number of these IT qualifications, it is prudent to teach text-based programming from Year 7. We found that teaching text-based programming from the start of the secondary phase ensured students were confident when they embarked on their GCSE in computer science. The teaching of programming is also quite novel and is perceived positively amongst young children; few students have any experience of text-based programming at primary school and therefore it creates a similar starting point for all students. There is a temptation to teach block-based programming; however, I've found that with this approach, much greater differentiation is needed. Inevitably some primary schools will have taught extensively using Scratch or a similar block-based language and others will have only covered office applications. The pedagogy and resultant understanding of programming constructs is also mixed. Where students feel confident in block-based programming, many of these may have used blocks to create visually impressive animations or even games without understanding the logic behind their programs.

Once the aforementioned topics with crossover between the two main strands had been placed on the plan, the remaining units were interleaved roughly in order of precedence. Whitehead notes that the teaching of certain subjects will require necessary antecedence (Whitehead, 1922). In computing, it is not possible to teach about the CPU instruction cycle (Year 8 term 1) before we have learnt about the different components in a computer system (Year 7 term 1) for example.

It is evident that the curriculum map on the following pages is informed by the principles of cognitive psychology. It is distributed, spaced, interleaved and involves a summative test or a performance of understanding at the end of each unit. This curriculum map is also available in the eResources, and you are encouraged to modify it to match the specifications of your Key Stage 4 exam boards.

The need for Fertile Questions

> Your memory is not a product of what you want to remember or what you try to remember; it's a product of what you think about. ... Memory is the residue of thought.
>
> (Willingham, 2009)

In the introduction, we covered some of the fallacies of computing education. The busy classroom and the quiet classroom were seen as poor proxies for learning. The focus cannot simply be on what the students are doing, the focus needs to be on what the students are thinking about. In an influential paper on curriculum design and teaching, Yoram Harpaz argues the case for moving away from factory schools based purely on knowledge transmission and imitation, "According to the principle of imitation, student learning is the last link in a mimetic chain; scientists copy the world; curriculum experts copy the sciences; teachers copy the curricula; and students copy their teachers" (Harpaz, 2005). This view of teaching and learning is problematic, not only because facts can change but also because this emphasis is limiting. Computing does not live in a text book or on a revision website; it is one of the most dynamic subjects that students will encounter and we therefore need to ensure that our teaching encourages thinking. Harpaz argues that for effective learning to take place, students need to be involved in its process and the understanding of its process. Leamnson also states that effective learning relies on deep engagement and emotional involvement - a desire to find personal meaning in what is being taught (Leamnson, 2000).

Fertile Questions are a way of encouraging understanding rather than mere recall. True understanding is the ability to apply this knowledge in new situations; this is effectively what exams are designed to test. Ofqual, the qualifications and examinations regulator, states that "exam questions cannot be identical in successive years or examinations" (Ofqual, 2011). As teachers we would therefore be foolish to simply teach our specification's content based on past examination papers without checking for deeper understanding.

In making a case for Fertile Questions, Harpaz conducted a literature review and states that beyond merely listening, recalling knowledge and being compliant, effective learning which demonstrates understanding also has to have the following prerequisites:

1   Effective learning is an outcome of active construction - not solely a result of the passive absorption of contents.
2   Effective learning results from undermining a learner's existing cognitive schemes, concepts and action patterns.
3   Effective learning results from the echoing of learned content in the learner - when it answers questions that the learner has and satisfies their hunger for meaning.
4   Effective learning results from strong intrinsic motivation - not solely from extrinsic rewards or fear of punishment.
5   Effective learning occurs in a dialogic environment.
6   Effective learning entails engaging in authentic problems in an authentic context that is "real" and "urgent" for the learner.
7   Effective learning is advanced by ongoing informative feedback and when assessment is formative and sustaining.
8   Effective learning is a result of positive supportive attitudes and learning environments.
9   Effective learning is the result of a productive theory of learning, where learners relate their learning and achievements to effort rather than ability.

Myth: learning styles

It is worth noting that one of the prerequisites that was referenced in Harpaz's 2005 article is that of preferred learning styles. The theory states that learners have a preference for learning, either by presenting information in a visual, auditory or kinaesthetic form. However, cognitive psychology has since informed us that there is no evidence to suggest that students benefit from teaching which is catered to a student's preferred learning style (Coe *et al.*, 2014). Thomas and McDaniel's review of existing research actually found that, "tasks which facilitate the greatest memory benefits are those that force students to process information in multiple ways, creating several routes to that information, these tasks also seem to improve metacomprehension accuracy" (Thomas & McDaniel, 2007).

Table 1.1 Six basic characteristics of a Fertile Question (adapted from Harpaz, 2005)

1 Open	A question that does not have one definite answer but rather several different answers which may even contradict each other.
2 Undermining	A question that undermines the basic assumptions and fixed beliefs of learners. This may challenge common sense and lead to conflicts which lack simple solutions.
3 Rich	A question that requires grappling with rich content indispensable to understanding humanity and the world, that is impossible to answer without careful and lengthy research. This question may break up into sub questions.
4 Connected	A question relevant to the learner's lives, society and to the discipline and subject within which it was asked.
5 Charged	A question with an ethical and emotional charge able to motivate learning and inquiry.
6 Practical	A question that can be developed into a research question; a question about which information is available to students.

Having established several compelling reasons why we need Fertile Questions, we can now state what a Fertile Question is and how we can formulate a Fertile Question. For many years the focus has been on producing the "correct answer" however, this can lead to a culture of rote learning, where mistakes, errors and misconceptions are avoided and hidden by the learners rather than embraced by the teacher and corrected. A Fertile Question on the other hand has six attributes, as shown in Table 1.1:

A Fertile Question that fulfils these six criteria is evidently a more useful starting point for planning the Medium-term Plans and lesson plans because these questions encourage much deeper thinking about the roots of our subject. It is through these Fertile Questions that Harpaz believes we can begin to build "Communities of Thinking" (Harpaz, 2005). Knight and Benson state that it is through these Fertile Questions that we allow our students to demonstrate expert thinking and apply their knowledge to solve meaningful problems (Knight & Benson, 2014).

The matrix in Table 1.2 plots the 19 Fertile Questions from the five-year curriculum map (Figure 1.4) against Harpaz's six basic characteristics. The first thing that you will notice is that out of the 30 school terms, there are only 18 Fertile Questions. Following the principles of spacing outlined in the previous chapter, some Fertile Questions have been repeated. This also follows the model of an iterative spiral curriculum design promoted by Jerome Bruner (Bruner, 1960); as students revisit these fundamental Fertile Questions over the five years, their understanding will become deeper and they will become more invested in the question. The second thing worth noting is that developing a Fertile Question which meets all six of Harpaz's criteria is quite difficult. Very rarely does a question meet all six characteristics. However, where they do, the potency of the question is apparent. Where questions meet only one criterion, these have been rejected and revised to be more fertile (Table 1.3).

It is likely that Fertile Questions may change over the years. Harpaz states that whilst these questions may be formulated by the teacher initially, in advanced "Communities of Learning," the Fertile Questions will eventually be posed by the learners themselves. As the Fertile Question informs the Medium-term Plan, these questions can and should be referred to throughout the unit, in consolidation at the end of the unit and also in extending the capabilities of the high-attaining students in your class.

Table 1.2 Fertile Questions in computing

Fertile Question	Open	Undermining	Rich	Connected	Charged	Practical
How can we design the fastest computer system in the world?	✓			✓		✓
How can we accurately model the world using computer software?	✓	✓		✓		✓
How can we think more like a computer?	✓	✓	✓	✓	✓	✓
How can we produce robust programs which are effective and efficient?	✓			✓		✓
Can a computer be more intelligent than the human who programmed it?		✓	✓	✓	✓	✓
How can we write programs that never fail or crash?	✓	✓		✓		✓
Is there anything more important than a CPU inside a computer?	✓	✓				✓
To what extent is the online world more dangerous than the offline world?	✓	✓	✓	✓	✓	✓
How can we guarantee that your data (passwords, personal information and SnapChat photos) are not hacked when travelling across a network?	✓			✓	✓	✓
What types of problems are quicker to solve by writing a program and what types of problems are slower to solve?	✓	✓		✓		✓
Will the Internet slow down as it grows bigger and gets older?		✓		✓		✓
Have computers made the world better or worse?		✓	✓	✓	✓	✓
Which software is most important at an intelligence agency such as MI5?	✓			✓		✓
How do computers represent, store and process anything in 1's and 0's?	✓	✓				✓
How do media companies use computers to construct their products?	✓			✓		✓
How can we query a large data set using a programming language?	✓					✓
Is there anything we cannot represent using 0's and 1's?	✓	✓				✓
How does theoretical knowledge help us become better computer scientists?	✓			✓		✓

Table 1.3 Rejecting and re-writing Fertile Questions

Rejected Fertile Question	Revised Fertile Question
Are we ever safe online?	To what extent is the online world more dangerous than the offline world?
What is more important, hardware or software?	How can we write programs that never fail or crash?
How can we solve problems with programs?	What problems are quicker and easier to solve by writing a program?
What problems are quicker and easier to solve by writing a program?	What types of problems are quicker to solve by writing a program and what types of problems are slower to solve?

Chapter 1 summary

1 Computing consists of three strands: computer science, information technology and digital literacy. Although the term 'digital native' is frequently used to describe our students, it is a somewhat misleading label; computing does need explicit teaching and subject-specific pedagogy.

2 In order to design a successful curriculum, we must first understand what it means to be an expert in computing.

3 Cognitive psychology can greatly inform curriculum design. Many of the principles are counter-intuitive. However, extensive research tells us that for a curriculum to be successful it needs to be spaced, interleaved and include frequent practice testing.

4 The curriculum is best structured around problems to be solved. The best way to frame lessons are through carefully designed Fertile Questions.

Note

1 The model is somewhat simplified for the purposes of this chapter; Baddeley states that working memory can be broken down into four components (Baddeley, 2000).

References

Anderson, R. O., 2011. Brain, mind and the organization of knowledge for effective recall and application. *LEARNing Landscapes*, 5(1), pp. 45-61.
AQA, 2016. *AS and A-Level Computer Science Specifications*. Manchester, UK: AQA.
Atkinson, R. C. & Shiffrin, R., 1968. Human memory: a proposed system and its control processes. In: K. Spence & J. Spence, eds. *The Psychology of Learning and Motivation*. New York: Academic Press, pp. 89-195.
Baddeley, A. D., 2000. The episodic buffer: a new component of working memory? *Trends in Cognitive Science*, 4(11), pp. 417-23.
Baddeley, A. D. & Hitch, G., 1974. Working memory. *The Psychology of Learning and Motivation: Advances in Research and Theory*, 8. New York: Academic Press, pp. 47-9.
Bagge, P., 2014. *Computer Science Terminology for Primary Teachers*. [Online] Available at: http://code-it.co.uk/csvocab [Accessed 27 November 2014].

Bahrick, H. P. & Phelps, E., 1987. Retention of Spanish vocabulary over 8 years. *Journal of Experimental Psychology: Learning, Memory, and Cognition*, 13, pp. 344–9.

Bangert-Downs, R. L., Kulik, J. A. & Kulik, C.-L. C., 1991. Effects of frequent classroom testing. *The Journal of Educational Research*, 85(2), pp. 89–99.

Bjork, E. L. & Bjork, R., 2011. Making things hard on yourself, but in a good way: creating desirable difficulties to enhance learning. In: M. A. Gernsbacher, R. W. Pew & L. M. Hough, eds. *Psychology and the Real World: Essays Illustrating Fundamental Contributions to Society*. New York: Worth Publishers, pp. 55–64.

Bjork, R., 2014. *Applying Cognitive Psychology to Enhance Educational Practice*. [Online] Available at: http://bjorklab.psych.ucla.edu/research.html [Accessed 18 February 2014].

Bruner, J., 1960. *The Process of Education*. Cambridge, MA: Harvard University Press.

Carpenter, S. K., Cepeda, N. J., Rohrer, D., Kang, S. H. K. & Pashler H., 2012. Using spacing to enhance diverse forms of learning: review of recent research and implications for instruction. *Educational Psychology Review*, 24(3), pp. 369–78.

Cepeda, N. J., Rohrer, D. & Pashler, H., 2006. Distributed practice in verbal recall tasks: a review and quantitative synthesis. *Psychological Bulletin*, 132(3), pp. 354–80.

Code.org, 2014. *Unplugged Computational Thinking*. [Online] Available at: http://code.org/curriculum/course3/1/Teacher.pdf [Accessed 27 November 2014].

Coe, R., Aloisi, C., Higgins, S. & Major, L. E., 2014. *What Makes Great Teaching*, Durham: The Sutton Trust.

CSTA, 2011. *Operational Definition of Computational Thinking for K-12 Education*. [Online] Available at: https://csta.acm.org/Curriculum/sub/CurrFiles/CompThinkingFlyer.pdf [Accessed 2014 18 June].

Deans for Impact, 2015. *The Science of Learning*, Austin, TX: Deans for Impact.

Department for Education, 2013. *National Curriculum in England: Computing Programmes of Study*. [Online] Available at: https://www.gov.uk/government/publications/national-curriculum-in-england-computing-programmes-of-study [Accessed 26 July 2016].

Didau, D. & Rose, N., 2016. *What Every Teacher Needs to Know about Psychology*. 1st ed. Woodbridge: John Catt Educational Ltd.

Dorling, M. & Woodman, A., 2015. *Skills and Knowledge Audit Tool*. [Online] Available at: http://tools.quickstartcomputing.org/secondary/audit-tool/ [Accessed 1 April 2017].

Dunlosky, J., Rawson, K. A., Marsh, E. J., Nathan, M. J. & Willingham, D. T., 2013. Improving students' learning with effective learning techniques. *Psychological Science in the Public Interest*, 14(1), pp. 4–58.

Ebbinghaus, H., 1885. *Memory: A Contribution to Experimental Psychology* (Henry A. Ruger & Clara E. Bussenius, trans. 1913). New York: Teachers College, Columbia University.

Harpaz, Y., 2005. Teaching and learning in a community of thinking. *Journal of Curriculum and Supervision*, 20(2), pp. 136–57.

Kemp, P., 2014. *Computing in the National Curriculum - A Guide for Secondary Teachers*. 1st ed. s.l.:Computing at School.

Knight, O. & Benson, D., 2014. *Creating Outstanding Classrooms*. London: Routledge.

Leamnson, R., 2000. Learning as biological brain change. *Change*, November/December, pp. 34–40.

Learn That Foundation, 2005. *Wrong Answer*. [Online] Available at: https://www.learnthat.org/pages/view/wrong-answer.html [Accessed 29 October 2016].

Lloyd, S., 2015. *Subject Audit for Computing Teachers*. [Online] Available at: http://community.computingatschool.org.uk/resources/3250 [Accessed 27 July 2016].

Miller, G. A., 1956. The magical number seven, plus or minus two: some limits on our capacity for processing information. *The Psychological Review*, 63(2), pp. 81–97.

Nuthall, G., 2007. *The Hidden Lives of Learners*. Wellington: NZCER Press.

OCR, 2016. *A Level Computer Science Specification H446*. Cambridge: OCR.

Ofqual, 2011. *GCSE, GCE, Principal Learning and Project Code of Practice*. Coventry, UK: Ofqual.

Papert, S., 1980. *Mindstorms*. New York: Basic Books, Inc.

Pearson, 2017. *BTEC Nationals: Information Technology*. [Online] Available at: http://qualifications.pearson.com/en/qualifications/btec-nationals/information-technology-2016.html#tab-1 [Accessed 17 April 2017].

Perkins, D. N., 2009. *Making Learning Whole*. San Francisco: Jossey-Bass.

Selby, C. C. & Wollard, J., 2014. *Refining an Understanding of Computational Thinking*, Southampton: University of Southampton.

Sentance, S., Waite, J., Bragg, T. & Rickus, N., 2017. *Secondary Master Teacher Subject Knowledge Audit*, London: CAS London CRC.

The Learning Machine (TLM), 2016. *Computing Qualifications*. [Online] Available at: https://theingots.org/community/Computing_qualification_info_units [Accessed 27 July 2016].

The Royal Society, 2012. *Shut Down or Restart? The Way Forward for Computing in UK Schools*. London: The Royal Society.

Thomas, A. K. & McDaniel, M. A., 2007. Metacomprehension for educationally relevant materials: dramatic effects of encoding-retrieval interactions. *Psychonomic Bulletin and Review*, 14(2), pp. 212–18.

White, D., 2016. *Computer Science Pedagogy*. [Online] Available at: http://ispython.com/computer-science-pedagogy/ [Accessed 27 March 2016].

Whitehead, A. N., 1922. *The Rhythm of Education*. London, Training College Association.

Willingham, D., 2013. *Better Studying = Less Studying. Wait, What?* [Online] Available at: http://www.danielwillingham.com/daniel-willingham-science-and-education-blog/better-studying-less-studying-wait-what [Accessed 31 July 2016].

Willingham, D. T., 2009. *Why Don't Students Like School?* San Francisco: Jossey-Bass.

Wing, J. M., 2006. Computational thinking. *Communications of the ACM*, 49(3), pp. 33–5.

Wing, J. M., 2008. *Computational Thinking: Two and a Half Years Later*. [Online] Available at: http://www.cs.cmu.edu/~CompThink/seminars/wing/index.html [Accessed 21 March 2016].

Zagami, J., 2013. *Computational Thinking*. Brisbane, QLD: EduTechPress.

2 Medium-term planning

From our curriculum maps and Fertile Questions, we can then start to build a Medium-Term Plan which in turn will inform our lesson plans. Knight and Benson advise planning backwards from a unit's end outcomes (Knight & Benson, 2014). If we know what students need to know and to be able to do at the end of the unit, we can form a series of assessment objectives for that four- to six-week unit of work. Example outcome statements from a Year 8 unit on networks might be:

- I can explain the different types and topologies of networks.
- I can explain the key differences between a wired and wireless network technologies.
- I can explain how the Internet works.

Based on these three assessment objectives, we can plan more granular statements which must be met in order for a student to be deemed to have mastered this objective from the unit of work. These granular statements will naturally vary in complexity based on a student's stage of mastery for each overarching assessment objective.

At Greenwich Free School, Corinne Flett structured her Medium-Term Plans in science as a sequence of lessons going from surface-level knowledge to deep learning. We would expect most students to start a unit of work in the first stage of mastery which equates to 0-25 per cent of the objective being mastered.[1] The first few lessons should start by assessing and building on what students already know. Cognitive psychology tells us that students learn by referencing and building on what they already know (Wiliam, 2011; Deans for Impact, 2015; Didau & Rose, 2016). If students have no frame of reference, they will not be able to access the unit. Once we know what our student's existing knowledge and reference points are, we can start to plan the lesson activities which will enable them to build on their prior knowledge, skills and understanding.

A student may start in stage 1 at the emerging stage of mastery with the ability to name some network devices they are familiar with from home or school, for example a modem, router, hub and Wi-Fi adapter. In stage 2, students will be able to state the differences between a LAN and a WAN as their knowledge and understanding reaches the developing stage. In stage 3, student's knowledge and understanding is secure and they can explain the factors affecting the performance of a network; and finally in stage 4, students will be able to explain the roles of routers, switches, servers and NICs in a network. A more detailed Medium-Term Plan which demonstrates this is shown in Figure 2.1.

Each lesson takes the students on a journey through the Fertile Question towards mastery. Knight and Benson note that it is worth having a lesson question, so that each lesson's content is transformed into a series of problems to be solved (Knight & Benson, 2014).[2] Each lesson and its associated learning activities should encourage students to think like experts and eventually lead us to our end point of the unit which is addressing the Fertile Question through a final *performance of understanding*.

Summative assessment: performance of understanding

The concept of a performance of understanding was introduced by David Perkins and Tina Blythe to underline the importance of understanding in the learning process; as a teaching perspective it takes us beyond the recalling of knowledge and routine skill (Perkins & Blythe, 1994). A performance of understanding can be differentiated from other formative and summative assessments in that the performance can take any form as long as the activity demonstrates the student's current understanding by producing compelling evidence of where that student is in relation to the learning objective(s) for the unit. The performance should deepen the student's understanding by addressing the Fertile Question (Moss & Brookhart, 2012). In computing, a performance of understanding might take the form of a program with comments, a piece of extended writing or a series of relevant exam questions. The following selection of Medium-Term Plans for computing (Figures 2.1-2.5) is based on a template developed by Corinne Flett (Head of Science at Greenwich Free School) following the work of Oliver Knight (Knight & Benson, 2014). The selection includes one Medium-Term Plan from each year group – a full set of editable Medium-Term Plans are available in the eResources which accompany this book.

The Medium-Term Plans at Key Stage 4 (most notably the programming ones) build upon a Key Stage 3 predecessor. Comparing a Year 7 programming Medium-Term Plan with a Year 11 one, the use of spacing in the curriculum design will become apparent. The iterative nature of the curriculum is also evident; the same concepts are revisited at greater depth with additional content and concepts added to students' existing knowledge and understanding. Should any teacher or student walk into your lesson, they should be able to locate themselves within the Medium-Term Plan and therefore identify what comes next in the sequence of learning.

The system established at Greenwich Free School uses assessment objectives to calculate a percentage of mastery; each assessment objective (which is derived from the national curriculum and exam board specifications) can be split into four stages, where stage 1 is a novice with an emerging level of understanding and stage 4 is an expert who has achieved mastery of the objective. By assessing to what extent each student has achieved each assessment objective, a student is placed in a stage of mastery from 1 to 4. This can be used to calculate an overall percentage of mastery for each unit. Each unit's percentage can be compared and a running mean can also be calculated at any point in the year. In formulating predicted grades, we can then simply match the percentages from these units to the grade boundaries for any terminal examination.

GFS Computing Medium Term Plan

Subject: Computing

Unit title: Computer Systems

Fertile question: How can we design the fastest computer system in the world?

Notes

Class: 7

Levels:

Context of this lesson:

Before this lesson:

Next lesson:

I can explain the basic systems architecture in Von Neumann Architecture

Stage 1 Emerging 0–25% mastery	Stage 2 Developing 26–50% mastery	Stage 3 Secure 51–75% mastery	Stage 4 Mastered 76–100% mastery
1A – I can name different hardware devices 1B – I can recall the term input or output device 1C – I can recall the term storage device 1D – I can recall the names of different software	2A – I understand the terms hardware and software 2B – I understand what the difference between an input and output device is 2C – I can recall one storage device 2D – I can recall a variety of input and output devices	3A – I can define a computer system 3B – I can describe the purpose of RAM in a computer system 3C – I can explain the need for secondary storage 3D – I can state the purpose of the CPU as the processor of data and information	4A – I can explain how a variety of computer systems work using Von Neumann Architecture keywords 4B – I can explain how the amount of RAM in a personal computer affects the performance of the computer 4C – I can explain the need for virtual memory 4D – I can explain why data is represented in computer systems in binary form

Figure 2.1 Medium-Term Plan for Year 7 – computer systems.

GFS Computing Medium -Term Plan

Subject: Computing
Unit title: Networks
Fertile question: Will the Internet slow down as it grows bigger and gets older?

Notes

Class: 8
Levels:
Context of this lesson:
Before this lesson:
Next lesson:

Stage 1 Emerging 0–25% mastery	Stage 2 Developing 26–50% mastery	Stage 3 Secure 51–75% mastery	Stage 4 Mastered 76–100% mastery
I can explain the different types and topologies of networks			
1A – I can name some network devices	2A – I can explain the difference between a LAN and a WAN 2B – I can state the hardware needed to connect stand–alone computers into a Local Area Network 2C – I can state some factors that affect the performance of networks 2D – I can identify a star and mesh topology	3A – I can explain the factors that affect the performance of networks 3B – I can explain the pros and cons of a star and mesh topology 3C – I can explain the pros and cons of different transmission media	4A – I can explain the roles of servers, routers, switches, WAPs and NICs
I can explain the key differences between a wired and wireless network technologies			
1C – I can name some devices needed to create a wireless network	2E – I can explain how WiFi works and the devices necessary for wireless signals	3D – I can explain the need for encryption across a network 3E – I can explain the need for different Wifi frequencies and channels	4B – I can explain how the different wireless encryption methods work
I can explain how the Internet works			
1D – I can name some devices on the Internet	2F – I can state that the internet is a worldwide collection of computer networks	3F – I can explain the roles of the different hardware devices on the Internet: Modems, Routers, DNS Servers, Web Servers	4C – I can explain DNS 4D – I can explain how web hosting works 4E – I can explain what Cloud Computing is and how it has affected individuals and organisations.

Figure 2.2 Medium-Term Plan for Year 8 – networks.

GFS Computing Medium-Term Plan

Subject: Computing
Unit title: Intro to Spreadsheets
Fertile question: Can we accurately model the world using software?

Notes
Class: 9
Levels:
Context of this lesson:
Before this lesson:
Next lesson:

Stage 1 **Emerging** 0–25% mastery	**Stage 2** **Developing** 26–50% mastery	**Stage 3** **Secure** 51–75% mastery	**Stage 4** **Mastered** 76–100% mastery

I can use a range of forumla and functions to model a real–world problem

Stage 1	Stage 2	Stage 3	Stage 4
1A – I remember to start all formula with an equals sign	2A – I can use grid references in my formula	3A – I can use Goal Seek to find a target value	4A – I can use 3D references across multiple sheets
1B – I can use arithmetic symbols to perform calculations	2B – I can use conditional formatting to highlight values	3B – I can use IF Statements to produce conditional outputs	4B – I can use a range of advanced formula such as COUNTIF, VLOOKUP
1C – I can use auto functions such as AutoSum	2C – I choose appropriate formatting, e.g. currencies, data formats	3C – I can use Validation to limit values on cells	

I can use spreadsheet tools to format data and predict data trends

Stage 1	Stage 2	Stage 3	Stage 4
1D – I can create a chart to visualise data	2D – I can choose an appropriate chart for continuous or discrete data	3D – I can plot complex charts with secondary axis such as climate charts	4D – I can interpret data and provide a detailed analysis from my model
1E – I can label my chart to provide meaning and context	2E – I can format my spreadsheet so that it is appropriate for audience and purpose	3E – I can add trendlines to predict trends	4E – I can create a menu system using Macros

Figure 2.3 Medium-Term Plan for Year 9 – spreadsheets.

GFS Computing Medium-Term Plan

Subject: Computer Science
Unit title: Algorithms/Programming Techniques
Fertile question: How can we think more like a computer?

Notes_

Class: 10
Levels:
Context of this lesson:
Before this lesson:
Next lesson:

Stage 1 Emerging 0–25% mastery	Stage 2 Developing 26–50% mastery	Stage 3 Secure 51–75% mastery	Stage 4 Mastered 76–100% mastery
I can understand a range of algorithms			
1A – I can decompose some of the tasks into their component parts 1B – I can name some searching or sorting algorithms	2A – I can decompose a problem into clearly defined component parts 2B – I can explain how different searching and sorting algorithms work 2C – I can interpret an algorithm in flowchart or pseudocode form	3A – I can correct or complete partially completed algorithms in flowchart and pseudocode form 3B – I can design detailed algorithms in both flowchart and pseudocode form to represent the solution to a problem	4A – I can explain which algorithms are more efficient for a given data set
I can create programs using a range of techniques			
1C – I can use three basic programming constructs to control the flow of a program: Sequence, Selection and Iteration and comment on these accordingly 1D – I can use basic string manipulation including concatenation, casting, formatting.	2D – I can identify different data structures including arrays, 2D arrays and dictionaries 2E – I can identify different data types (int, real, Boolean, character and string)	3C – I can use basic file handling to store and retrieve data 3D – I can use a variety of data structures when solving problems including arrays, 2D arrays and dictionaries 3E – I can choose the correct data type for a given problem 3F – I can use arithmetic and boolean operators appropriately to solve a problem	4B – I can create efficient and elegant programs using functions, sub programs (procedures) and other programming techniques to create structured, re-usable code 4C – I can combine different data types confidently (int, real, Boolean, character and string) 4D – I can use file handling to append and search for data

Figure 2.4 Medium-Term Plan for Year 10 – algorithms/programming techniques.

GFS Computing Medium-Term Plan

Subject: Computer Science
Unit title: Programming
Fertile question: How can we think more like a computer?

Notes

Class: 11
Levels:
Context of this lesson:
Before this lesson:
Next lesson:

I can demonstrate a range of programming techniques

Stage 1 Emerging 0–25% mastery	Stage 2 Developing 26–50% mastery	Stage 3 Secure 51–75% mastery	Stage 4 Mastered 76–100% mastery
1A – I can identify and use variables, operators, inputs, outputs and assignments	2A – I can use basic string manipulation	3A – I can use suitable loops including count and condition controlled loops when appropriate	4A – I can create efficient and elegant programs using functions, sub programs (procedures) and other programming techniques to create structured, re-usable code
1B – I have attempted to program a solution to solve component parts of the task using few of the techniques identified	2B – I can comment and explain how my code works	3B – I can use different types of data, including Boolean, string, integer and real appropriately in solutions to problems	4B – I can import modules and libraries and use these appropriately to solve a given problem
1C – Code may be minimal, disorganised or hard to follow	2C – I have attempted to program a solution to most component parts of the task using several techniques	3C – I can use basic file handling operations	4C – I can develop a program which handles exceptions and errors including both invalid and erroneous data
1D – Component parts of the task may be trivial, incomplete, or not attempted	2D – A good range of techniques are used appropriately, giving a working solution to most component parts of the task	3D – I can define and use arrays (or equivalent) as appropriate when solving problems	4D – There is an attempt to program solution to solve all of the task using most of the techniques listed
	2E – Some sections of the solution may be inefficiently coded, although basic functionality is mostly successful	3E – I can create an effective program that does not have any syntax or logical errors when it is run	4E – The task is clearly broken down into its component parts, with reasons given, and there is a clear correspondence of the design with the final code
	The task is mostly complete, but it may be limited in its scope	3F – The task is clearly broken into its component parts and there are links to the design	

Figure 2.5 Medium-Term Plan for Year 11 – programming.

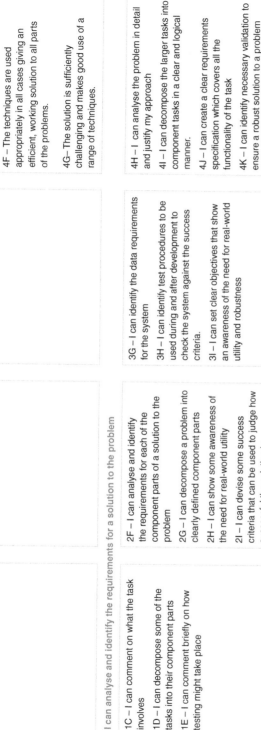

I can analyse and identify the requirements for a solution to the problem

1C – I can comment on what the task involves

1D – I can decompose some of the tasks into their component parts

1E – I can comment briefly on how testing might take place

1F – I can plan solutions to some of the component parts of the task

1G – I can create a limited outline describing the intended approach to some parts of the task

1H – I can create a brief outline of a solution

I can design algorithms and choose suitable data types and data structures

2F – I can analyse and identify the requirements for each of the component parts of a solution to the problem

2G – I can decompose a problem into clearly defined component parts

2H – I can show some awareness of the need for real-world utility

2I – I can devise some success criteria that can be used to judge how successful the solution is.

2J – I can create a flowchart or pseudocode to partially solve a problem

2K – I can design the user interface including suitable input and output formats and navigation methods for the system

2L – I can discuss how testing will take place

3G – I can identify the data requirements for the system

3H – I can identify test procedures to be used during and after development to check the system against the success criteria.

3I – I can set clear objectives that show an awareness of the need for real-world utility and robustness

3J – I can design detailed algorithms in both flowchart and pseudocode form to represent the solution to a problem

3K – I can identify suitable variables and other data structures

3L – I can use appropriate data types in the system

3M – I can create a test plan with some test data

4F – The techniques are used appropriately in all cases giving an efficient, working solution to all parts of the problems.

4G– The solution is sufficiently challenging and makes good use of a range of techniques.

4H – I can analyse the problem in detail and justify my approach

4I – I can decompose the larger tasks into component tasks in a clear and logical manner.

4J – I can create a clear requirements specification which covers all the functionality of the task

4K – I can identify necessary validation to ensure a robust solution to a problem

4L – I can describe appropriate validation for the system to ensure the input is sanitised

4M – I anticipate misuse and design my solution defensively with planned destructive testing to prevent errors and ensure the solution is robust

4N – I can give reasoning for the design of my user interface

4O – I can recognise patterns and plan functions/sub programmes to produce structured, reusable, modular code

4P – I can produce a detailed test plan and testing strategy which includes valid, invalid, boundary (extreme) and erroneous data.

Figure 2.5 Continued

1I – I can show that the solution works using evidence H	2M – I can choose sensible variable names	3N – Testing shows that the solution works
	2N – I can explain the solution using suitable annotation, comments and evidence of development	3O – There is record of the resources used
	2O – I can show an understanding of the relevant information by presenting evidence of the development of the solutions	3P – I can show an understanding of the technical terminology/concepts that arise from the investigation through analysis of the data collected
	2P – I can demonstrate testing and refinement of the code during development.	3Q – I can use the terminology/concepts surrounding the topic and contained in the information collected correctly when it comes to producing analysis in the supporting script

4Q – I can use the terminology/concepts surrounding the topic and contained in the information collected fluently when it comes to producing analysis in the supporting script
4R – I can show detailed evidence of development
4S – I can show detailed evidence of systematic testing and refinement showing that all parts of the code work as required
4T – I can organise my code well and provide detailed comments and annotation to explain the function of the code
4U – I can produce a detailed record of resources used and I can present my report in a coherent and structured format. All information is relevant and substantiated

1J – I can produce a report covering some aspects of the investigation	2Q – I can produce a full report covering all aspects of the investigation	3R – I can state the pros of the solution and the evidence that I have presented
1K – I can provide evidence to show that post-development testing has taken place	2R – I can present the information in a clear form which is understandable by a third party and which is easily navigable using a Table of Contents, Headings and page numbering	3S – I can complete testing with a test plan which covers all major success criteria. This evidence is detailed and shows remedial action where necessary
	2S – I can show some evidence of testing many parts of my solution using my test plan and test data	3T – I can use some specialist terms in my written report
	2T – I can provide evidence to show how the results of testing have been compared to the original creiteria	3U – I can present a conclusion to the report
	2U – I can present my evaluation in a relevant, clear, organised, structured and coherent format	

4V – I can perform destructive testing to deliberately try to uncover errors and improve the robustness of the program
4W– I can critically appraise the evidence and how this relates to the success criteria.
4X – I can highlight unresolved issues and suggest future improvements to my program
4Y –I can use specialist terms correctly and appropriately when evaluating the solution against all the success criteria
4Z – I can justify my conclusions based on the evidence provided

Subject: Computer Science

UPN	Name	Tags	FFTD 20 Target	% Mastery Target	% Mastery (The figure in this column is the figure to enter into SIMS)	Progress Indicator	I can explain how the CPU works	I can understand and use logic diagrams, truth tables and logical operators to solve problems	I can explain the different types and topologies of networks	I can explain the key differences between a wired and wireless network technologies	I can explain how the Internet works
							Autumn 1		Autumn 2		
							56.91489	60.48387	71.42857	71.42857	67.85714
W203XXXXXXX	Student 1	EAL	5+	64	70.0	Above	2	3	3	3	3
F2032XXXXXXX	Student 2	PPG SEN Support	6	70	80.0	Significantly Above	3	2	3	4	4
E2032XXXXXXX	Student 3	EAL	8	88	85.0	On	4	4	3	3	3
N203XXXXXXX	Student 4	PPG	4	52	55.0	On	2	3	2	2	2
Q209XXXXXXX	Student 5	PPG	6-	67	60.0	Below	2	2	3	3	2
P203XXXXXXX	Student 6	PPG	6	70	75.0	Above	2	3	4	3	3
V203XXXXXXX	Student 7	PPG	5+	64	45.0	Significantly Below	1	2	2	2	2

Figure 2.6 Example progress tracker for Year 8 computer science (developed by Alec Chapman, data manager at Greenwich Free School).

'In this example tracker, Student 1 has been assessed across five objectives. As there are four stages of mastery, the maximum score is four for each objective. Given that there are five objectives, the student can score a maximum score of 20 across the five objectives. This student has scored 14 out of 20, which gives 70 per cent. Their mastery target percentage is based on an FFTD 20 Target of 5+ (In GCSE grades one through nine). The percentage for a 5+ has been set at 64 per cent based on historical data. This student is therefore "above" the expected level of progress.

Mastery percentages are more valid than the abolished national curriculum levels as this system based on mastery percentage allows students and teachers to track their progress in granular detail on student progress trackers. It allows for easy comparison between units and is an objective measure based on what a student understands and what the student can or cannot do. National curriculum levels were fraught with problems; a student's target was often simply a sub-level higher than their previous national curriculum level. National curriculum levels also lacked detail and granularity, nobody knew what a level 4C was or meant, it wasn't consistent within schools and certainly wasn't consistent across schools. A target level which is simply a sub-level higher than a student's prior level ignores the fact that learning is not linear and that students may be better at some units than others.

A system based on mastery percentages is less open to manipulation; it accepts that all students are at different stages of mastery for different units and it allows teachers and leaders to set more meaningful and realistic targets for their students. These personalised targets ensure students feel a sense of achievement when they are on or above their expected target; it encourages a growth mindset as opposed to a fixed mindset which simply focuses on which students get the highest national curriculum levels. Finally, as students can see exactly what stage of mastery they achieved for each assessment objective, it is clear what they need to do next in order to improve their mastery of a given objective and unit.

An example progress tracker developed by Alec Chapman (data manager at Greenwich Free School) is included above in Figure 2.6 to show how mastery stages are converted into percentages.

Baseline tests

We can define learning as a relatively permanent change in thinking, knowledge and skills (Atkinson *et al.*, 1993). However, in order to establish whether learning has actually occurred, baseline tests that establish what students already know are essential (Nuthall, 2007). Ausubel and Atherton go as far as stating that the most important determinant of learning is what the learner already knows (Ausubel, 1968; Atherton, 2013). Baseline tests are useful in computing because Key Stage 2 data from primary schools often does not indicate how much of the primary computing curriculum has been covered.

There are several computing baseline tests available, the most popular being TLM's free computing baseline test at www.theingots.org, which has been taken by over 170,000 pupils. Whilst an external baseline offers automated marking, objectivity and a large sample size, if you design your own internal baseline, the granularity of results mean that you can use these results to build progress trackers and develop differentiated activities and sequences of lessons. A time-saving option for Years 8-11 would be to simply use an end-of-year exam as a baseline for the next year. However, it is advised to have these end-of-year exams externally moderated by a partner school to ensure that the tests are robust, representative of the national curriculum and accurately marked.

Whilst some students may respond negatively to the concept of testing, I have found it useful to let students know that all tests (that are not terminal exams) are essentially the same as an eye test. One of the main reasons for taking an eye test is to diagnose any possible problems with a person's vision and to administer a correcting prescription. Unlike (say) a driving test, it is not possible to pass or fail an eye test, it is purely diagnostic and aims to help you see clearly. This analogy can be applied to all end-of-unit (and baseline) tests in education; they are there to help the teacher to identify misconceptions and areas of weakness so that he or she can help students "see" and understand the subject better. Once students understand the rationale for tests, you will often find them less anxious, less motivated to cheat and the tests will usually be more reflective of a student's understanding and learning.

Chapter 2 summary

1   The starting point for a Medium-Term Plan should be the end point for the unit of work. What should students understand and be able to do at the end of the unit? From this point, you can plan backwards and create assessment objectives.

2   In order to assess the extent to which an assessment objective has been met, it is useful to devise granular statements, stating exactly what a student should know and be able to do at each stage of mastery.

3   The Medium-Term Plan allows you to address a Fertile Question through a sequence of lessons which build progressively.

4   Students should be taught how to use the Medium-Term Plan to locate themselves within the unit of work. They should be able to assess their current level of mastery and therefore what they need to do or learn next in order to improve their level of mastery.

5   A mastery percentage can be calculated for each unit and a target percentage can also be set to motivate students.

Notes

1   A mastery percentage for a unit is a much more accurate and robust method than the abolished national curriculum levels which existed up until 2015.

2   Lesson questions are covered in detail in Chapter 3.

References

Atherton, J. S., 2013. *Learning and Teaching*. [Online] Available at: http://www. learningandteaching.info/teaching/advance_organisers.htm [Accessed 18 February 2016].

Atkinson, R. L., Atkinson, R. C. & Smith, E. E. B. D. J., 1993. *Introduction to Psychology*. 11th ed. Fort Worth, TX: Harcourt Brace Jovanovich.

Ausubel, D. P., 1968. *Educational Psychology: A Cognitive View*. New York and Toronto: Holt, Rinehart and Winston.

Deans for Impact, 2015. *The Science of Learning*. Austin, TX: Deans for Impact.

Didau, D. & Rose, N., 2016. *What Every Teacher Needs to Know About Psychology*. 1st ed. Woodbridge: John Catt Educational Ltd.

Knight, O. & Benson, D., 2014. *Creating Outstanding Classrooms*. London: Routledge.

Moss, C. M. & Brookhart, S. M., 2012. *Learning Targets: Helping Students Aim for Understanding in Today's Lesson*. Alexandria, VA: ASCD.

Nuthall, G., 2007. *The Hidden Lives of Learners.* Wellington: NZCER Press.

Perkins, D. & Blythe, T., 1994. Putting understanding up front. *Educational Leadership*, 51(5), pp. 4-7.

Wiliam, D., 2011. *Embedded Formative Assessment.* Bloomington, IN: Solution Tree Press.

3 Lesson planning

Lessons do not sit in isolation and expert teachers focus on sequences of learning rather than individual elements. This sequence of lessons is informed by the curriculum and medium-term planning that was covered in the previous chapter. However, practically speaking teachers are still faced with the challenge of subdividing a unit of work into individual lessons. This chapter covers some research-based strategies that all teachers should know about and adopt. The first strategy worth considering is the lesson question.

The lesson question

The content and learning activities that we set are not perceived as important and relevant purely because they exist in the national curriculum; lessons are perceived as important when they relate to the lives of our students. Nuthall recommends that lessons and activities need to focus on solving a major question or problem that is significant in the discipline and in the lives and culture of the students (Nuthall, 2007). Note that this does not mean designing all your resources around your local football team or latest pop-music sensation (Hattie and Donoghue, 2016). Willingham advises that when we try to make activities based on a student's direct interests this is likely to lead to distraction and irrelevant cognitive load (Willingham, 2009). Hattie and Donoghue support the notion of ensuring that content and outcomes have inherent value. In their research citing 28 meta-analyses from 1,304 studies into a student's *will* or desire to learn, the perceived value of a task was ranked second highest after student's self-efficacy. Clearly students need to value what they are being presented with and they need to be nurtured to encourage them to believe that they can complete the lesson tasks.

We know that learning is not simply the filling of a pail or the recalling of facts. Ultimately, we wish for students to understand the meaning of the information that they are learning so they can apply it in new scenarios. In order to derive meaning, the tasks should require explanation and elaboration. Linked to the Fertile Question should therefore be a lesson question that provides a clearly defined context and encourages higher-order thinking. By having a clearly defined context, we reduce demand on working memory. To enhance engagement, the question could be episodic and address a current social issue, news event, video or scientific finding (Anderson, 2011). The lesson question should encourage students to ask referential questions demanding students to explain "why" and "how" something works rather than simply "what", "where" or "when" questions which rely on recall (Deans for Impact, 2015).

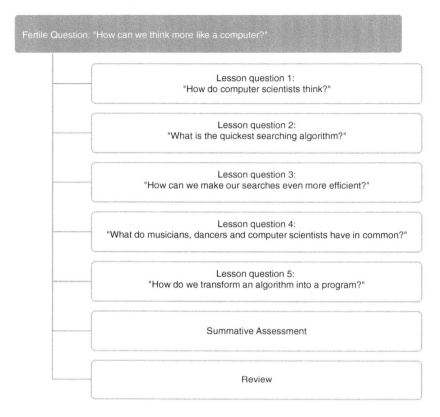

Figure 3.1 The lesson questions are informed by the Fertile Question in the MTP.

It is these referential questions which provide students with an inherent value for the lesson. By addressing the lesson question, students are encouraged to think more deeply and give their opinion or explain their reasoning thereby demonstrating their current level of understanding.

Some lesson questions can be pre-planned based on the previous lesson and the current Fertile Question. However, other lesson questions will occur organically; a student might ask, "If we are trying to design a faster mobile phone and we know that RAM makes computer systems faster, why can't phones have 128GB of RAM in the same way that a desktop might have?" This is a truly engaging lesson question and one that might not have been pre-planned based on the Medium-Term Plan. However, it is certainly worth investigating further so the following lesson's activities could ask students to compare mobile phone architecture and memory management with the typical architecture and memory management in a desktop computer.

One final technique is to encourage students to link their answer(s) to the lesson question back to the Fertile Question. Linking back to the Fertile Question enables them to see how this individual lesson is a small part of the big picture. Anderson argues that by revisiting a contextual theme, we provide a road map of where we are going and where we are now (Anderson, 2011). Fertile Questions can be expressed as a visual map such as a mind map or network diagram of ideas. This encourages the interconnected thinking that is required in Hattie and Donoghue's deep learning phase. Anderson proposes that these multi-modal representations (verbal, visual, psychomotor) also serve to help students organise information, reduce cognitive load further and enable multimode encoding in memory; all of these combined help to improve recall.

Table 3.1 on page 57 applies the aforementioned concepts to form some example lesson questions. These lesson questions are based on the Fertile Question and the complexity of the question is informed by the formative and summative assessment data on the students' current stages of mastery.

Applying cognitive psychology to lesson planning

In 2009, Hattie published *Visible Learning*, a book based on over 800 meta-studies which explored the effect of over 100 teaching strategies and "influences". By 2015, he had ranked the 195 effects to determine which "influences" had the greatest positive or negative effects. As an update to his books, Hattie released a review article in 2016 with Gregory Donoghue which argued that learning is the process of moving through three different phases from a surface learning phase to a deep learning phase and ending with a phase of transfer (Hattie & Donoghue, 2016). The paper reviewed 228 meta-analyses containing 18,956 studies and found that different teaching strategies were best suited at different phases of learning. For example, "exploring errors and misconceptions" in the surface learning phase is likely to have a moderately negative impact on learning. Yet the research showed that the same technique has a positive impact on learning in the transfer phase. Table 3.2 outlines ten effective teaching strategies for each of the different phases of learning.

Hattie and Donoghue advise that these strategies should not be used discretely on a lesson-by-lesson basis but that these strategies should be combined and embedded in worthwhile content. This can be justified in learning binary representation of numbers. A student may start with surface learning through the review of base ten denary numbers before using *rehearsal* to practice various conversions from binary to denary. In the same lesson, the student may *self-question* "Why is binary used instead of denary?" The student may also question if it is possible to represent any number in binary, for example decimals and numbers exceeding 255. Towards the end of the lesson, the teacher might explore *new contexts* in which that binary can be used, for example how the same binary string might be used to represent not only a number but also a character using the American Standard Code for Information Exchange (ASCII) character set or a picture using a grid. This method of thinking and reflecting applies to all topics; as a student explores new content and contexts they are likely to make links to existing content. In order to make the content meaningful, it is useful to engage in a discussion about the application of this content to new scenarios.

It is worth noting that *pausing to detect similarities and differences* for the transfer of skills in new domains and *understanding patterns* have a striking parallel to "pattern recognition" as outlined in relation to computational thinking in Chapter 1. The key difference here is that computational thinking focusses on the similarities whereas Hattie emphasises the importance of recognising differences too. This makes sense, when a student encounters a different computational problem, they may believe they can use previous data structures and

Table 3.1 Computing lesson questions matched to Fertile Questions

Fertile Question	Example Lesson Questions
How can we design the fastest computer system in the world?	1. Why does my phone get hot when it has been running for a long time? Why does cooling my computer speed it up? 2. Why does my phone and tablet boot up in seconds, yet my desktop takes up to a minute? 3. Why are Apple computers more expensive than PC's with equivalent hardware? 4. Why did Intel and AMD stop increasing their CPU clock speeds and started to build CPUs with more cores instead? 5. Why does magnetic and optical storage still exist if solid state drives are so much quicker?
How can we accurately model the world using computer software?	1. How can scientists use spreadsheets to complete their experiments? 2. How are computers used to forecast the weather? 3. Are there any office-based jobs which do not require the use of a spreadsheet? 4. How can a business use spreadsheets to increase its profits?
How can we think more like a computer?	1. How do algorithms shape the way we live? 2. How can we make our programs more intelligent? 3. Is it better for computers to think more like humans or for humans to think more like computers? 4. How might we apply computational thinking to problems outside of computer science? 5. How can we design the fastest searching algorithm for a given data set? 6. When should we write a procedure or a function?
How can we produce robust programs which are effective and efficient?	1. Which types of problems can computers solve quicker than humans? 2. What are the best practices of expert programmers? 3. How can we make fewer errors when programming? 4. Why do we need machine languages? 5. How does a computer understand a high level language like Python?
Can a computer be more intelligent than the human who programmed it?	1. How can we make our computer do what we want? 2. How can we make our programs appear to be intelligent? 3. How can we make our own game using Python? 4. To what extent can a computer think? 5. How can we make our programs more efficient?
How can we write programs that never fail or crash?	1. How can we plan our programs to reduce the chance of errors and crashes? 2. How can we handle any user input sensibly? 3. Does letter-case matter? 4. How can we save time by re-using code?

Table 3.1 Continued

Is there anything more important than a CPU inside a Computer?	1. How does a CPU process instructions? 2. How do we decide which is the best CPU architecture? 3. How many computers do I have at home? 4. Why do we need so many different types of memory? 5. Will Solid State Drives replace all other types of storage?
To what extent is the online world more dangerous than the offline world?	1. How can I make my password more secure? 2. What threats exist online? 3. Why do people behave differently online? 4. What do I need to know about Sexting and the law? 5. What data and information is on my digital footprint?
How can we guarantee that your data (passwords, personal information and snapchat photos) are not hacked when travelling across a network?	1. How do computers communicate with each other? 2. Why is my Internet connection so slow?! 3. What do all the devices on the Internet do? 4. How has Cloud Computing changed the world? 5. How safe is WIFI? 6. How do data packets know where to go? 7. What are the different threats posed to networks? 8. How can I ensure that my data is secure?
What types of problems are quicker to solve by writing a program and what types of problems are slower to solve?	1. How can we use a program to solve a mathematical problem? 2. Can a computer generate a truly random set of numbers? 3. How can we use random numbers to build computer games? 4. What are the alternative data structures to variables and when should we use them?
Will the Internet slow down as it grows bigger and gets older?	1. Why do most companies use a network of computers? 2. What is the best topology for a given business's network? 3. How am I able to access all my files from any school computer? 4. What is the difference between the Internet and the school network? 5. When I am on the Internet at the same time as my mum, is there any chance that my webpages will go to my mum's tablet and her webpages appear on my laptop? Can the webpages we request get muddled up? 6. How does the Internet deal with Skype, Email, the WWW and online game traffic differently? 7. How does Wifi work? 8. How has Cloud Computing changed the world? 9. How can the same webpage look different on a desktop, a tablet and a phone? 10. How can I edit any webpage on the WWW?

Continued

Table 3.1 Continued

Have computers made the world better or worse?	1. Who was right in the privacy case between Apple and the FBI? 2. What are the negative environmental impacts of technology companies and how are companies like Intel reducing their environmental impact 3. Why is Wikileaks so controversial? 4. How have computers been used by armed forces and terrorists? 5. How does technology affect cognitive development? 6. Following lawsuits from Apple, Microsoft and Samsung, can original ideas still exist in computing? 7. What is the best thing to do with old pieces of technology? 8. Will Computers create more jobs or make more people unemployed? 9. How can Computers help people with specific needs? 10. How is technology used to produce music? 11. How do social media companies use your data?
Which software is most important at an intelligence agency such as MI5?	1. What are the different purposes of systems software? 2. Are all operating systems essentially the same? 3. How do utility system software increase performance? 4. Will Open Source software overtake proprietary software in the next ten years? 5. Computing legislation-What are the implications of breaking the law?
How do computers represent, store and process anything in 1's and 0's?	1. How can we represent any number using just 0s and 1s? 2. How can we represent any word using just 0s and 1s? 3. How do computers deal with different languages e.g. English, Chinese and Russian? 4. How can we represent any image using just 0s and 1s? 5. Why do we not use binary to represent colours on the web?
How do media companies use Computers to construct their products?	1. How can I make a memorable logo? 2. To what extent are images in magazines edited? 3. Why do all fashion magazines follow a similar layout?
How can we query a large data set using a programming language?	1. How do banks store details of all their customers? 2. How can we quickly find a single record amongst millions? 3. How can we be more specific in our searching?
Is there anything we cannot represent using 0's and 1's?	1. How can the same binary string represent either a number, letter or image? 2. How can we represent sounds using 1s and 0s? 3. Why do DJs still use Vinyl LPs and CDs?

Table 3.2 Ten strategies for effective learning (adapted from Hattie & Donoghue, 2016)

	Surface learning (Encoding content and underlying skills for later retrieval)	Deep learning (Relationships between different content and extensions of ideas)	Transfer (The proficiency to apply learning to new problems and situations)
1	Developing strategies to integrate with previous learning and prior knowledge	Elaborating and re-organising existing ideas and materials	Pausing before addressing new problems to detect similarities and differences between the old and the new problems
2	Providing students with success criteria	Reflection through self-monitoring of learning strategies	Understanding patterns in the transfer before applying the strategies to new tasks
3	Outlining and transforming	Self-talk and self-questioning	Modifying existing schema with new ideas and ways of thinking
4	Mnemonics	Developing their own success criteria and self-evaluating against these	Developing new success criteria
5	Summarising	Seeking help (explanations, hints and examples) from peers or their teacher	Experiencing different contexts
6	Targeted deliberate practice	Thinking aloud and other metacognitive strategies to explain their thinking	Receiving feedback and revising knowledge based on feedback
7	Rehearsing over time (spacing) and adjusting this based on feedback	Evaluative listening and classroom discussion	Engaging in productive failure
8	Memorisation during consolidation	Problem-solving teaching	Efficient problem solving
9	Cognitive load: Overlearning to reduce demands on working memory	Encouraging students to deliberately activate prior knowledge and then make further relations and extensions	Systematic inquiry based on theory-building and disconfirmation rather than simply following processes for how to find some result
10	Learning how to seek, interpret and act on feedback	Peer tutoring	Exploring errors and misconceptions

algorithms, where in fact this novel problem may require a novel way of thinking. The student may need to investigate using a dictionary or a two-dimensional list and a more complex algorithm.

Hattie also emphasises the need to teach students to stop and think before addressing new tasks. Too often, students will want to rush to write the program or build the relational database before actually planning it carefully and thinking about how this problem might be similar or different to their prior problems.

A final point worth reflecting on is the importance of success criteria and feedback. Both of these feature in all three phases. However, their use evolves. Hattie suggests that teachers should set success criteria in the surface phase; however, as students develop their thinking, these success criteria can be set by the students. This is somewhat mirrored by the practical assessments at GCSE and A levels where students are required to set their own success criteria. Feedback is also critical and is not only something which needs to be explicitly taught, but it should be a fundamental part of a computing classroom's culture; this will be discussed in more detail in Chapter 4.

The lesson plan

It is likely that every school will have their own lesson plan pro forma. Despite the fact that Ofsted no longer require lesson plans to be submitted and many schools are also adopting similar policies, the rationale for the lesson plan remains the same and that is to offer a framework for thinking about your lesson in depth. I would therefore advise you to consider using a lesson plan to structure your thoughts, particularly for new topics. In recent years, partly as a protest against management and Ofsted, there has been a rise in the popularity of five-minute lesson plans or quick fixes. I have tried most of these and it is no surprise that the teaching and learning following a five-minute lesson plan is not going to be as good as one that is completed in more detail in (say) 15–45 minutes.

Lesson planning is likely to have the greatest impact on teaching and learning. For some years there will be a mismatch between a teacher's subject content knowledge and their pedagogical content knowledge. As we learn how to best teach our subject, we will continuously develop our pedagogical content knowledge both consciously and sub-consciously. We will find out what works and what does not work. Shulman, who coined the term 'pedagogical content knowledge' (PCK) in 1986 refers to this development over time:

> Within the category of pedagogical content knowledge I include, for the most regularly taught topics in one's subject area, the most useful forms of representation of those ideas, the most powerful analogies, illustrations, examples, explanations, and demonstrations - in a word, the ways of representing and formulating the subject that make it comprehensible to others. Since there are no single most powerful forms of representation, the teacher must have at hand a veritable armamentarium of alternative forms of representation, some of which derive from research whereas others originate in the wisdom of practice.
>
> (Shulman, 1986)

In order to teach better, we need to understand our student's thinking. As experts in a given field, we can often fall into the expert's trap when we are teaching. The expert's trap is to assume

GFS LESSON PLAN

Teacher: W Lau	Subject: computing	Set/Year: 8W
Lesson: 6	Class & Room: COMP1	Number on roll: 23
Focus of lesson: *(Concept and target knowledge)* Improving understanding of how networks and the internet works. Focussing on keywords and hardware devices. Target knowledge: That modems/routers are necessary for Internet access and wireless routers and access points can be used to achieve Wifi.	Date: 22/2/17	**Student data:** (Numbers) HPA: 2 SEN: 6 EAL: 7 PPG: 10
	Lesson question: How can we improve our understanding of networks? **Fertile Question: Will the Internet slow down as it grows bigger and gets older?**	

Links to prior learning:	*Lesson objectives:*
From summative assessment: Most pupils know some network vocabulary and keywords. However, the accuracy of use varies greatly. Some pupils can explain how the Internet works, others have not grasped how all the devices come together to form a working network. The Do Now should clear up the main misconceptions.	By the end of the lesson pupils **must, should and could** Must: be able to identify different network topologies Should: be able to explain the roles of different devices on the network Could: explain how the Internet works and how a WiFi network works

Time	Lesson structure
	Do Now: connections to prior learning and lesson focus. *(Engage, intrigue, motivate)*
7 mins	Pupils match the keywords to labels on the diagram of the train
7 mins	**Main body of the lesson. Activation phase:** *(Input and accessing new information)* Explain why certain questions are necessary and the importance of review
28 mins	**Main body of the lesson. Demonstration phase:** *(Learners demonstrating understanding of new knowledge – Mastery.)* Students working independently based on tasks which are precisely targeted Students should be using subject-specific language to talk about their thinking Students should be developing their autonomy and expertise to monitor their working Students should be asking questions and working independently through the worksheets which are increasingly complex

Figure 3.2 Example lesson plan for Year 8 review lesson.

10 mins	**Plenary – Review and consolidate.** *(Pupils seeing the progress they have made, seeing their learning in a new light, placing their knowledge into the big picture – making connections)*
	Exit ticket: Pupils reflect on the fertile question and can also explain things which they understand better after the first review lesson:
	Scripted questions:
	Pupil C: State one correction which you have made today?
	Pupil E: Can you tell me what the role of the Modem is in a network?
	Pupil V: Can you tell me how the Internet deals with so much traffic?
	Follow up: So do you think the Internet will slow down as it gets bigger and grows older?
	Pupil B: Would you like to accept, challenge or extend?

Assessment/Homework

Assessment through roaming and checking in the demonstration phase and cold calling in consolidation. Books will be marked before tomorrow's review lesson.

Differentiation and Intervention Strategies

Targeted pupils	EAL, SEN, HA, etc.	Level	Nature of intervention. *(Based on IEP strategies where appropriate)*
Pupil B	VI	5B	Pairing with Pupil R, Sat at front, Size 24pt
Pupil C	SLCN	5C	Pairing with Pupil S (HA) and resources
Pupil D	ASD	5A	Pairing with Pupil T and resources
Pupil E	DYS	5B	Pairing with Pupil U, Seated at front
Pupil F	PD	5C	Pairing with Pupil V (HA), Sat at front
Pupil G	DYS	5B	Pairing with Pupil W and resources
Pupil V	HAP	5A	Encouraged to move onto Extension sheet
Pupil U		5A	

Pupil progress and understanding: *Reflect on the lesson before discussing the lesson with the person observing. Include in this section any pupil misconceptions or miscues that will need to be addressed at the beginning of the next lesson.*

EBI

WWW

Figure 3.2 Continued

too much prior knowledge and to fail to make explicit the knowledge that is implicit to us. The key here is to pre-empt misconceptions; Mark Guzdial, professor at the College of Computing at Georgia Institute of Technology encourages computing teachers to complete the performances of understandings and assessments themselves, whilst trying to predict the most-likely wrong answers and distractors – the most commons ways in which students might fail or misinterpret a question (Wolfman, 2014). His practice is based on Philip Sadler's research at Harvard University which found that the strongest science teachers could predict their pupils' misconceptions:

> If teachers are to help students change their incorrect beliefs, they first need to know what those are … The results showed that students' scores showed the most improvement when teachers were able to predict their students' wrong answers.
>
> (Reuell, 2013)

Rather than thinking like an expert, it is necessary for us at the lesson planning stage to think like a novice. Shulman (1986) goes on to add the importance of this way of thinking:

> [Teachers need to have an] understanding of what makes the learning of specific concepts easy or difficult: the conceptions and preconceptions that students of different ages and backgrounds bring with them…if those preconceptions are misconceptions, which they so often are, teachers need knowledge of the strategies most likely to be fruitful in reorganizing the understanding of learners.

The previous lesson plan template (Figure 3.2) attempts to offer a framework for thinking about the lesson in a way that will maximise learning through a logical sequence of activities. For trainee teachers or newly qualified teachers, it would be beneficial to use this lesson-planning template to start with. Over time, this framework will become somewhat internalised and as good planning habits develop, it will no longer be necessary to complete a lesson plan for every single lesson and the teacher will start to concentrate more on the sequence of lessons. However, for topics which a teacher is unfamiliar with, I would certainly use a template to structure your thoughts and the lesson-planning process.

Planning with teaching assistants

A teaching assistant (TA) is a highly skilled practitioner who specialises in supporting students with special educational needs and disabilities (SEND). Given that computing teachers will only see a student for one or two hours a week and TAs can spend up to six hours a day working with the same student, TAs will have many strategies in their teaching toolkit to help you support your SEND students. Ideally, you will meet with your TA(s) at the same time every week during a mutual planning, preparation and assessment (PPA) period to discuss the week's lesson(s). This gives you time to explain any computing terminology and skills. You should spend this time demonstrating the process of constructing the product and the finished product.

In a confident and supportive relationship, these meetings will become a two-way conversation, where the TA will interject with suggestions for how you may adapt the resource or how he will adapt the resource for the learner (Radford, *et al.*, 2015). At both St Marylebone Church of England (CE) School and Greenwich Free School, I've been lucky to work with many TAs who have proactively taken my lesson resources and produced scaffolded resources for SEND students. This illustrates the power of a strong Teacher/TA relationship where everyone benefits. The teacher is the subject expert and may know how to differentiate to an extent, but the TA will offer precise insight into where the SEND student(s) may struggle and what interventions can be put into place to support the student(s).

If you cannot meet on a weekly basis, even meeting for 30 minutes once a fortnight or emailing your lesson resources a week in advance is better than the TA arriving with no prior knowledge of the lesson. If you are emailing resources for the TA to adapt, always do so at least three days in advance. Teaching assistants in most of the schools that I have worked at do not have as much PPA time as classroom teachers and so emailing a day in advance is unrealistic. It does not allow the TA enough time to ask any questions or indeed put together good resources.

In some classrooms, the TA may arrive at the lesson without being briefed and therefore will have little subject knowledge or context of the lesson. There may be many reasons for this, it may be that you have been too busy to meet with your TA before this lesson or the TA may be a last-minute supply TA. In these cases, the teacher should at least speak to the TA in the first ten minutes of the lesson, to brief them on which students will require intervention and what strategies to use including potential pitfalls. Having exemplars from previous years or classes will also help the TA understand the end goal for the lesson. If a TA is not provided with any resources or direction to support the neediest students, the SEND students are likely to make significantly less progress than their peers from a similar starting point. In an effective classroom where a consistent and supportive relationship with a TA has been developed, TAs will help ensure that SEND students can access the curriculum and achieve the same results as their peers with a similar starting point.

The four-part lesson

The previous lesson plan was structured around four phases; this is based around the Accelerated Learning Cycle popularised by Alistair Smith (Smith, 2001). The remainder of this chapter discusses how this four-part structure can be used to plan computing lessons.

The connection phase

Extensive research by Ausubel, Hunter, Nuthall and Rosenshine state that we should start any learning episode by connecting to a student's prior learning (Ausubel, 1968; Hunter, 1982; Nuthall, 2007; Rosenshine, 2012). I would suggest that in the majority of lessons, this connection is made using what Doug Lemov refers to as a 'Do Now'. Since 2005, Lemov has been researching high-performing teachers and the techniques that they have used to achieve

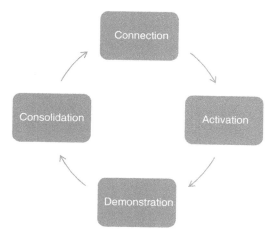

Figure 3.3 A four-part lesson can be structured around the Accelerated Learning cycle (adapted from Smith, 2001).

excellent student outcomes' (Lemov, 2015). One of the most commonly used techniques is the Do Now. The Do Now is an activity that ensures a consistent start at the beginning of every lesson and allows the teacher to connect to prior knowledge. It is also an excellent opportunity to develop the habit of frequent low-stakes testing which strengthens neural pathways and interrupts the process of forgetting. An example of an effective Do Now may be a series of multiple-choice questions as these allow for the uncovering and subsequent correction of misconceptions in prior learning. Multiple-choice questions are also useful as they allow for the interleaving and spacing of content from a variety of topics.

> While the brain is not a muscle that gets stronger with exercise, the neural pathways that make up a body of learning do get stronger. Periodic practice arrests forgetting, strengthens retrieval routes, and is essential for hanging onto the knowledge you want to gain.
>
> (Brown *et al.*, 2014)

Lemov states that the Do Now should be delivered in the same way every lesson, for example it could be on the board before students enter the classroom or already at desks. I like to hand the Do Now out on a printed sheet at the door, thus allowing me to combine two of Lemov's techniques together; a greeting at the door (what Lemov calls a 'Threshold') alongside a printed Do Now for students to complete. There are four criteria to ensure a Do Now is focussed, efficient and effective:

1   Students should be able to complete the Do Now without any direction from the teacher or discussion with peers. This helps establish a self-managed habit of productive work.
2   The activity should take three to five minutes to complete.
3   The activity should require a written response to ensure that it is rigorous and engaging. As the act of writing is observable, it enables teachers to see what students are thinking and holds students to account.
4   The activity should preview the day's lesson and/or review the previous lesson(s).

An example Do Now is shown in Figure 3.4 below and a bank of these are available in the eResources which accompany the book. Whilst you may wish to design your own questions for your Do Nows, it is also worth using the free bank of questions at www.DiagnosticQuestions. com. This is a crowd-sourced platform which many CAS teachers have contributed to. The result of this collaboration is over 2,500 questions which are available for teachers to create their own diagnostic quizzes. These questions have all been expertly designed in collaboration with CAS, the National Association of Advisors for Computers in Education (NAACE), Cambridge Assessment and the Centre for Evaluation and Monitoring (CEM). These questions would be perfect for a Do Now or any other low-stakes diagnostic test.

The activation phase

Following the Do Now in the connection phase, the teacher may wish to launch the lesson question or present a stimulus to create further intrigue, engagement and motivation. Once the students understand "why they are here and why the lesson is important", the teacher

---

Quick Quiz 12/12/2016

1) Which of the following is an INPUT device :
A) Memory Stick
B) Web Cam
C) DVD
D) Hard Disk Drive (HDD)

2) Which of these is an OUTPUT device:
A) Microphone
B) Monitor
C) Webcam
D) Barcode Scanner

3) What is the purpose of the CPU (Choose the BEST answer):
A) It processes instructions and data
B) It outputs things to the monitor
C) It is the brain of the computer and does all the thinking
D) It cools down the rest of the computer with its fan

4) What is the OUTPUT for the program below when the user INPUT is "James":
name=input("what is your name?")
print ("Hello", name)
       A) Hello, James
       B) Hello James
       C) Hello, name
       D) Hello name

4) Colours can be stored in hexadecimal in the following format: RedRed-GreenGreen-BlueBlue. What colour is: 99-00-AA

5) What is one advantage of using a network?

6) What is the difference between a WAN and a LAN?
(Choose two)
A) A WAN offers wireless Internet access
B) A WAN is spread over a large geographical area or across several buildings
C) A LAN is slower than a WAN
D) The Internet is an example of a WAN

 Figure 3.4 Example Do Now for a Year 8 lesson.

can then move onto the activation phase. It is in this second phase that the teacher needs to plan how they will model the thinking required to solve today's lesson question. Examples of effective modelling may be the teacher talking through a segment of exemplar code which the students will build on or it might be by comparing a selection of pupils' written work of varying quality. Whilst it is tempting to only show the best work to students at this phase, Sadler advises that we should present exemplars of varying quality so that teachers can explain to students the differences between high-quality exemplars and lower-quality ones (Sadler, 1989). Royce Sadler's research shows that by seeing a range of responses, students will eventually be able to make judgements about each piece of work and distinguish which pieces are of a high quality and why some examples are better than others. Students can then apply this in their own work. Organising these exemplars requires time and preparation prior to the lesson; doing so during the lesson would be inefficient and impact upon the pace of the lesson.

During the activation phase, the teacher's modelling should ensure that students have a clear conceptual framework before the main tasks are launched. It is here that Collins *et al.* advise that we think out loud to make our thinking visible for the learners (Collins *et al.*, 1991). The cognitive apprenticeship that Collins *et al.* discuss in their paper is particularly important in computing where the expert has a large amount of tacit knowledge and skills alongside the domain knowledge that is readily available online and in textbooks. Unless these implicit habits and ways of working and thinking are made explicit, we are likely to lose our students in the modelling process.

Here are a few examples of how a teacher might externalise a process or activity which is usually internalised and completed silently and intuitively:

1   Web authoring: A teacher may model the process of creating a paragraph with a <p> tag in HTML. They might then comment on a good habit which is to add the closing HTML tag as soon as the open <p> tag is created.
2   Video editing: The first thing we might do is save our project to an external drive and configure the autosave settings and scratch disks. We may then import our opening and closing clips so we can build inwards from the start and end points.
3   Image editing: We may duplicate layers and then create new mask layers for each new effect that we apply.
4   Spreadsheet modelling: In our formula, teachers will want to encourage the use of references at all times and discourage the use of hardcoded values – the latter will seem more natural to students as this is what they are used to when they write equations in maths.
5   Programming: naming our variables with lower-case letters and either underscores (or camel-casing depending on the standards for that language). This is counter-intuitive for many students as proper nouns are usually capitalised in the English language. However, introducing capital letters increases the likelihood of syntax errors and the infamous error message "x is not defined" where *x* is the name of a variable with incorrect letter casing.
6   Truth tables: When composing a truth table for a circuit or series of logic gates, the input values simply follow a sequential binary sequence; for example for two inputs, 0-0, 0-1, 1-0, 1-1, for three inputs this becomes 0-0-0, 0-0-1, 0-1-0, 0-1-1, 1-0-0 and so on.[2]

All of these work flows and internalised habits are not necessarily habits that students will read about in textbooks or online, nor are they habits which students will figure out by themselves intuitively. As a computing teacher, you will have your own areas of expertise (we can't be experts in everything!) and this hidden tacit knowledge that you have built up over years of experience must be shared verbally with your students, otherwise their journey towards mastery and becoming an expert in that topic will be greatly hampered.

The expert's trap is to attempt to teach something without explaining it fully. As someone who may be at the fourth stage of competence (see Figure 3.5), the expert is at risk of failing to empathise with their novice students and therefore assume too much prior knowledge. The expert may feel as though their practical demonstration speaks for itself. Even when teaching something as visual as animation, it is important to talk through all of your steps.

As we narrate our thinking out loud, Knight and Benson state that it is imperative that we use subject-specific language that equips learners to address the Fertile Question (Knight & Benson, 2014). We cannot be casual with our use of language because all of our students' assessments will expect them to use accurate technical language.[3] The transition from the activation phase to the demonstration phase is often the best place to frame the lesson's content into a problem to be solved.

The demonstration phase

The demonstration phase, as the name suggests, should allow students to demonstrate their understanding. This might be initially through co-construction and there may be some scaffolding at first; however, eventually the tasks should become progressively more challenging and lead to some form of independent practice. Like the Do Now, a demonstration phase

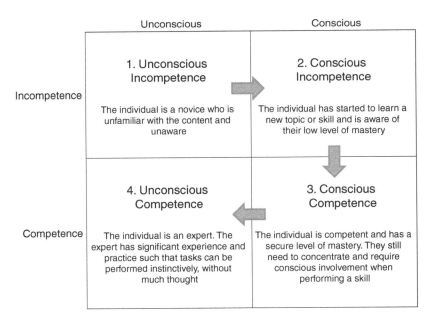

Figure 3.5 Four stages of competence. Adapted from Noel Burch and P. G. Bailey (Gordon Training Ltd, 2016; Bailey, 2011).

should have a low threshold and a high ceiling. The initial tasks may be procedural and involve recall, repetition of a skill and comprehension, whilst the latter tasks will involve increasingly higher-order thinking skills such as analysing, evaluating and creating. Whilst the demonstration phase may have a set of tasks, during the delivery of the lesson, the teacher should punctuate this phase with formative assessment[4] check-ins and feedback to ensure students are on the right track and working towards the lesson's aims and addressing the lesson question.

The actual lesson activities will be discussed in the next chapter as these will vary depending on the lesson topic and students' current stages of mastery.

The consolidation phase

In the final phase of the lesson (the consolidation phase), students should be given the opportunity to reflect on their work and compare it to the success criteria and the exemplars from the initial phases. To what extent does their thinking and learning demonstrate that they have addressed the lesson question and achieved the lesson's objectives? Students may be asked to reflect on the Fertile Question at this stage and be asked to think about where they are going next. If students have progress trackers and curriculum maps to hand, they should be able to see what comes next and where they are roughly on their journey towards mastery. If your computer suite has classroom management software, for example Lanschool, iTalc or Netsupport, the teacher may wish to showcase work at this stage and ask for evaluative comments from the rest of the class.

In the previous lesson plan, you will notice scripted questions. These are useful for lessons with a long demonstration phase and therefore a short consolidation phase. It is worth planning some questions in advance and to target these to specific students so that you get a broad range of responses at varying levels of questioning. Weaker students may be simply asked *what* they did, *how* did they perform a certain task or to *what* extent they met the objectives, whilst students with high prior attainment (HPA) may be asked *why* we should follow a certain approach. Higher-order questions should stretch students by requiring generalisation, analysis or evaluation.[5]

If the students have completed at least two lessons in a unit, it may be worth using another of Doug Lemov's tools, an 'exit ticket', to assess a student's current level of understanding. An exit ticket consists of one to three questions that enable you to check the level of understanding at the end of the lesson. These can be A5 or A4 in size (I wouldn't recommend much smaller) and give the teacher valuable data on the individuals in the class. It is yet another form of low-stakes testing and can be marked quickly by the teacher to identify common mistakes and misconceptions. These can be addressed in the Do Now in the next lesson. Thus the four-part lesson cycle restarts with the data from the consolidation phase feeding into the connection phase of the next lesson.

As teachers become more comfortable with their pedagogical content knowledge and more confident in the classroom, the teacher may feel that it is no longer necessary to have an explicit four-part lesson every lesson and the lesson structure may be more nuanced and less rigid. At this level of teacher expertise, the teacher will move away from individual lesson plans and focus more on the sequence of lessons in their Medium-Term Plan. The structure for this sequence of lessons, which is based on four decades of research by Barak Rosenshine will be introduced in the next chapter.

Lesson narrative

Rarely should a lesson exist in isolation, but rather it will be clearly part of a lesson sequence as specified in the Medium-Term Plan. The Fertile Question is likely to be addressed in some form and the lesson is guided by an explicit lesson question or learning objective(s). This is backed by the research of John Hattie; citing 800 meta-analyses of 50,000 research papers, Hattie states that in order to make the teaching visible for students, learning goals need to be challenging and explicit (Hattie, 2009). The narrative and structure of the lesson are important as it helps students navigate their way through the problem to be solved. The narrative also adds a rationale or a why. In computing lessons, the lesson question or Fertile Question can be added into the lesson before or after the activation phase - it explains the rationale of the lesson to the students; that is, why the lesson is important. Without a clear lesson narrative, the lesson risks becoming 30-60 minutes of "doing". We know from the cognitive psychologist Daniel Willingham that *memory is the residue of thought* (Willingham, 2009) and in order to encourage thinking rather than the mere completion of tasks, there need to be problems to be solved and students need to feel that they are in your lesson for a valid (learning) reason. As each lesson has a clear narrative, students can make explicit links to prior learning and see the bigger picture.

Whilst it makes sense to fit the lesson narrative into the four-part model, it is worth mentioning that the four-part lesson is a supporting structure and not a constraint. In some lessons, the teacher may not go through all four parts; the lesson of a unit may well be entirely about connection and students may not do much independent practice. However, later lessons will probably involve all four parts. Likewise, in the last lesson of a unit students may be reviewing an assessment (performance of understanding) and therefore most of the lesson may be spent consolidating what they have learnt.

Chapter 3 summary

1   Every lesson should be planned with two things in mind: students' prior knowledge and the desired end point.
2   Students are motivated by relevance and will want to know "why this lesson is important". One effective way of creating intrigue and motivating students is through a lesson question.
3   In order to plan effective lessons, we must think like a computing novice and anticipate what misconceptions, misunderstandings and preconceptions students may have.
4   Lesson content and tasks should be framed as problems to be solved with a focus on student thinking.
5   A consistent four-part lesson cycle allows for structured learning through the previewing of content, modelling, independent practice and review.
6   Task design should consider the phase of learning; different types of tasks are effective for surface, deep and transfer learning.

Notes

1   Lemov's work is primarily based in the US and it is particularly impressive because it is based on thousands of observations of schools, classrooms and teachers whose results buck the trend of pupil outcomes being inversely correlated to household income. Based on these observations he compiled a list of techniques which many of these expert teachers used. On the surface, some teachers may be sceptical given the context of the writing. However, these techniques have been used successfully in some of the most successful schools in the UK across all subjects.

2   Whilst this habit is easily taught, it is also a difficult one to forget and when students encounter Karnaugh maps at A-Level they have to be taught that the sequence is 00, 01, 11, 10.

3   In the UK, the keywords and definitions that students are required to learn for their GCSE and A-Level exams are often based on the British Computer Society glossary of computing.

4   Also known as 'Assessment For Learning' (AFL).

5   Expert teachers of computing will have developed the skills to empathise with their students who may think like novices. They will use scripted questions to pre-empt and address student preconceptions, misconceptions and misunderstandings throughout the entire lesson. For teachers that use presentation software such as Powerpoint or Keynote, it is useful to add these scripted questions into the notes sections of slides. This ensures that when you redeliver the lesson the following year or when a peer delivers the lesson, the scripted questions are there ready for you to reuse.

References

Anderson, R. O., 2011. Brain, mind and the organization of knowledge for effective recall and application. *LEARNing Landscapes*, 5(1), pp. 45–61.

Ausubel, D. P., 1968. *Educational Psychology. A Cognitive View.* New York: Holt, Rinehart and Winston.

Brown, P. C., Roediger, H. L. & McDaniel, M. A., 2014. *Make it Stick: The Science of Successful Learning.* Cambridge, MA: Belknap Press of Hardward University Press.

Collins, A., Holum, A. & Seely Brown, J., 1991. Cognitive apprenticeship: making thinking visible. *American Educator: The Professional Journal of the American Federation of Teachers*, 15(Winter), pp. 38–46.

Deans for Impact, 2015. *The Science of Learning*, Austin, TX: Deans for Impact.

Gordon Training Ltd, 2016. *Learning a New Skill Is Easier Said Than Done.* [Online] Available at: http://www.gordontraining.com/free-workplace-articles/learning-a-new-skill-is-easier-said-than-done/ [Accessed 23 December 2016].

Hattie, J., 2009. *Visible Learning.* London: Routledge.

Hattie, J. A. & Donoghue, G. M., 2016. Learning strategies: a synthesis and conceptual model. *npj Science of Learning*, 10 August. Available at: https://www.nature.com/articles/npjscilearn201613

Hunter, M., 1982. *Mastery Teaching.* El Segundo, CA: TIP Publications.

Knight, O. & Benson, D., 2014. *Creating Outstanding Classrooms.* London: Routledge.

Lemov, D., 2015. *Teach Like a Champion 2.0.* San Francisco: Jossey-Bass.

Nuthall, G., 2007. *The Hidden Lives of Learners.* Wellington: NZCER Press.

PGBailey, 2011. *Unconscious Incompetence.* [Online] Available at: https://www.flickr.com/photos/pgbailey/6429568067 [Accessed 23 December 2016].

Radford, J., Bosanquet, P., Webster, R. & Blatchford, P., 2015. Scaffolding learning for independence: clarifying teacher and teaching assistant roles for children with special educational needs. *Learning and Instruction*, 36(2015), pp. 1–10.

Reuell, P., 2013. *Understanding Student Weaknesses.* [Online] Available at: http://news.harvard.edu/gazette/story/2013/04/understanding-student-weaknesses/ [Accessed 3 August 2015].

Rosenshine, B., 2012. Principles of instruction: research-based strategies that all teachers should know. *American Educator,* Issue Spring, pp. 12-39.

Sadler, D. R., 1989. Formative assessment and the design of instructional systems. *Instructional Science*, Issue 18, pp. 119–44.

Shulman, L. S., 1986. Those who understand: knowledge growth in teaching. *Educational Researcher*, 15(2), pp. 4-14.

Smith, A., 2001. *Accelerated Learning in the Classroom.* 5th ed. Stafford: Network Educational Press Ltd.

Willingham, D. T., 2009. *Why Don't Students Like School.* San Francisco: Jossey-Bass.

Wolfman, S., 2014. *CS Education Zoo Episode #6: Mark Guzdial.* [Online] Available at: https://www.youtube.com/watch?v=z1oTtPECHZI [Accessed 1 August 2015].

Part 2
Delivery

4 Research-based instructional principles

The previous chapter looked at how cognitive science can inform the planning of lessons. In this chapter we will continue by looking at further research into the teaching of lessons. In a review of research from cognitive scientists, master teachers and cognitive supports spanning four decades, Barak Rosenshine presents ten research-based instructional principles that all teachers should use (Rosenshine, 2012). These are as follows:

1 Lesson starts: Begin a lesson with a short review of previous learning.
2 Present new material in small steps with student practice after each step.
3 Ask a large number of questions and check the responses of all students.
4 Provide models.
5 Guide student practice.
6 Check for student understanding.
7 Obtain a high success rate.
8 Provide scaffolds for difficult tasks.
9 Require and monitor independent practice.
10 Engage students in weekly and monthly reviews.

These steps are summarised in Figure 4.1. The rest of this chapter uses Barak Rosenshine's Principles of Instruction to outline how a typical lesson would be delivered according to the students' current stages of mastery.

Emerging stage of mastery

In the first lesson of (say) a six-lesson unit of work, the majority of students will be in the "Emerging" stage of mastery, understanding between 0 and 25 per cent of the concepts required to reach mastery. The lesson should start with a Do Now, a review of prior knowledge which allows students to connect to this lesson's content. Following the Do Now, the teacher should then model the thought processes for the new concept or skill. Collins *et al.* state the importance of making the teacher's thinking visible by thinking out loud in the process known as 'Cognitive Apprenticeship' (Collins *et al.*, 1991).

In applying Cognitive Apprenticeship to computing, many of the tasks we perform involve implicit steps or thinking. An example of this is closing a tag in HTML as soon as we open it.

We would model this by stating that "HTML Tags generally occur in pairs and therefore it is good practice to create a closing tag immediately after creating an opening tag". Later in the lesson, the teacher would check that students have internalised this habit by modelling the creation of (say) a paragraph, opening a <p> tag and then asking students, "As I've opened the <p> tag here, what should I do immediately, before I even write my paragraph?" The teacher should expect any student to be able to tell them that a closing </p> tag should be created. Unless we make these implicit habits explicit, our students will be lost as they will not be able to make the invisible conceptual leap that exists in the minds of their expert teachers.

The teacher will follow up teacher modelling with a worked example, presenting a finished product so that students know "what a good one looks like". This is the model which they will judge their work against. They will know if they are on the right track by referring mentally or literally to the teacher's model. Based on Rosenshine's research, for new material the construction process should be broken down into small steps with student practice after each step. If for example, students are studying spreadsheets, students should not be presented with four different functions to use in formulae along with formatting and the creation of graphs in one lesson. Rather, the first lesson might focus on arithmetic operators and a spreadsheet might be designed which allows for the practice of individual arithmetic operators before moving onto formulae which combine several operators and brackets.

For each of the lessons, Rosenshine advises that students should be attaining a high success rate in their guided and independent practice. Students should be attaining success rates of 80 per cent on their practice tasks. One way to gauge what the class's current success rate and level of understanding is is to stop the students after a set amount of time, model the correct processes and solutions on the board and ask students to mark their own

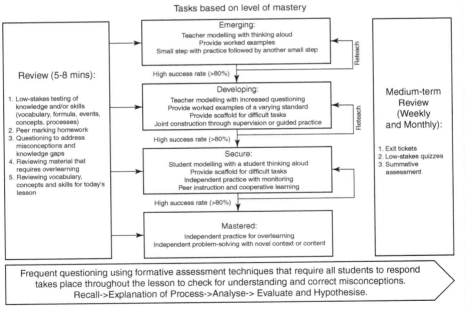

Figure 4.1 Lesson flow based on Barak Rosenshine's Principles of Instruction (Rosenshine, 2012)

work. At the end of this modelling and self-assessment, pupils may be asked to raise their hand if they achieved 50 per cent, 60 per cent, 70 per cent, 80 per cent or more. If it is clear that students have achieved a high success rate, the teacher can launch the next task or increase the complexity of the current task. Likewise, if it is clear that very few have achieved a high success rate, then the teacher may want to clarify some misconceptions.

Developing stage of mastery

By the end of the first lesson, students should be developing a sense of mastery and at this stage teacher modelling should be punctuated with increased questioning. The process of modelling at this stage will involve the deconstruction of the task, activity or process. Royce Sadler who has researched this area extensively advises that exemplars should be used during the modelling process and that these should be authentic pieces of student work of varying quality (Sadler, 2002).[1] John Sweller is another highly respected researcher who has spent over 30 years researching Cognitive Load Theory. During this time, he has also written extensively about worked examples versus problem solving. In a recent essay, professor Sweller discusses the benefits of showing highly variable worked examples (Sweller, 2016), referencing the work of Paas and Van Merriënboer (Paas & Van Merriënboer, 1994); he states that learners who encounter highly variable worked examples learn more than those shown more similar worked examples. The differences in quality allow students to truly understand what is meant by 'quality'; it makes abstract specifications and criteria more concrete. There is no substitute for exemplars; Sadler emphatically states that exemplars convey messages that nothing else can.

Effective modelling

Modelling is the process by which we deconstruct a task, activity or process and then reconstruct it for students to understand; how we explain to enable understanding. Successful modelling is invariably intertwined with expert questioning (Baxter *et al.*, 2016).

As an expert teacher, you may assume that students already have a certain level of prior knowledge. The key behind effective modelling is to assume nothing. As you model a process, if you are unsure if students are already familiar with a process, you may choose a student to talk you through the process. If it becomes apparent that this process needs modelling fully, then you should proceed to do so using either the projector, classroom management software, a pre-recorded video tutorial or a document camera (visualiser). The following table (Table 4.1) summarises when and how each method should be used.

In the second or third lesson of the unit, the teacher should still be providing scaffolding for difficult tasks. However, the intention should be that the scaffolding will be removed once the students achieve a high success rate. At this point, students should have the opportunity to complete joint construction through supervision or guided practice. This guided instruction and collaboration is supported by Pearson and Gallagher's Gradual Release of

Table 4.1 Modelling tools and techniques

Technique	Usage	Special notes
Projector	Useful when modelling procedural tasks for 1-10 minutes prior to task launch. If you are modelling a process in an office application or IDE for programming, you should use the zoom tool to ensure that the text is readable from the back of the room.	This is best done whilst students are still at their desks. If you feel the need to use the screen magnifier, it may be best to use classroom management software to broadcast your screen instead, as some students find the magnifier confusing and disorientating.
Classroom management software	Useful for intervention modelling to the whole class or a small selection of students during the demonstration phase. This is mainly used to clarify a common misconception or mistake. Classroom management software can also be used to showcase live exemplars from your classroom. This is another method of narrating the positive and building momentum and lesson pace.	For a complete solution I recommend *Lanschool, Netsupport, Impero* or *Ranger* which all involve annual subscription. If you simply need screen monitoring and showcasing (without the ability to launch programs and control web access remotely), the freeware *iTalc* is usable. However, it does require separate configuration for each teacher's account. For Apple iPads, *Explain Everything* is a great tool for showcasing and live recording too.
Pre-recorded video tutorial	Best suited for highly technical or procedural tasks with many steps. The pre-recorded video tutorials reduce cognitive load and ensure the modelling is entirely differentiated. Students can access these tutorials independently as part of the SPOT or 3B4Me framework. It is ideal when students have a wide range of abilities and skillsets and are working on different practical skills at different times.	For Windows, I recommend the free program Open Broadcaster Software. For Mac, I recommend using the pre-installed screen recorder in Quicktime Pro. The recorded videos can be stored on a network drive or uploaded to YouTube. It is important to narrate your videos as you record them. The aforementioned software both allow synchronous voice recording.
Document camera (Visualiser)	For modelling handwritten work in books. This might include showcasing exemplars, model answers or talking through a worked example. The document camera can be used to annotate student's work and to demonstrate the marking process prior to peer-marking. It is useful to have a bank of student exercise books from previous years with exemplars so that students can see the required standard of both content and presentation prior to the demonstration phase. The document camera can also be combined with screen recorder software so that the modelling process can be replayed at any time from the bank of pre-recorded video tutorials.	It is recommended to buy a document camera with a light and auto-focus. Epson, iPevo, aVer and Elmo are all reputable brands. If you do not have a budget for a dedicated document camera, you can also use free mobile apps such as Kinoni Epoccam (ios/Windows/Android) or Droidcam for Android. The advantage of using an app is that the visualiser becomes a wireless tool allowing you to roam around the classroom and showcase student work wirelessly. The disadvantage of using a mobile app is that unless you have a tripod, the presentation can suffer from shakiness and motion blur.

Responsibility Model (Pearson & Gallagher, 1983) along with Lewis and Wray's research into literacy (Lewis & Wray, 2000) and Gibbons's work on reading, writing and language acquisition (Gibbons, 2002). As students develop their level of understanding, it is worth closing the lesson with a formative assessment in the form of an exit ticket or low-stakes quiz.

Secure stage of mastery

By the third or fourth lesson in a six-lesson unit, in order for modelling to be truly effective, we need to encourage students to analyse the exemplars and form their own opinions of quality; by being able to judge quality accurately, students will be able to judge and improve the quality of their own work during independent practice. After initial teacher modelling, To and Carless recommend critical peer dialogue as an effective way of students participating in this deconstruction and reconstruction process (To & Carless, 2016). To and Carless found in their research that peer dialogue and critique can provide a more supportive environment for peers to ask questions about an exemplar, thus greatly increasing participation. For reserved students and students who may still fear failure in front of a whole class, a pair or a small group discussion allows students to make their opinions without the fear of judgement from their peers. One area worth guiding students with is identifying weaknesses in exemplars as students generally gravitate towards identifying strengths and rarely identify weaknesses.

Teacher guidance is certainly required during the modelling process particularly during the early stages of a unit of work when it is highly likely that the teacher is the only expert in the room. When a teacher is leading a discussion about an exemplar, possible questions might be:

- Who is the intended audience for this piece of work? How has the student ensured their work is user friendly and suitable for the audience and purpose?
- How many marks would you give this student and why?
- What keywords and technical vocabulary has this student used? What technical vocabulary should a student be using in this answer?
- What might be a more efficient way of doing this?
- What data structure could they use for this data set?
- State three things you would do to improve this program/poster/report/essay/answer.
- State three strengths of this program/poster/report/essay/answer.
- What feedback would you give this student to improve their work?
- This piece of work scored five out of seven; what is missing to ensure the student gets full marks?
- Are there any questions you wish to ask about the exemplars?
- Why do you think the student has used this formula here? Can you explain their thinking?
- What is the graph trying to show? How successfully has the student done this? How could it be improved?
- If you were to pick out the strongest sentence or argument from this paragraph, what would it be?
- What did you like about this film trailer?
- What three techniques has the student used effectively to communicate the genre of their film to the audience?

- List the graphic design rules and principles each of these exemplars have used.
- What are the similarities between the different exemplars?
- How might this exemplar be better or weaker than your own?
- Can you summarise the key differences between the three exemplars we have looked at this morning?

The use of teacher-led modelling, peer discussion and individual deconstruction can take place during any unit of work. These varying methodologies do not necessarily need to take place in a linear sequence as the benefits of each methodology can be reaped regardless of the stage of mastery. However, one key finding based on experience and the literature review is that the choice and range of exemplars do need to be planned in advance (Figure 4.2).

As students move from novice to expert, the guidance provided to students should be gradually reduced (Renkl & Atkinson, 2003). Whilst problem solving is one of the key elements of computational thinking and is one of the skills encouraged by Knight and Benson (Knight & Benson, 2014) and Nuthall (Nuthall, 2007), Sweller and researchers who have built on his Cognitive Load Theory have found that problem-solving tasks are not suitable for novices during their initial stages of cognitive skills acquisition as they will experience cognitive overload (Sweller, 2016). Once a novice has developed their understanding and skills through varied worked examples, these learners's intrinsic cognitive load will decrease, allowing them to be exposed to problems which they are required to solve. Renkl and Atkinson go on to state that these initial problem-solving tasks will require scaffolding. Through the gradual fading of both worked examples and scaffolding, students should complete problem-solving tasks independently.

Rosenshine notes that whilst independent practice should be extensive and successful in order for skills and knowledge to become automatic, this independent practice should still involve monitoring. Brief monitoring of no more than 30 seconds is appropriate. However, formative assessment can also be used to check the understanding of the whole class.

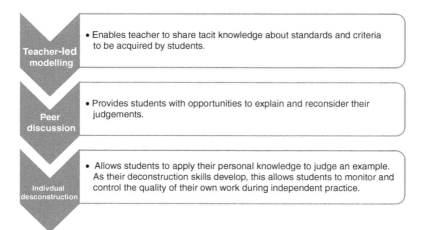

Figure 4.2   Modelling methodologies (based on Carless & Chan, 2016; Sadler, 2002).

The expert teacher does not simply follow a rigid lesson structure and plan; the expert teacher will elicit feedback through frequent questioning and formative assessment techniques throughout the lesson and adapt their instruction accordingly.

> An assessment functions formatively to the extent that evidence about student achievement is elicited, interpreted, and used by teachers, learners, or their peers, to make decisions about the next steps in instruction that are likely to be better, or better founded, than the decisions they would have taken in the absence of the evidence that was elicited.
>
> (Kingsbury *et al.*, 2011)

The use of formative assessment strategies by teachers is similar to the strategies employed by football managers, pilots and heart surgeons. Whilst all the aforementioned professionals approach their operations with a plan, this plan is adapted in real time. In aviation, when a pilot checks their instruments and discovers that they have deviated from the flight plan's destination, the pilot makes a course correction. The pilot checks these instruments regularly, not just towards the end of the flight. Similarly, in teaching, expert teachers should be regularly checking that their students are on track to meet their destination and if not, the teacher should introduce a form of intervention to change their student's trajectory and ensure a high success rate. The formative assessment should not take place only at the end of the lesson as this does not leave sufficient time to offer immediate corrective feedback for students to act on. An expert teacher's classroom is a responsive classroom and the corrections to the lesson delivery are made throughout the lesson.

At this secure level of mastery, teachers can also rely on peers to provide feedback, correction and instruction. Pair programming is an example of a cooperative learning and peer instruction which is supported by research and industry (Williams & Kessler, 2002) (Hannay *et al.*, 2009) (Denner *et al.*, 2014) (Franklin, 2015). The theory behind pair programming is that the programmer (driver) is required to think aloud and the observing peer (navigator) should review the program, offering advice and feedback based on the driver's programming and thought processes. As both students regularly switch roles after timed intervals, their shared knowledge and understanding allows them to achieve more than if they were to program separately. This technique will be discussed in more detail later in Chapter 6.

Mastery

The Gradual Release of Responsibility model (Pearson & Gallagher, 1983) states that students should move from teacher-led learning to student-led learning. At this final stage of mastery, Rosenshine states that independent practice is necessary in order to build fluency. The teacher plays an increasingly passive role with much less intervention and much more observation and monitoring.

Learners at this stage should be independent in their thinking and application of knowledge and skills. The independent practice in the form of overlearning is what leads to fluency and automation. Rosenshine's research suggests that the material used in independent practice may involve slight variations in the material covered during guided practice. In a computing classroom, these variations might involve subtle changes in context or content, for example re-designing a poster for a different audience or using a similar selection algorithm for slightly different conditions.

At the end of each unit of work, there should also be a summative assessment which tests the students' stages of mastery by asking them to apply their skills or knowledge to a new scenario or context. These assessments should be conducted in exam conditions and should mirror the assessment requirements at GCSE or A level as closely as possible. In many cases, exam boards will release their old exam papers and also supply some specimen exam papers for new specifications. Teachers are encouraged to use these official materials wherever possible to ensure that the assessments are rigorous, accurate and appropriate.

Following a summative assessment, students should spend at least one lesson reviewing their assessment. It is here that the teacher should design resources and activities to correct misconceptions and misunderstandings. Some teachers like to have a digital mark book which directly feeds into a personalised learning checklist (PLC) for each student. Dr Jasper Green (network lead for science at Ark Schools) suggests an alternative approach which is marking an assessment with mark scheme at hand and annotating this mark scheme with misconceptions; it soon becomes apparent where the common misconceptions are for a certain unit and what these misconceptions are (Green, 2016). Indeed, a combination of the two techniques can be used to record and analyse misconceptions.

Before students start their corrections, students could also be given the opportunity to reflect on their learning and current level of understanding. Figure 4.3 gives an example of a reflection sheet for a database unit which is used during the Do Now and revisited as a plenary activity in the consolidation phase:

<u>**Do Now: Databases end-of-unit review**</u>   **21/04/2017**

Topics covered:

Adding data to a **table**   Creating a printable **report**
Searching using **queries**   **Formatting** a form/report
Adding data using a **form**   to make it look appealing.

Look at your mark sheet and the topics above, then complete the section below:

Two things which I did well in:	Two things I need to improve on:
1	1
2	2

What grade do you think your teacher will give your work?

   Figure 4.3 Assessment reflection sheet.

To be completed **after** the review lesson: What skills did you work on improving during the review lesson?

1. _____
   _____
   _____
   _____

2. _____
   _____
   _____
   _____

Figure 4.3 (Continued)

This chapter has discussed research-based principles of instruction at different stages of mastery. It should be apparent to the reader that depending on the students' stages of mastery, the level of intervention, scaffolding and teacher dialogue changes to ensure that students have the tools to become more independent and responsible for their own learning. The following chapter will outline effective actions, habits and routines in the computing classroom.

Chapter 4 summary

1 Every lesson should begin with a short review of previous learning.
2 The type of modelling, exemplars, teacher guidance and practice depend on the students' stages of mastery.
3 The amount of scaffolding, guidance and modelling is gradually reduced (faded) and teacher responsibility is reduced to ensure that students become more independent on their journey towards mastery.
4 Overlearning through independent practice leads to fluency and automaticity.
5 Frequent questioning using formative assessment techniques that require all students to respond should take place throughout the lesson to check for understanding and correct misconceptions.

Note

1 If you are completing Non-Examination Assessment (NEA) or coursework, it would be considered malpractice if you showed actual examples of the same assignment; in these you should use a parallel task which tests similar skills and techniques as the live assessment whilst varying in context and content to avoid malpractice.

References

Baxter, M., Knight, O. & Lau, W., 2016. *GFS Teaching Handbook*. London: Greenwich Free School.
Carless, D. & Chan, K. K. H., 2016. Managing dialogic use of exemplars. *Assessment and Evaluation in Higher Education*, 20 July, pp. 1–12.

Collins, A., Holum, A. & Seely Brown, J., 1991. Cognitive apprenticeship: making thinking visible. *American Educator: The Professional Journal of the American Federation of Teachers*, 15(Winter), pp. 38–46.

Denner, J., Werner, L., Shannon, C. & Ortiz, E., 2014. Pair programming: under what conditions is it advantageous for middle school students? *Journal of Research on Technology in Education*, 46(3), pp. 277–96.

Franklin, J. P., 2015. *Perceptions by Young People of Pair Programming When Learning Text Languages*. London: Axsied/King's College London.

Gibbons, P., 2002. *Scaffolding Language, Scaffolding Learning*. Portsmouth, NH: Heinemann.

Green, J., 2016. *Question Level Analysis in Science*. [Online] Available at: http://thescienceteacher.co.uk/question-level-analysis/ [Accessed 29 December 2016].

Hannay, J. E., Dybå, T., Arisholm, E. & Sjøberg, D. I., 2009. The effectiveness of pair programming: a meta-analysis. *Information and Software Technology*, 51, (2009) pp. 1110–22.

Kingsbury, G. G., Wiliam, D. & Wise, S. L., 2011. *Connecting the Dots: Formative, Interim and Summative Assessment*. College Park, Maryland: Northwest Evaluation Association (NWEA).

Knight, O. & Benson, D., 2014. *Creating Outstanding Classrooms*. London: Routledge.

Lewis, M. & Wray, D., 2000. *Literacy in the Secondary School*. London: David Fulton Publishers Ltd.

Nuthall, G., 2007. *The Hidden Lives of Learners*. Wellington: NZCER Press.

Paas, F. G. W. C. & Van Merriënboer, J. J. G., 1994. Variability of worked examples and transfer of geometrical problem solving skills: a cognitive load approach. *Journal of Educational Psychology*, 86(1), pp. 122–33.

Pearson, P. D. & Gallagher, M. C., 1983. The instruction of reading comprehension. *Contemporary Educational Psychology*, 8(3), pp. 317–44.

Renkl, A. & Atkinson, R. K., 2003. Structuring the transition from example study to problem solving in cognitive skill acquisition: a cognitive load perspective. *Educational Psychologist*, 38(1), pp. 15–22.

Rosenshine, B., 2012. Principles of instruction: research-based strategies that all teachers should know. *American Educator*, Spring, pp. 12–39.

Sadler, D. R., 2002. Ah! … so that's 'quality'. In: P. L. Schwartz & G. Webb, eds. *Assessment: Case Studies, Experience and Practice from Higher Education*. London: Kogan Page, pp. 130–36.

Sweller, J., 2016. Story of a research program. *Education Review*, 10 February, 23, pp. 1–19.

To, J. & Carless, D., 2016. Making productive use of exemplars: peer discussion and teacher guidance for positive transfer of strategies. *Journal of Further and Higher Education*, 40(6), pp. 746–64.

Williams, L. & Kessler, R., 2002. *Pair Programming Illuminated*. Boston, MA: Pearson.

5 Actions, habits and routines in the computing classroom

Whilst the previous chapter discussed the lesson start, practice, modelling and review at the various stages of students' mastery, this chapter will deal with actions, habits and routines of expert computing teachers. It is first worth differentiating between these three sets of behaviour. An action is the most basic unit of behaviour, it can be performed once or occasionally. A habit is an action which is repeated frequently enough that it becomes automatic. As teachers, there are some actions which only need to be performed once a year, perhaps at the start of the academic year and there are others which need to be internalised as a habit to ensure that the classroom runs efficiently. Teachers do not think consciously about them, this is what makes habits so powerful (Andrews, 1903). Lastly, some habits and actions will be performed regularly in a particular order, this sequence of actions and habits becomes routine. Routines may require more conscious effort than individual habits, however the steps always remain the same. Expert computing teachers use routines in their everyday practice and also design routines for their students to follow.

This chapter is divided into the following sections of actions, habits and routines:

1. Classroom culture
2. Behaviour management
3. Lesson pace
4. Differentiation
5. Questioning
6. Formative assessment
7. Marking and feedback.

Classroom culture

Building the culture of the classroom should be the focus of any teacher's first few lessons. It is not worth rushing into dense content during this time. Once you have established a positive learning culture in the classroom and your students are highly motivated and trusting, it will be possible to teach practically any computing topic. The aim is to create a positive, productive environment where everyone (the students and the teacher) is willing to take risks. Due to the computer lab being a specific learning environment, students will need to be inducted and trained into how they should conduct themselves within the lab. I will now outline my first few lessons for building a positive learning culture.

Your first computing lessons

I will start my first lesson as I intend to start all my lessons, greeting my students on the door with a printed Do Now. This Do Now is different to most of the others I will use in the future because there is very little on this Do Now concerning computing. The Do Now is all about the student: This is where information can be gathered about the students, where we instil good habits and show that we care and that for some tasks in school, there are no right or wrong answers, the teacher wants to know what the student thinks and feels. There are two versions of the initial Do Now. One is based on the work of Tyler Hester and I have used it successfully with all my classes (Hester, 2012).

The modified version of this is reproduced in Figure 5.1; I produced a separate version for each year group and these are available as modifiable templates in the eResources. It is worth noting that quite a few of the techniques and material that I use for my first lesson are inspired by Tyler Hester's "first lessons" video series. He has a wealth of experience teaching in challenging urban environments and his educational philosophy and resources are certainly worth looking at and adapting. They are freely available here: www.agapemanagement.org.

The second Do Now (Figure 5.2) is one I have used with my tutor groups and it could be used if you join a school mid-year (say) as a long-term supply teacher. It enables you to establish a relationship with your group and it puts the learner at the centre of the first lesson, thereby serving the same purpose. It is a low-threshold task which greatly facilitates a calm start to the lesson. Students should be able to write about themselves in silence, which means you have time to take the register and circulate around the room to check on student's answers and to narrate all the positive things you are seeing.[1]

This second Do Now first appeared on Dan Meyer's first day wikispace: www.firstday.wikispaces.com. I personally came across this on Twitter and a resource named *32 Ways to Get to Know Your Class*, www.tinyurl.com/32IceBreakers. I modified it to include British spellings and I changed a few boxes based on my experience of teaching in London schools. It is also included as an eResource.

In the first lesson, you should use a seating plan; this can be displayed on the board and also can be printed out so that you can instruct students where to sit. Seating plans should be data led and designed to maximise learning. At Tudor Grange Academy, Simon Brown explained how the school uses a system whereby weaker pupils are always sat next to a stronger pupil or a highly motivated pupil. From experience, I would use baseline data to pair high prior attaining (HPA) pupils with middle prior attaining (MPA) pupils. Lower prior attaining (LPA) pupils should always be paired with a MPA or HPA pupils. This is so that students can benefit the most from each other. The weaker pupil is always able to ask their neighbouring peer for assistance and the higher attaining pupil benefits from having to explain a concept which solidifies their understanding.[2]

If pupils have hearing or visual impairments, as in SEND, they should be seated near the front. As a teacher in a new school, I would speak to the head of year to see which students

Name: _____
Period: _____

Student Survey for Mr. Lau's Computing Class

Directions: For me to be the best teacher that I can be, it is helpful for me to know things about you. Take about eight minutes and complete the survey below for yourself.

Part I: What you do

What do you like to do in your free time?

In my free time, I like to _____
_____

I like doing this because _____
_____

Another thing that I like to do is _____
_____

I like doing this because _____
_____

Part II: Your goals

What do you want to do when you graduate from secondary school?

When I graduate from secondary school, one thing I want to do is _____
_____

I want to do this because _____
_____

Part III: Year 6

How good was your teacher last year? Circle a number.

1 --------------------- 2 --------------------- 3 ----------------------- 4 ----------------------- 5 -------------------------6

Bad   Not that great   Only OK   Pretty Good   Good   Great

Explain why you circled the number above:

I circled the number _____ above because _____
_____

How much Computing did you learn in school last year? Circle a number.

1 --------------------- 2 --------------------- 3 ----------------------- 4 ----------------------- 5 -------------------------6

Nothing   Not that much   A little bit   A good amount   A lot   A Huge

                                                                                                        Amount!

Explain why you circled the number above:

I circled the number _____ above because _____
_____

Figure 5.1 Do Now for an introductory lesson.

Describe what you think you will learn about in Computing? _____

_____

Part IV: Year 7

How much do you want to succeed in Computing this year? Circle a number.

1 ----------------------- 2 -------------------- 3 ---------------------- 4 --------------------- 5 ----------------------- 6

| I don't want to | Not that much | A little bit | Quite a bit | A lot | I really want |
| to succeed | | | | | |

Explain why you circled the number above:

_____

_____

What else should Mr. Lau know about you?

_____

_____

_____

_____

If you finish early, draw a picture of yourself doing something that you love in this space.

Figure 5.1 Continued

work well with each other, which students need to be monitored closely at the front of the room and which students can be trusted to sit at the back of the room without distracting their peers or going off task. Wherever possible, I would leave two desk spaces at the front of the room empty as these can be used for front-table targeted intervention in your lessons. This technique is discussed at the end of this chapter in the formative assessment section.

For consistency, pupil desks can be numbered (see Figure 5.3). I number the desks in decimal and their binary-equivalent forms from 0–31. Computers are also numbered from 0–31 and pupils should sit at these seats for all lessons in the computer lab. This ensures an efficient entry/exit and also increases accountability for pupils to look after their desk and computer. I generated these labels using tables in a word processor and these were laminated, trimmed and then stuck onto the tables and monitors respectively. I liked the idea of having binary as well as decimal numbers on the labels as it exposes students to number systems and specifically the binary representation of numbers from the very first lesson. I also think that starting the numbering with zero is also a benefit because computer scientists generally start counting from zero rather than one. Getting students immersed in an environment whereby they are thinking like a computer scientist from an early age pays dividends; it makes introducing counters in for loops, array indexes, hexadecimal colour codes, ASCII and unicode values much easier later on.

Having welcomed the students with the Do Now and allowed them sufficient time to complete this activity, I would introduce them to the agenda for the day[3]:

1 Computing induction
2 Practising how we work together respectfully and by following instructions for the first time
3 Password security
4 Your books: details, covers, contents, sticking in your student survey
5 The exit routine: the book algorithm.

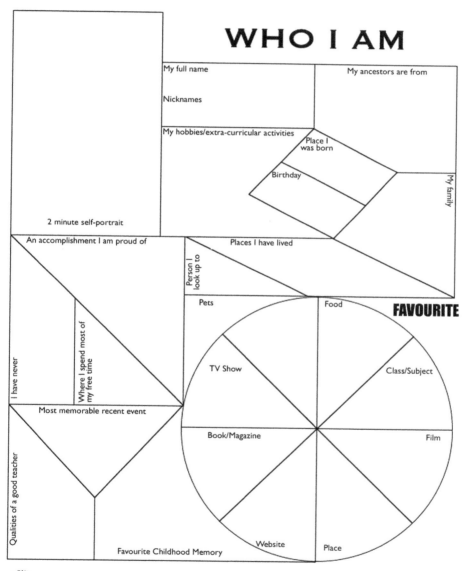

Figure 5.2 An alternative Do Now for an introductory lesson.

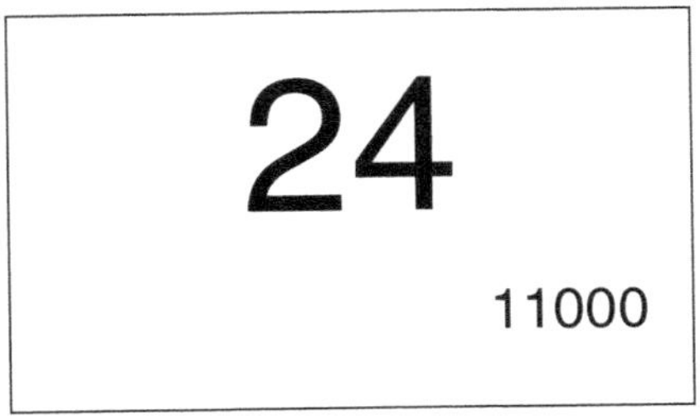

Figure 5.3 An example of a desk label for the computer lab.

The computing induction explains the rationale; that is, the 'why' for the year. This is based upon Simon Sinek's leadership book *Start with Why* (Sinek, 2009). It is here that I sell the subject; this is usually reinforced by news articles and statistics about digital skills and job adverts for jobs in computing. During this short induction, you should also establish your role: as a teacher you are there to help your students. I remind them that I act out of respect and love. When I give instructions, it is not out of spite or hate, it is not because I enjoy being in control, it is to ensure that everyone can learn in the most effective and efficient way. At this point, I set the high expectation that I will expect the best from each of my students regardless of their background or household income. I enforce that at the age of 18, they should be able to choose whether to work or continue studying at a college, by way of an apprenticeship scheme or at university. I follow this up with rights which I believe students should have in my classroom:

1 The right to learn
2 The right to be heard
3 The right to be respected.

I explain that we are all here for the same reason; we come to school to learn. We come to school to have a positive experience. Nobody comes to school wanting to be disrespected and so from day one, if a student acts in a way which does not allow their peers to have the three rights listed, they will receive a warning and then detention as per the school's behaviour system. Your school will operate their own behaviour system and it is worth familiarising yourself with these so that you can apply them consistently in your classroom. If you are new to the school or new to teaching, the best way to see how the behaviour system is implemented is to go and watch a few experienced teachers teach their lessons. You will quickly pick up what the cultural norms of your school are.

I go into explicit detail as to what I expect and I try to keep this as simple as possible. Figure 5.4 is an A3 poster that I designed based on the work of Bill Rogers (Rogers, 2011). At the bottom of Figure 5.4 are five simple rules; these are based on the school rules and experience in the classroom. I would advise not having chairs with casters; however, if you have them in your classroom, consider getting standard classroom chairs for the student desks and keep the office chairs at the computers; this clear separation will stop students from wheeling around the classroom! The last rule regarding eating and drinking applies to

We all have a **right** to be **respected**

To enjoy **respect** in this classroom:
- We all **share** the same **place**, **space** and **reason** for being here together.
- We all **share** the same fundamental **feelings**; it's about the way we treat one another here.
- Safety is more than physical safety (people's **feelings**, personal **space**, **property**).

No touching   Do not wheel around   Do not throw equipment   Be Kind   No eating or drinking

Figure 5.4 Example poster for rules and routines in the computer lab.

bottled water too; if students desperately need to drink water, they can do so in the doorway of the classroom. Over the past ten years, I've encountered too many liquid-damaged computers and I think the best rule is to not allow any food or drink in the computer lab. This rule can be explained by telling the students that food and drink is banned in all the labs in the school, including the computing labs. According to Bill Rogers, the rules have to be clear and enforceable; provided the rules are explained in the first lesson and there is a rationale for each rule, students rarely protest. Issues arise when you decide to "invent rules on the spot" or when you try to introduce rules in the middle of the year. By establishing clear rules in the first lesson and being certain about what you will or will not accept in your classroom, it provides a safe and consistent environment for students to learn and thrive.

I finish this section of my lesson by explaining what rewards students are to expect if they meet and exceed my high expectations. The first reward has to be learning, learning is its own reward. As students invest in themselves, they should get a good feeling about knowing they have done their best and learned something new. This, accompanied with regular and specific praise from the teacher, lays the foundation for building strong intrinsic motivation. The next level of rewards can be based on your school reward system; we use house points in school and I also have a top ten poster for each year group based on two categories: growth and scholarship (Tables 5.1 and 5.2). Growth is based on the percentage of improvement from their baseline and scholarship is based on the highest summative assessment scores.

Depending on the culture you wish to create, some teachers will have a final level of rewards based on gifts at the end of each term or academic year. Whilst these can be bought with your department budget, technology companies and universities are often willing to donate gifts. Careers events, technology fairs and your own social network are also a great source of free promotional items. Whilst students are very happy when they receive extrinsic rewards, I personally find that intrinsic rewards and phone calls home have a much greater sustained positive effect than frequent extrinsic rewards.

Having established some ground rules, you can now begin inducting students into the processes for using the computer room and logging into the network. Given that students will need their usernames and passwords for many lessons, not just computing, it's worth going through password security with students. Historically, we asked students to create secure

Table 5.1 Example poster celebrating the top 10 students in terms of attainment

YEAR 11 SUPERSTARS–TOP 10 FOR SCHOLARSHIP

Rank	Theory Mock Spr 2	UMS %	Grade
I	Jacob Stafford	80	A1
2-	Ryan Smith	80	A1
2-	Ivan Hua	80	A2
4	Jessica Contento	80	A2
5	Nathan Dancey	70	A2
6-	Jude Asare	70	A2
6-	Samuel Maxwell	70	A3
8	Jacob Parkes	70	A3
9-	Jacob Petrou	70	B1
9-	Kyle Torpey	70	B2

Based on Spring 2 Mock Exams

Table 5.2 Example poster celebrating the top 10 students in terms of progress

GFS COMPUTING YEAR 11 RISING STARS
TOP 10 FOR GROWTH

Rank	Year 11	Progress %
1-	Alina Gordey	21
2	Jude Asare	8
3-	Jacob Parkes	7
3-	Oluwaseyi Ogunleye	7
5	Charlie Hills	6
6	Kyle Torpey	4
7-	Jacob Stafford	3
7-	Ryan Smith	3
7-	Vinay Vadukul	3
7-	Hakeem Karatu	3

Based on progress made in A451 Theory from Jan 2017 to Mar 2017

passwords using a mixture of cases, numbers and symbols. However, we found that too many students forgot their passwords, so we started to set out some criteria, the first one being that the password should be easy to remember and hard to guess.

Looking at Table 5.3, you will also see the technique 'think pair share', which involves students thinking in silence for 15–30 seconds, pairing up and discussing with their peers before being asked to share their thoughts. At the bottom of the slide, I've added in a technique for structured discussion used by Jo Parkes (Head of English at Greenwich Free School). In his classroom he has windows on one side of the classroom and a standard wall with no windows on the opposite side. In pair discussion, he will often use the term

Table 5.3 A think pair share activity for choosing a good password

The Password Dilemma

Passwords expire every 90 days. They have to have a capital letter. They have to have a number.

Think –> Pair –> Share

Which of these passwords are easy to remember, hard to guess:

A	B	C	D
Hello123	MikeSmith1	AirMax360!	RedDoor1!
Hello1234	MikeSmith2	AirMax360!!	RedDoor2!
Hello12345	MikeSmith3	AirMax360!!!	RedDoor3!

Odd numbers talk first

'window to wall' which means the person sitting closest to the window speaks first and the person sitting closest to the wall has to respond. Due to the layout in my computer lab, this was modified so that students sitting at odd-numbered desks spoke first. This structured discussion encourages accountability and also allows you to vary the discussion leader for each think pair share (swapping to even-numbered desks first for the next think pair share), thereby ensuring each person in a pair will have the opportunity to lead a discussion and one student is not allowed to dominate. At each stage, students are asked to justify their answers and their peer is asked to accept, challenge or extend (A-C-E) on their peer's initial response.

The aim of this activity is to encourage thinking and to introduce students to the concept of digital security. You may also choose to illustrate how effective the use of symbols can be by using the website: howsecureismypassword.net. This website illustrates how secure your password is and will update in real time as you type thus allowing you to compare the passwords in Table 5.3.[4] Based on the table, Person C and Person D have the strongest set of passwords. Both of these people have picked something meaningful and memorable to them whilst also being difficult for someone to guess. Neither Person C or Person D would need to write down their password to remember them.

Person D's password remains the same length for a longer period of time; the password can be changed nine times following a similar algorithm without increasing the length of the password. Person C's password whilst potentially easier to remember (they simply need to remember the number of exclamation marks they have following their memorable phrase), this could become unwieldy after six or seven password expirations and subsequent changes. In either case, changing the last symbol in the password every 90 days could result in memorable and short passwords.

Students are given the opportunity to log in and start creating folders in their user areas for each of their subjects or if they are waiting for others to login, they can spend that time finishing their Do Now student survey. I would allow five to ten minutes for this activity. Depending on your school's lesson length, the next part of the lesson may need to be started the following lesson.

From experience, A4 exercise books serve as useful notebooks for revision and I highly recommend using them as opposed to going paperless and taking all notes online. There are two reasons for this: First, most programmers and professionals who work with computers still keep a notebook. Often it is easier to work on a computer whilst referring to a notebook, rather than switching between several word-processed documents on the computer.[5] Second, most GCSE computer science courses are now 80 per cent theory and these theory exams are handwritten. Digital note taking has its place, tools such as Google Keep and Microsoft OneNote are excellent tools for curating a range of digital content. However, students still need to be able to write answers legibly, concisely and without the support of the World Wide Web. It is worth emphasising early on that computing is not all about computers and there will be lessons where students do not use their computers at all. I try to emphasise that using the computer is not necessarily a reward, nor is work done on paper a punishment; the computer is simply a tool which allows us to think and express our thoughts and in many lessons, traditional pen and paper will be better tools for this.

> Computer science is not about machines, in the same way that astronomy is not about telescopes.
>
> (Fellows, 1991)

If you are to use exercise books, like any other traditional academic subject, it is worth setting out your expectations for presentation and layout. The slides in the eResources go into more detail about my preferences and these can be tweaked according to your school's policies. In short, I would expect a table of contents and page numbers. Each piece of work needs to be dated with an underlined title and pupils should write using one colour pen, self/peer mark in another colour pen and they should not use red pen at all. I allow students to decorate their books with a computing theme. This helps build a positive culture as students are given ownership of their book; it also ensures students do not confuse their computing book for another subject's book of the same colour. Examples of beautifully decorated books are also in the eResources.

If this brings you close to the end of the lesson, it is worth introducing students to their first algorithm or routine. This algorithm's main purpose is to ensure that your classroom runs efficiently and time is rarely wasted in distributing and collecting resources. Put simply, the "book algorithm" is planned by the teacher and is based on the shortest and most efficient path for students to pass their books so that they are collected in one pile; ideally this pile should be located near to where the books are usually stored. In the diagram in Figure 5.5, students are instructed to pass their books to their right (your left) along the row. Once the last student in the row is reached, this student forms a pile of books, they can then pass these books towards desk 7; that is, forwards or backwards. The student at desk 7, Morgan in this case, is responsible for taking the books to the allocated space on the windowsill.

In order to get a sense of positive competition, students are informed that they will be timed and their time will be logged on the leader board at the front of the room. There are only two rules: Books must be passed in silence and they cannot be thrown. If students break any of the two rules, their time does not count. If necessary, the algorithm can be repeated with the student survey sheet. The record time for the room in the diagram is 7.85 seconds and provided

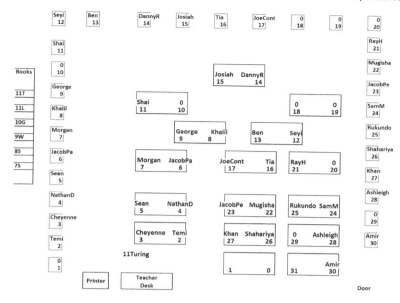

Figure 5.5 A typical classroom layout for a computer lab.[6]

this routine is practised at the end of every lesson, it becomes automatic by the end of the first term.

Should you have time remaining, you may wish to follow Tyler Hester's first lesson series where he continues to talk about himself and his philosophy of education. In the past, I have often talked about my past students as many have graduated from universities, apprenticeships and training schemes. Many are currently working or pursuing further studies in a variety of fields including computer science, accounting, finance, law, film, animation, fashion, art, real estate, education and medicine. Speaking about past students enables your current students to relate to people from a similar background and of a similar age. It also helps students see the bigger picture and they realise that by studying computing, it is possible to follow a wide range of career paths.

As mentioned previously, the purpose of the first few lessons is to establish the culture of your classroom. It is here that you set what your high expectations are and explain how you wish for the classroom to be run. It is worth spending two to three hours planning these first few lessons. Students need a teacher that is confident, engaging and respectful and this is established in the first few lessons (Rogers, 2011). The amount of time invested in planning these lessons is worthwhile as you can reuse the same lesson for multiple year groups and classes. The following section will cover strategies which ensure this positive learning culture is sustained throughout the year.

Sustaining the positive learning culture

If the student is faced with sources of stress in an educational context which go beyond the positive challenge threshold—for instance, aggressive teachers, bullying students or incomprehensible learning materials whether books or computers—it triggers fear and cognitive function is negatively affected.

(CERI, 2008)

In order to maximise learning, we need to sustain an environment where students feel safe. Public verbal praise should far outweigh the number of warnings, sanctions and negative interactions. The positive interactions should primarily focus on effort rather than outcome in order to nurture a growth mindset within the classroom (Dweck, 2006). Many of the strategies for establishing the initial positive environment are covered by Doug Lemov and Paul Bambrick-Santoyo in their various books (Lemov, 2010; Lemov, 2015; Bambrick-Santoyo, 2016). In preparation for your first few classes, in the previous section I have covered most of the rules and routines which you might wish to use for your students. The following section includes routines and techniques which you will want to use consistently and frequently in all your lessons to ensure good habits are formed.

One basic routine involves how you will get your students' attention when they are using the computers. Ideally, all your students' screens will face inwards to the centre of the room, thereby making it easier for you to monitor students' learning and progress. However, one unavoidable drawback of this typical layout is that all students will have their back to you when they are on their computers; therefore the visual signals that you may have in your teacher toolkit to regain students' attention are unlikely to work. I generally do a countdown (as per the school's policy); teachers operating in a school without a consistent policy may wish to use other audio cues like a calming wind chime. On your chosen signal, request students to turn their monitors off and look at or "track" you. If you have classroom management software and you are stopping your students to model a process from your computer or another student's computer, it is best to use this software to broadcast directly to the students' screens. If your school uses laptops instead of desktops, you can ask your students to close their screen halfway or to 45 degrees; this ensures your students are focussed on you as they can no longer see their work. Closing the lid halfway means their computers avoid going into sleep or hibernate mode, thereby making the transition back to independent practice much smoother. Training your students in this simple yet effective technique is essential; as with all routines this needs teacher modelling first and then student practice. You need your student's full attention and if they can still see material on their screen, their attention will be somewhere else and they won't be able to process your instructions. Taking away distractions reduces cognitive load, thereby allowing for more effective teaching and learning.

Another routine to establish is that of *one voice*. The routine explains itself, only one voice; that is, only one person should be heard at any one time during teacher or student questioning. This links back to the rules about respect from the previous section. The best technique to establish one voice is Doug Lemov's strong voice. The strong voice guidelines state:

1 The teacher stands still and faces their students, maintaining strong eye contact.
2 The teacher adopts a formal pose and does not walk around the room when delivering instructions.
3 The teacher uses a formal register (tone and word choice).
4 The teacher uses economy of language.
5 Do not talk over students – pause if you are interrupted.

6   Do not engage in student's off-task questions – keep their focus on topic.

7   Quiet power – If anxious, speak deeper, rather than faster and louder.

(Lemov, 2010; Bambrick-Santoyo, 2016)

The most important part of the strong voice technique is part 5, not talking over your students. By refusing to talk over students, you demonstrate to them the level of respect that is expected during *one voice*. It reinforces the philosophy that everyone has the right to be heard and that because you respect your students, you will not interrupt them and likewise they should not interrupt you or their peers.

Many behaviour management books and courses will talk about 'least invasive intervention' or 'praising in public and reprimanding in private' (Rogers, 2011). This is another key technique required to sustain a positive environment; nobody responds well to public humiliation. When a student is doing something incorrectly, you might first start by publicly praising their surrounding peers for meeting your expectations, for example, "Well done, I can see Jamie-Maie, Giacomo and Susie using cell references in their formula." There is a small chance that this does not correct a student's off-task behaviour or incorrect method for completing a task. If that is the case, you may point to a student's screen and quietly prompt them, for example by asking them how they could improve the formula so that it always updates automatically if the values in the cells change. Many novice teachers will make the mistake of loudly and publicly pointing out the mistake from afar. This should be avoided. If you notice several students making the same mistake, perhaps that is the time to intervene by stopping the whole class, modelling the incorrect method and then asking a student to correct the method and explain why (in this case) cell referencing is better than using data values in a formula.

There will be times when a student does something which is dangerous or they contravene your classroom rules in a serious manner, for example they make violent physical contact with a peer. In this case, you may need to shout to begin with to bring a quick stop to the behaviour; however, in most cases it is best to try to remain calm to diffuse the situation. Rarely is it useful to shout in your lesson; students need to see that you are in control and calm at all times. If you shout often, you leave few other tools in your toolkit to escalate to when a student's behaviour continues to deteriorate or if there is a more serious incident.

Rogers advises that we should always start our corrections with the least intrusive method first and try to be non-confrontational. In order to sustain the positive environment, it is important to keep the fundamental respect in a classroom intact. Never ask "why" a student is misbehaving; this rarely has an answer which will help you resolve the situation. The aim must always be to restore and maintain calmness, order and focus. If there is a major incident in the classroom and you feel your stress levels rising, Rogers advises that you should calm yourself first and then calm your students (Rogers, 2011).

Behaviour management

Michael Linsin advises all teachers to have a classroom management plan (Linsin, 2011). At the start of this chapter, I devised a set of rules (shown at the bottom of Figure 5.4). You will want to devise your own rules which address every conceivable misbehaviour or disruption in your classroom.

Linsin has his own set of rules:

1   Listen and follow directions.
2   Raise your hand before speaking or leaving your seat.
3   Keep your hands and feet to yourself.
4   Respect your classmates and your teacher.

He states that your rules should make sense to students. They need to be fully enforceable, and they need to cover everything. He states that a good set of rules will have a refreshing lack of ambiguity, they will discourage arguing, complaining and finger pointing.

Having established a set of rules, it is important to establish a set of consequences. In schools with a strong behaviour management policy, this will be consistent across all classrooms and you will need to follow this consistently. If there is not a strong behaviour policy, you will need to devise your own set of consequences. It may include:

1   A verbal warning
2   A written warning
3   Detention
4   Removal from the classroom.

The consequences do need to be enforced, be clear when you are giving a student a warning and it is necessary to strike a balance between being minimally invasive and being assertive and clear. For the verbal warning, you should state what the student has done wrong, deliver the warning and move straight on, do not allow for this to take up time or time for them to answer back. Provided you do not leave a pause for an expectant retort, the student will generally not argue back. If a student does argue with you, state calmly that you can discuss this at the end of the lesson. At the written or verbal warning stage, it might be worth changing the seating plan slightly; the student who has misbehaved may be moved to the front desk or away from their peers. This isolation in itself is enough to give students a bit of time to reflect whilst remaining in the lesson. The aim of a teacher must be to keep all their students in their classroom and learning unless a student is particularly disruptive or it is unsafe for a student to remain in the classroom. It is vital to remain calm throughout the process of escalation through the consequences.

Generally, when I get to the detention stage I will ask the student to speak to me at the end of the lesson so I can then inform them of their detention. By informing students of someone's detention in the middle of a lesson, you will risk creating an antagonistic and negative situation which could disrupt the learning for the rest of the class. A student may inevitably ask if they have detention and I would simply reiterate that you will speak to them at the end of the lesson. In many schools, students may be removed from lessons or sent out from lessons if their behaviour does not improve; use this technique sparingly and with caution; using it often diminishes the seriousness and devalues the technique. However, do not feel as though you are weak if you use this last step; strong senior leaders and pastoral teams will never reprimand you from following a system consistently. Using the consequences in a measured fashion is a sign of a strong teacher.

Classroom incident reflection

Name: _____

Form: _____

In the space below write down your account of what happened in Mr Lau's lesson.

How did Mr Lau feel when the problem occurred?
_____
_____

How did the rest of the class feel when the problem occurred?
_____
_____

How might this problem have impacted you?
_____
_____

How might this problem have impacted those around you?
_____
_____

Why has Mr Lau set the detention? Did he do this to annoy you?
_____
_____

What can you do to ensure this doesn't happen again?
_____
_____

What can Mr Lau do to ensure this doesn't happen again?
_____
_____

Is there anything you can do to make amends?
_____
_____

Sign your name here: _____

Today's date: 21/04/2017

Figure 5.6 Classroom incident reflection form.

When speaking to students at the end of the class or at detention, Rogers advises that students should be offered a chance to give their version of events, asked what classroom right was affected (e.g. right to learn, to be heard or to be respected) and what they can do differently next time. Jessica Dumbreck, 2i/c science at Greenwich Free School, devised the following set of questions which have been made into a reflection form which can be completed in silence at the start of detention (Figure 5.6). A written reflection is my preferred method as it encourages introspection and empathy rather than immediate antagonistic dialogue and debate.

GFS Restorative Justice Record

Name: _____

Form: _____

In the space below write down your account of what happened:

What happened?

_____
_____
_____

What were you thinking or feeling at the time?

_____
_____

Has anything happened before or since?

_____
_____

What were your thoughts or feelings then?

_____
_____

Has anyone else been affected?

_____
_____

What are your thoughts and feelings now?

_____
_____

What do you need now?

_____
_____

Sign your name here: _____

Today's date: 19/9/2016

Figure 5.7 Restorative Justice Record for reflection prior to a restorative conversation.

The follow-up to this form would be a restorative conversation about how their learning was impacted, how the feelings of others were affected and how we can move on and ensure the same mistake does not happen again. The next time you see the student, they should be given a fresh start. You cannot hold grudges or take things personally, no matter how severe the level of disrespect. In severe cases, you may ask for a head of year or senior leader to chair the restorative conversation. An alternative template for an extensive restorative conversation is provided in Figure 5.7.

The selective use of praise when some students are not meeting expectations is known as narrating the positive and falls under Lemov's technique positive framing. Positive framing sees students in the best light and gives them the benefit of the doubt. By narrating the positive, we can build momentum in the classroom; simply stating that you can see 80 per cent of students with their monitors off and then 85 per cent and then 90 per cent will quickly ensure everyone complies and meets your expectation. You should only continue when you have 100 per cent compliance; anything less than 100 per cent suggests that it is okay for students to ignore your instructions and the percentage of compliance will begin to slip for other tasks (Lemov, 2015). Our students will all generally conform and converge towards social norms when in a group (Smith & Mackie, 2007): This is because they will want to feel a sense of connectedness. It is the teacher's job to establish what these social norms are. If the social norms involve a noisy and disrespectful classroom, the students will collectively conform to this to feel part of the connected group. However, if you can create positive social norms and remind students of these frequently and publicly, you are likely to achieve and sustain a positive learning environment.

At times, you may feel as though the classroom is becoming noisy and unruly. The first thing to remember is that a silent classroom can be a poor proxy for learning. Silence could be a sign of apathy, boredom, confusion or a lack of trying for fear of failure. To gauge what the level of engagement is and to see if any hotspots in your classroom need addressing, Lemov advises the teacher to position themselves in a corner of the room, which he refers to as 'Pastore's perch' (named after an expert teacher, Patrick Pastore). In Figure 5.5, Pastore's perch would be in between the door and desk 30. By standing here rather than at the teacher's desk or in the middle of the room, you decrease the angle in which you need to scan from 180 degrees to 90 degrees. From this position you can pause and examine what is actually happening in your room. You can now ask yourself:

- Do some students need some recognition through public praise?
- Which students are working co-operatively?
- Does the seating plan need to be changed?
- What task is the majority working on? Can this be used to narrate the positive and build momentum for students which have slowed down or become disengaged?
- Do you need to have a quiet word with a certain hotspot in the room?

Clearly a lot of this section is based on the work of Lemov and Bambrick-Santoyo, and I highly recommend reading their books. However, if I were to highlight one final technique which encourages a growth mindset in students it would be Lemov's 'No Opt Out'. The technique simply states that "I don't know" is never a valid answer and the end point for a questioning sequence should always end in the student delivering the correct answer. In order to maintain high expectations, you may acknowledge a reluctant student by stating, "I know you don't know, but I want to know what you think." If a student is still uncertain, you may give them a multiple-choice set of answers or you may ask if he or she wishes to "phone a friend". Even if he or she gets the answer wrong, you would always go back to the student and ask them to repeat the correct answer and you should praise them for delivering the correct answer. Although this seems somewhat unnatural at first, it enforces the notion that not trying is not acceptable and the student can still be praised for eventually getting to the correct answer, even if this is with the help of his or her peers. Students should develop the habit of attempting to answer questions rather than fearing that they may get ridiculed by their peers for incorrect answers.

No opt out is backed by research into the generation effect by cognitive scientists Rosalind Potts and David Shanks. In their studies, even when students generated a wrong answer, as long as the students were provided with corrective feedback, the students still benefited more than when they were simply told an answer (Potts & Shanks, 2013). The generation effect in many cases introduces desirable difficulty (Bjork & Bjork, 2011) by requiring the student to think and recall. The benefits of the generation effect and no opt out cannot be underestimated.

Lesson pace

Lesson pace is an area which needs particular attention in the computing classroom. Given that in the majority of schools, lessons are less than 60 minutes long and the time is unavoidably lost during practical tasks and general administration (logging in/out, loading programs, saving, troubleshooting, debugging, re-drafting), it is vital that pace is maintained and lesson time is used wisely. A few key habits will greatly facilitate lesson pace.

If you have planned to deliver a practical lesson using computers, you should ensure that all computers and monitors are switched on before the lesson. Waiting for computers to boot, resume from hibernation or download updates will greatly impact lesson pace. Likewise, if it is the first lesson in a unit of work, it is worth checking that all the necessary software is correctly installed on all the devices at least a week before the lesson. This task is relatively straightforward if you have classroom management software and a school technician. If these are not in place, you could train a group of student technicians and ask them to help you with these audits.

If students need their exercise books, these should ideally be handed out before the lesson. If you are teaching consecutive lessons, the books for the next lesson can be handed out during the consolidation phase of the previous lesson. The book algorithm described at the start of this chapter should ensure that the books are already roughly in sequence. Some teachers ask students to label their books with their desk number; however, as the seating plan is likely to change a few times during the year based on assessment data this might not be worthwhile.

Worksheets including Do Nows and exit tickets should be printed and trimmed before your lesson. Ideally, they would be printed at the start of the day. Having prepared all the resources (hardware, software and hardcopy), you will feel much more relaxed for the start of the lesson. Operating under stress generally results in rushed and inefficient working practices.

The Do Now ensures a calm and consistent start to the lesson and is a good opportunity to check the learner's current understanding. In most cases, it should take between five and eight minutes. A valid exception would be a Do Now activity that asks for students to review their work based on teacher feedback. Whilst the Do Now is taking place, the teacher should take the register and continue to roam the room to check for understanding and gauge what misconceptions might exist. The teacher can also narrate the positive things he or she is seeing and encourage task compliance. Using a countdown timer is one way to ensure the Do Now does not unnecessarily take up too much lesson time.

Whilst I would promote direct instruction for most lessons, teacher input needs to be concise. Teachers need to demonstrate an economy of language whereby they use as few words as necessary when explaining and giving instructions. Teachers can further ensure that lesson pace is maintained by punctuating their input with targeted questions. Computing lends itself well to punctuating with cold call (see page 108) questioning, particularly during teacher modelling. As a teacher completes one step of the task (say) creating a graph in a spreadsheet or a line of code in a program, the teacher can stop and ask questions such as:

1 "What should I do next to ensure the graph is meaningful?"
2 "What is missing from the graph?"
3 "What is missing from the end of this line of code?"
4 "Looking at the pseudocode, what comes next?"
5 "What is the name of the variable in this line?"
6 "How do we add a 'line of best fit' to this graph?"
7 "What do I need to click on to get axis labels?"
8 "Why might a graph be more useful than the original table of data?"
9 "What validation could you ask to ensure the data is sensible?"
10 "Is this now correct?"

All of these questions require students to pay close attention to the teacher modelling a process. If you fall into the habit of modelling without punctuated questions, students may also develop the habit of switching off during the teacher demonstration. However, if students expect that there will be a question to punctuate each step, then they will start to develop better observational habits.

Formative assessment will be covered in more detail in the following pages; however, it is worth noting that real-time data gleaned through formative assessment can quickly inform the teacher of hurdles which he or she may not have anticipated. Likewise, asking students how many tasks they have completed can give you a very clear visual indicator of class progress and can inform you of when the next piece of whole-class modelling or intervention needs to take place. Ten minutes into a demonstration phase, I might stop students and ask them to

"put your hands up if you have completed task one ... keep your hands up if you have completed task two ... and let's see who is on task three ..."

I would then roughly comment on this in terms of a percentage of the class; this in itself helps drive lesson pace in a positive way. Occasionally, a student may be procrastinating, spending too much time on unnecessary formatting or talking to their peers and the student will not be particularly motivated if you say, "James, why are you still on task 1?" Yet, when James hears that everyone has completed task two and 70 per cent of the class are on task three, this implicitly suggests that he needs to improve his pace. Highlighting the positives in your classroom is a much better motivator than highlighting the negatives, and AFL allows you to provide evidence for positive progress.

Differentiation is another significant area in itself and entire books have been written about this area of pedagogy. I can highly recommend *How to Differentiate Instruction in Mixed-Ability Classrooms* (Tomlinson, 2001) as a short yet comprehensive book on differentiation techniques. In terms of lesson pace, the tasks that you plan should be progressively more difficult and there should be an extension task at all times. However, there may be instances whereby despite careful planning, students are significantly ahead of or behind where you expect them to be. Do not be afraid to adjust the extension task throughout the lesson. Of course, this is also a great opportunity to praise students for their outstanding progress.

In terms of developing a solid routine for lesson planning, I would always recommend that the last step in the lesson planning process for a computing teacher should be to complete all the tasks that they have planned for their students themselves. There are several reasons for this:

1   You will uncover hidden bugs in your planned tasks and solutions.
2   You will have a worked example ready for a student who misses a lesson in a series of lessons.
3   Your worked example can be given to the teaching assistant, thereby allowing them to support learners more effectively.
4   Your worked example can be modified and used as a resource for students with low prior attainment (LPA) or a SEND.

Whilst working at St Marylebone CE School, we developed the routine of completing each other's lessons and assessments. We found that even the wording of the tasks could be open to misinterpretation. We also noticed that some tasks were over-planned or under-planned in terms of the time allocated and adjustments could be made before the lesson was delivered.

Differentiation

Differentiated Instruction is a teaching philosophy based on the premise that teachers should adapt instruction to student differences. Rather than marching students through the curriculum lockstep, teachers should modify their instruction to meet students' varying readiness levels, learning preferences and interests. Therefore, the teacher proactively plans a variety of ways to "get it" and express learning (Tomlinson, 2001).

Differentiation should become a habit rather than an afterthought or bolt-on to the lesson planning and delivery process. However, Tomlinson admits that the mere act of differentiation is itself difficult and in forming good differentiation habits and routines, it may be worth differentiating with the class you find easiest to work with. Some differentiation requires very little preparation whilst other techniques are much more involved. In this section I hope to cover a wide variety of techniques which can be used in the computing classroom.

In computing, I find the use of video tutorials a worthy investment in time. These tutorials can be made using free software such as Open Broadcaster Software (OBS). The act of making these tutorials allows the teacher to practice the skill and complete a process or task whilst narrating their thinking aloud for their students. If there are any bugs or idiosyncrasies with the software being used, it will be picked up at this stage and learners can be warned of these and given strategies to combat these issues. Once recorded, these tutorials can be reused for multiple classes for several years. Examples of YouTube tutorials that I use in my lessons can be found at www.tinyurl.com/WLauPyTutorials. Whilst observers often assume that these are most beneficial for low-prior-attaining students, I actually find them an excellent resource for the middle- and high-prior-attaining students. By allowing students to access these tutorials independently, it provides time for the teacher to work one-to-one with the weaker students in the class.

Jane Waite warns that video tutorials, step-by-step worksheets and structured online learning guides (commonly used when teaching programming) can result in students becoming overly dependent on these scaffolds (Waite, 2017). In many cases, students simply copy techniques procedurally without understanding how and when to use them in new contexts. It is therefore important that the tutorials do not provide a complete solution to a specific problem, but rather provide a generic guide to a particular technique (e.g. using a for loop to repeat a set of steps or using the clone brush in Adobe Photoshop). Pan *et al.*'s research into using videos as scaffolding tools states that videos should include key terms, knowledge, skills and resources and that in doing so, these videos may also help reveal related procedures, structures or mechanisms for coping with and resolving problems (Pan *et al.*, 2012). These types of tutorials also reflect the nature of learning in the Information Age. Videos are frequently used to supplement computing courses, and whilst teachers should be careful about how much support to provide in these videos, this medium cannot be ignored.

Wood *et al.* advise that the support provided by scaffolding should ideally be provided on an as-needed basis and faded as learner competence increases (Wood *et al.*, 1976). I have found that students are generally very good at self-regulating their use of these video tutorials. As students become more familiar with a technique and as students move towards mastery, students become less reliant on the video tutorials, relying instead on the automatic recall of techniques and applying these to the problem at hand.

If tutorials are not appropriate for a task because it is more open-ended, for example a graphic design task, Tomlinson advises that students are given anchor activities. These activities are self-directed tasks which students automatically move to when they have completed a directed task; they differ from a lesson's extension task in that they do not necessarily follow the lesson's prior content-based activity. In computing, this might be the creation of quizzes for self-testing, a research task on a new piece of technology or the creation and subsequent updating of a digital portfolio. Once again, these tasks result in the teacher being free to assist students who are working at a slower pace.

Doug Lemov cites the use of the front table in a classroom. Rather than having a static seating plan, the front table can be used to bring a small group of students forward to do a more thorough check for understanding before they start a task (Lemov, 2015). Students can be asked lower-order thinking questions such as:

1   "What program will you open first?"
2   "Where will you find the source images?"
3   "What's the first step I need to take?"
4   "What should I do after I have done _____ ?"
5   "Where will I find the tutorials if I get stuck?"

The front table technique can also be adapted for high-prior-attaining students to introduce an advanced skill or to launch an extension task. When designing a series of tasks, these tasks should become progressively more difficult and the extension task should always require higher-order thinking. The extension task should require new ways of thinking, rather than simply doing "more of the same".

Scaffolding strategies should be provided to ensure that students can access work in their zone of proximal development (ZPD). In mixed ability settings, differentiation is essential and should stretch students with high prior attainment and support those with low prior attainment. Table 5.4 summarises the different ways that a computing teacher may differentiate in a computing classroom.

For students with SEND, it may be necessary to provide more specialised differentiated resources. In Chapter 3, we discussed how to effectively plan with a Teaching Assistant (TA). From experience, there will be times when you do not have a regular TA attached to your class or do not have a mutual free PPA period in which to meet, I would therefore advise you follow the steps outlined below.

First, at the beginning of the year print out your class's datasheet. Go through all the students with SEND, some may be visual or hearing impairments. An adjustment to the seating plan may be required to seat them at the front where they can clearly see you speaking. This is essential for students with visual and auditory impairment as many will depend on lip-reading to hear you. If you spend a lot of your time facing the board as opposed to facing your students, adjustments to your teaching stance will need to be adopted.

For students with visual impairment, it will be necessary to check with your special educational needs coordinator (SENCO) what size fonts this student can read. In some cases, students will require size 24 font. On some occasions, I would recommend enlarging an existing A4 resource onto A3 paper using a photocopier; however, it is important to be discreet with this as many students will not want adverse attention drawn to them. Some students may prefer size 24 font on A4 paper and this is worth discussing with a student individually. The colour of the paper may also need to be changed. Students with dyslexia may request their work to be printed on blue, buff or pink paper. It is useful to have transparent A4 document wallets or acetate sheets in these colours. These are readily available from most stationers and supermarkets. Having these to hand means that if you forget to print on a particular colour, you can quickly resort to using a transparent wallet or acetate.

I would next look through the notes for all of your other SEND students. Your SENCO may have added notes on your school's management information system (MIS). However, if

Table 5.4 Methods of differentiation for computing

Topic	Differentiation method		
	Differentiation by content or resource	Differentiation by process or support	Differentiation by product
Programming	**Stretch**: Include extension tasks which rely on multiple data types and data structures **Scaffold**: Provide partially completed programs and/or printouts	**Stretch**: Provide tutorials to introduce a skill which the student needs to adapt for their own program **Scaffold**: Spend more time one-to-one, checking student syntax and adding comments in the code where changes may be necessary	**Stretch**: Ensure the program uses self-defined procedures and functions to minimise redundancy and encourage code re-use **Scaffold**: Provide a simplified checklist of requirements or a simplified rubric
Databases	**Stretch**: Create a database from scratch, importing data from an external file **Scaffold**: Provide a ready-made database with some query templates as examples for students to modify	**Stretch**: Students to draw their own entity-relationship model before completing their database **Scaffold**: Provide planning templates for queries or entity-relationship models	**Stretch**: Construct a relational database model and perform queries which require the use of logical operators and wildcards **Scaffold**: Perform queries on a relational database model
Spreadsheets	**Stretch**: Use spreadsheets with multiple worksheets that require 3D referencing **Scaffold**: Provide a partially-completed spreadsheet which requires some data entry	**Stretch**: Use named references, absolute and relative cell referencing **Scaffold**: Provide video tutorials and helpsheets which explain how functions work	**Stretch**: Students asked to perform analysis and make inferences based on the results **Scaffold**: Students are asked closed questions which require simple interpretation of results
Print Publications	**Stretch**: Give a design brief for a more challenging (unfamiliar) audience **Scaffold**: Provide a bank of high-quality images for students to use on a template	**Stretch**: Cover advanced image editing techniques including the use of masking and curves **Scaffold**: Provide more regular feedback with regards to layout and design principles	**Stretch**: Design derivative publications based on student's original design, e.g. versions, campaigns or adverts to be integrated within the finished product. **Scaffold**: Design a derivative publication based on a commercial design, e.g. Advert or magazine cover

Continued

Table 5.4 Continued

Web Publications	**Stretch**: Include HTML, CSS and Javascript **Scaffold**: Provide a website template for students to modify	**Stretch**: Allow an open process where students are guided towards Javascript dynamic content and CSS menus where they can choose how to enhance their website **Scaffold**: Provide video tutorials for different techniques accompanied with printed worksheets Encourage the use of embedded elements such as Youtube videos, social media streams and other widgets	**Stretch**: A multi-page website with internal hyperlinks and interactive elements **Scaffold**: A single webpage with hyperlinks to external sites and embedded widgets
Video projects	**Stretch**: Students to produce their own raw footage for a challenging brief, e.g. in low light conditions, requiring pans, tilts and significant amounts of continuity shots, e.g. shot-reverse shot **Scaffold**: Provide a bank of appropriate stills, titles and video clips	**Stretch**: The workflow would incorporate using key frames for editing audio and transitions The workflow could be extended further to include colouring, grading and visual effects **Scaffold**: Use of simple editors such as Movie Maker or iMovie. Helpsheets which guide students with the importing of video clips and general work-flow	**Stretch**: Finished video may include student's own edited sounds, complex transitions and titles. The latter would be produced using motion graphics software **Scaffold**: Finished video will use built-in titles and effects
Research / Theory content	**Stretch**: Ask fertile questions which require a balanced argument **Scaffold**: Provide suitable websites as starting points, e.g. BBC Bitesize, Teach-ICT, SimpleWiki.	**Stretch**: Require Harvard referencing using citation tools in the word processor **Scaffold**: Provide a partially complete bibliography and either gap fills or writing frames for students to complete	**Stretch**: Students may be asked to write an extended written report **Scaffold**: Students will complete comprehension-style questions and can be asked to present their work as a presentation, an audio or video recording

these are missing, a head of year or form tutor will usually be able to tell you about specific strategies for your SEND students. Many SEND students will have developed an attainment gap over the years due to their SEND. I would advise pairing SEND students who have low prior attainment with a supportive student of middle prior attainment. If the attainment gap is too steep, the students will be hindered by each other's pacing and level of understanding. A student with slightly higher prior attainment will be able to support their peer and benefit from this supportive relationship. In my experience, the maxim, "You don't fully understand a discipline until you can explain it to a novice" holds true.

Finally, as recommended in the earlier section on lesson pace, I would ensure that you have completed a worked example of the product for the lesson in advance. As a last resort, you can share your worked example on a networked drive for students to access. You would only need to provide this for students with low prior attainment rather than for the entire class, and if the student managed to reproduce the worked example, you can give them an extension task which will encourage higher-order thinking and will boost their confidence further.

As the lesson unfolds, the support that you provide for students with SEND may also differ. Students with visual impairment will benefit from using the magnifier tool, most operating systems have a high-contrast mode and most programs also have a zoom function. Students with slower processing or working memory impairments may benefit from reduced cognitive load. This can be provided in several ways. A high-effort method would be to provide scaffolded worksheets and tutorials for every lesson. This may be necessary for some learners with severe learning difficulties. However, for students with moderate or mild learning difficulties, these may result in the student becoming overly dependent and they may feel like they are not sufficiently challenged. Remember that tasks need some desirable difficulties, otherwise students will not be required to perform much cognitive processing and thus learning will be minimal.

A low-effort method for intervention is to write notes to the students. This can be done on a mini-whiteboard or on sticky notes. Some autistic students will arrive to your lesson with a Now-Next-Later visual aid; this is useful for structuring steps for students to follow. In my classroom, I used a large roll of transparent acetate (the type that is used to protect large display boards) to transform a lot of my walls into writable, dry-wipe erasable surfaces. I have found that writing short instructions, explanations, worked examples and algorithms on these covered walls or on the windows around the classroom is an effective way of differentiating when providing one-to-one support. Students can refer to these written notes throughout the lesson and it is a great way to reduce cognitive load. For students with high prior attainment, I would reduce the level of support by perhaps demonstrating a technique and asking them to take notes in their books.

Simmons and Hawkins state (2015) that it would be unrealistic to use all these methods of differentiation in every lesson. I agree with their advice; the differentiation you provide will require adjustment and you will find the right mix of differentiation strategies once you get to know your students individually rather than simply differentiating based on your class datasheet. Over time, you will be able to strike a fine balance in your differentiation strategies to ensure that your lessons are accessible and suitably challenging for all the learners in your classroom.

Questioning

> In a thinking classroom, teachers plan their questioning in ways that will promote differentiation, challenge, independence of thought, alongside opportunities to think together, share views and ideas and discuss or explore the differences in their thinking. Questioning will need to be planned to promote and model such thinking and to guide the learning task.
>
> (Gast, 2014)

We already know that prior knowledge is the foundation upon which we build new ideas, concepts and knowledge; however, this level of knowledge and understanding is constantly changing throughout our lessons. We cannot assume that everything the teacher says or does means that students fully understand a concept or skill. Therefore, questioning is an important habit to form as it allows us to constantly check our students' understanding.

Questioning elicits data which can be used to determine what you should do next in your lesson. It allows you to gauge whether you can move on or whether further instruction or clarification is required to correct a misconception. When used effectively it will punctuate your lesson, maintain a lesson pace and keep your students engaged. Teachers should punctuate their lessons (particularly phases where modelling is involved) with questions. By maintaining a dialogue with the students during modelling, you enable them to go on a journey with you and there will be more buy-in and better understanding. Without questioning, the modelling becomes like a sales talk demonstration with the teacher unable to gauge whether their students truly grasp the tacit knowledge behind the deconstruction and reconstruction of a model.

Questioning can take various forms. One form of questioning is the cold call. In this simple method championed by Lemov (Lemov, 2015), a student is chosen to assess their level of understanding rather than choosing students who offer an answer with their hands up.[7] Cold-calling using this method and combined with Lemov's no opt out is a powerful way to instil a culture of learning, where everybody is expected to answer at any time. Another form of questioning is to introduce randomisation; this can be done by writing students' names onto lollipop sticks. You could also give each student a lollipop stick to write their name on at the beginning of the year. Lollipop sticks are fairly cheap and robust; however, if you do not have a department budget, you may wish to simply populate a spreadsheet with your students from each class. If this is printed in size 18 font with cell borders and onto card, it will ensure the name tags can be easily trimmed and read out.

When a student gives an answer, you have four possible choices:

1 Stretch them with a more difficult follow-up question.
2 Ask the class if they would like to accept, challenge or extend (ACE).
3 Cold-call another peer to ask if they would like to accept, challenge or extend (ACE).
4 Scaffold the student towards the correct answer if it is not 100 per cent correct.

Dylan Wiliam claims that in some classrooms, the questioning fails to engage the whole class. A lot of questioning is done in a table-tennis fashion, bouncing questions backwards and forwards to the same student – this type of questioning is often referred to as initiation-response-evaluation (IRE) (Wiliam, 2011). Wiliam also states that without a sense of randomisation, teachers will often simply pick a student with high prior attainment (HPA) who has their hand up and when they give the correct answer, the teacher incorrectly assumes that the whole class has understood the concept. The alternative is to structure questioning more like basketball, where the question is bounced around the classroom, the ACE framework of questioning allows for this. Wiliam also documents a technique called 'pose, pause, pounce, bounce'. A question is posed, there is a five-second pause (similar to Lemov's wait time technique), a student is chosen at random and their answer is then bounced onto another random peer for further comment.

At many schools that have adopted 'Teach-Like-a-Champion' techniques, students could also be taught to use seat signals to give an audible sign of their thoughts. Students could be asked to click if they agree, wave if they disagree or put their hand up if they wish to extend the answer. Any student giving a seat signal may be called upon for a contribution and it is clear already what type of contribution they wish to make. If 70 per cent of students are clicking to an incorrect answer, the teacher knows that this is a common misconception. If there are one or two students who are waving and challenging this answer, it is worth choosing one of these students to hear their alternative viewpoint; perhaps they can correct the misconception for you. If this technique works for you, you can train your classes to use seat signals for all questions at any time in the lesson.

Another form of questioning which we have already covered is think pair share. As previously mentioned, it is worth structuring this dialogue explaining how you wish for students to critique each other and stating who should start the discussion (e.g. an odd-numbered desk first). Think pair share is useful when the level of mastery in your classroom varies widely. Think pair share allows weaker or less confident students to voice their opinions in a safe (private) interaction with a peer initially and once their thoughts have been shared and clarified, any student in the class should feel confident enough to answer the question with a well-prepared response if called upon.

For questioning to be effective, we must consider not only who we question but what these questions are. If the aim is to gauge understanding and to encourage students to think more deeply, then the choice of questions must be carefully considered. Hopkins, Craig and Knight propose using Bloom's Taxonomy as a basis for structuring questions and moving beyond lower-order thinking questions which emphasise factual recall (Hopkins *et al.*, 2015). By considering Bloom's Taxonomy, questions can move towards higher-order thinking which emphasise understanding increasingly complex and abstract knowledge and contexts (Figure 5.8).

When asking questions, the teacher's intention should be one of expectant response. In order to ensure a response, teachers should combine wait time with careful phrasing and intonation. If a teacher asks, "Are there any questions?" and follows up immediately without waiting, "OK, good let's move on", the teacher risks creating a culture where students are afraid of asking questions. Whereas, changing the initial question to "Now is the time for questions, who would like to ask a question about the exemplar?" and waiting for five seconds, students are more likely to respond positively. An alternative question which Jo Parkes (Head of English at Greenwich Free School) uses combines wait time with think pair share. Following the deconstruction of a student's written answer, Jo would ask the students to "Speak to the person next to you for 30 seconds and decide on a question you would like to ask about the example". With both of these questions, students are encouraged and expected to ask questions. If you are asking students questions with a definite right answer, it is important that you embrace mistakes and keep a neutral reaction even if the answer is incorrect.

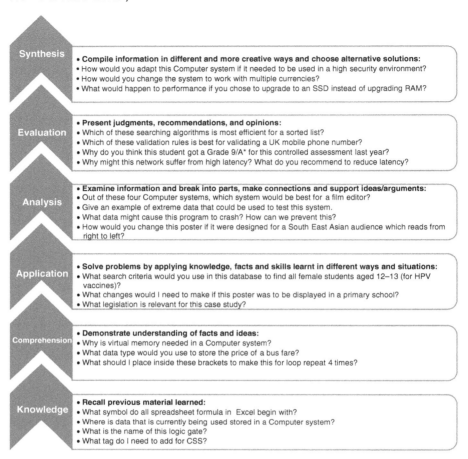

Synthesis
- **Compile information in different and more creative ways and choose alternative solutions:**
- How would you adapt this Computer system if it needed to be used in a high security environment?
- How would you change the system to work with multiple currencies?
- What would happen to performance if you chose to upgrade to an SSD instead of upgrading RAM?

Evaluation
- **Present judgments, recommendations, and opinions:**
- Which of these searching algorithms is most efficient for a sorted list?
- Which of these validation rules is best for validating a UK mobile phone number?
- Why do you think this student got a Grade 9/A* for this controlled assessment last year?
- Why might this network suffer from high latency? What do you recommend to reduce latency?

Analysis
- **Examine information and break into parts, make connections and support ideas/arguments:**
- Out of these four Computer systems, which system would be best for a film editor?
- Give an example of extreme data that could be used to test this system.
- What data might cause this program to crash? How can we prevent this?
- How would you change this poster if it were designed for a South East Asian audience which reads from right to left?

Application
- **Solve problems by applying knowledge, facts and skills learnt in different ways and situations:**
- What search criteria would you use in this database to find all female students aged 12–13 (for HPV vaccines)?
- What changes would I need to make if this poster was to be displayed in a primary school?
- What legislation is relevant for this case study?

Comprehension
- **Demonstrate understanding of facts and ideas:**
- Why is virtual memory needed in a Computer system?
- What data type would you use to store the price of a bus fare?
- What should I place inside these brackets to make this for loop repeat 4 times?

Knowledge
- **Recall previous material learned:**
- What symbol do all spreadsheet formula in Excel begin with?
- Where is data that is currently being used stored in a Computer system?
- What is the name of this logic gate?
- What tag do I need to add for CSS?

Figure 5.8 Encouraging questions which require higher-order thinking (adapted from Hopkins *et al.*, 2015).

If you have a clear tell when a student gives an incorrect answer, other students are unlikely to use the 'accept' in the ACE framework, thereby hiding common misconceptions in a class. Likewise, if you respond too negatively to incorrect answers, students may be afraid of offering answers in the future. In classrooms with a culture of error, where students embrace misconceptions and mistakes as stepping stones to improve, students are likely to take risks and develop their Growth Mindset (Lemov, 2015). The aim for any teacher is to develop a positive environment which empowers students and gives the teacher a clear view of the current understanding of the class, thus allowing for better intervention and instruction.

Formative assessment

The benefits of students receiving feedback have been well documented. However, often neglected is the feedback provided by students to their teachers. According to Hattie (2009), expert teachers seek feedback regularly to ascertain how much their students understand.

These expert teachers then use this feedback to make adjustments to their lesson rather than rigidly following the lesson plan. At Greenwich Free School, we aimed to achieve this by promoting a 'Responsive Classroom'. Working alongside Mike Baxter and Oliver Knight, we explored multiple formative assessment techniques with teachers for eliciting formative data from their learners (Figure 5.9). The teachers would then analyse the data to assess the extent of student understanding and respond to this data, addressing misconceptions, changing the lesson pace or learning tasks to support their students' progress.

If we wish to capture data in the moment to make real-time adjustments to the lesson, we would use one of the techniques in the immediate-term section. Dylan Wiliam refers to these

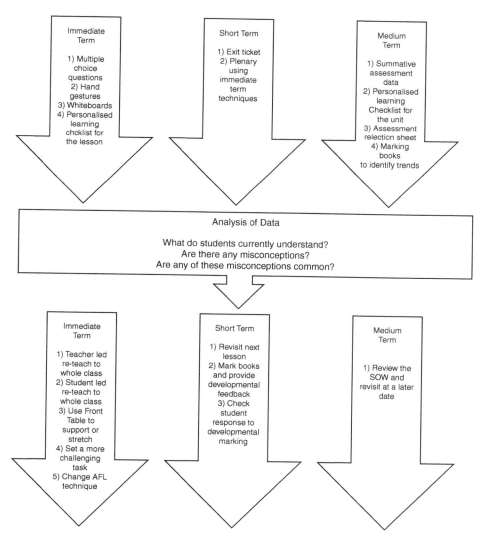

Figure 5.9 Formative assessment techniques in a Responsive Classroom (based on Baxter, *et al.*, 2017).

as "all student response systems", as they require all students to think and act and the result is visualised for the teacher to act on (Wiliam, 2011).

Multiple choice questions (MCQs) are a useful stimulus for students to visually vote and immediately inform you of their level of understanding. Ideally, these MCQs should be designed in advance[8]: the question stem for the MCQ may be lengthy, however the answers should be short. There should only be one correct answer and the question should not provide any hints or lead the learner to the correct answer. Ideally the incorrect answers (known as 'distractors') should each reveal a different common misconception that you predict some students will make. In terms of capturing these responses, there are several methods:

1   Coloured voting cards, for example white, red, amber or green. These are also known as traffic light or WRAG cards and most educational suppliers can print these in student planners if you wish to use them across the school.
2   Mini whiteboards – These can also be included as a glossy card insert in a student planner and students can be asked to write their answer or preferably A, B, C or D for clarity.
3   Four corners – Students can "vote with their feet" by moving to a labelled corner of the room which represents either answer A, B, C or D. They may be asked to convince others in their corner why the other answers are wrong.
4   Plickers – Currently a free app available for iOS and Android tablets and mobile phones. This app provides each student with a printable unique QR-style code which students hold up in different orientations to vote for A, B, C or D. The results are broadcast in real time to your computer and/or phone for further analysis.

Coloured voting cards are low maintenance and the speediest option and if you are new to these formative assessment techniques, I would recommend the voting cards first. Each answer is given a colour and students simply show you the colour corresponding to their answer. Mini whiteboards allow the students to write more detailed answers or draw diagrams which can be useful when you are covering topics such as logic gates, network topologies and algorithm flowcharts. Four corners are a great way to visualise learning as you can ask a spokesperson from each of the different answer groups to present their argument and after a student has given an answer, you can give the other students an opportunity to change their answer. This is visualised by students walking across the room to join a different group. Four corners are commonly used during ethical debates about IT use, where there is not necessarily a right answer. It's a great way to hear different viewpoints. From our experience, students are most excited by option four, Plickers. Piloted by Chris Speller and Jess Dumbreck at Greenwich Free School, it is used regularly in Science lessons at the school. Responses can take up to a minute to read, however the data that is produced is far more accurate than the other methods.

Hand gestures are a technique covered in Lemov's *Teach Like a Champion*. Students would be trained to use a certain hand gesture such as a click or a thumbs up if they agree with what someone else is saying or they may wave their hand if they disagree with their peer. Used across many charter schools in the US and also more and more schools in the UK, these hand gestures provide immediate visual feedback for the teacher and the learners. Clicks are a supportive way of agreeing with someone and it allows the teacher to acknowledge others who also have the same answer as a peer even though they may not have been chosen to offer the answer.

Whiteboards are often used during the Do Now or when a rough sketch or drafted answer may be required to visually see what students currently understand. Students are asked to show their boards after a countdown and a teacher may collect some boards and show these to the class using the document camera/visualiser. It's an excellent way to "see" current understanding and provides richer data where an MCQ is less appropriate.

Every unit's Medium-Term Plan (MTP)[9] can be used by students as a personalised learning checklist (PLC), or you may wish to isolate one section of the MTP and print this section out on a small A5 slip for students to self-assess their current level of understanding. Students may be asked to tick or annotate the PLC, and I usually encourage students to highlight the keywords which they do not yet understand.

If you only have 10–15 minutes left of your lesson, it will be difficult to use an immediate-term AFL technique. To assess understanding, you could instead revert to using an exit ticket. These were covered in Chapter 3 as exit tickets are usually pre-planned and printed before the start of the lesson. The key thing to remember is that for this to be truly useful, students should be told that this is a formative assessment. The marks from formative assessments are not published, these are not shown to parents and detention will not be issued for under-performance. The eye-test analogy that we used with baseline tests in Chapter 2 is useful here. Every student should write their name on the exit ticket and it should be completed independently and ideally in silence. These conditions ensure that the data that is gleaned is an accurate reflection of student understanding; if students are allowed to discuss and complete the exit ticket in pairs or as a small group, it is much more difficult to provide targeted intervention during the next lesson.

Any tasks that are completed independently provide an opportunity to offer formative developmental feedback even if it is not an assessment. Based on this work and the exit tickets, you may uncover new misconceptions which were not apparent from the immediate or short-term AFL techniques. A medium-term technique may be used every three to four lessons.

Analysing the data and choosing a response depends on whether there are common gaps in understanding. If the whole class understands something, then more challenging content and tasks will be necessary. However, in many cases it will be small groups or individuals who do not understand something. In the immediate term, a small group of students can be brought to the front table where they can be supported with a small group intervention, this might be remodelling a key skill or talking through a writing frame. As aforementioned, the front table may also be used to stretch students who have completed the learning tasks to a high standard. Advanced skills or independent tasks may be introduced at this point. If it is clear that one or two students fully understand a concept, you may wish to ask one of these students to reteach the whole class by remodelling a skill or re-explaining a concept to their peers. If it appears as though most of the class are uncertain, then it is best to reteach the material yourself.

Eliciting data from students is the easiest part of the habit as it is somewhat procedural. However, Wiliam (2011) notes that the most powerful (and perhaps the most difficult) part of formative assessment is the teacher's response to the data. The teacher actions generally involve modifying the activities to help pupils based on the initial assessment (Wiliam, 2011). The teacher must give feedback and the pupils must act on that feedback in order for the formative assessment to be effective.

Marking and feedback

Like other formative assessment techniques, the main aim of marking should be to provide feedback to learners which they can act on. Time also needs to be set aside to allow students to act on this feedback; this time should be planned as part of the unit of work.[10] Unless marking results in actionable, developmental feedback, it is likely the teacher will receive a poor return on their time invested into marking. A teacher should always ask themselves the question of "How long did it take me to mark this book?" and compare this to how long a student will spend acting on the teacher feedback. Teacher feedback can and should be a powerful contributor to student learning. Hattie and Donoghue cite "acting on feedback" as one of their top ten strategies in both the surface learning and transfer phases of learning (Hattie & Donoghue, 2016). The feedback should result in a student activity which requires students to think differently and improve on their prior knowledge and performance.

Marking is one of the many contributors to teacher workload and needs to be carefully managed to ensure it has the desired impact of improving students' learning. Marking books and classwork is one way of checking for understanding. However, I would advise marking selectively; I have seen many successful departments who only mark assessments and exit tickets. Do Nows can be peer or self-marked and marking classwork does not necessarily provide meaningful information on pupil progress. A student may have completed the classwork well because they received significant scaffolding and teacher support. Students may also have had some support from their peers and it is often difficult to ascertain how much support they have received. Conversely, well-designed assessments and exit tickets can provide a clear picture of student understanding and therefore of what gaps exist.

In many schools, the regular marking of books is compulsory and therefore good habits will ensure that the marking is not only completed, but it is done so to serve an effective purpose and it is completed efficiently. A time-saving technique is to sample six books, two high-prior-attaining, two low-prior-attaining and two middle-prior-attaining students. Based on these six books you should be able to cover the full spectrum of misconceptions and actions required for your entire class. Comments can then be codified using a symbol, coloured sticker or a checklist of skills, for example in Figures 5.10 and 5.11.

In the first example a student may simply have the following codes written in their book or coloured dot stickers with a similar code:

&
!
?
#

Some teachers may ask students to write down their feedback as a Do Now based on the marking codes. However, I personally feel as though this is a waste of time. I prefer the second version, where you print out a sticker with all the possible feedback on the sticker and you tick off the things that the student has already done well. The remaining tasks become their feedback and this directly informs the next lesson.

There may also be generic feedback which is used for any piece of work. At Greenwich Free School, we developed a school-wide system and this is codified as shown in Table 5.5. This table can be printed out and stuck into exercise books or folders at the beginning of the year or displayed as a poster in the classroom.

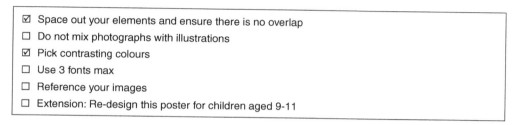

% Space out your elements and ensure there is no overlap
& Do not mix photographs with illustrations
@ Pick contrasting colours
! Use 3 fonts max
? Reference your images
Extension: Re-design this poster for children aged 9-11

Figure 5.10 Marking codes.

☑ Space out your elements and ensure there is no overlap
☐ Do not mix photographs with illustrations
☑ Pick contrasting colours
☐ Use 3 fonts max
☐ Reference your images
☐ Extension: Re-design this poster for children aged 9-11

Figure 5.11 Marking checklist.

As mentioned earlier, marking is a great contributor to teacher workload and as such, peer-marking and self-marking can also be used to mark homework such as past paper questions. This is a valuable exercise for students as they are given a mark scheme and they see how an examiner thinks and acts. They realise the importance of the accuracy of language, quality of written response, handwriting and the overall clarity of their response.

Midway through a teaching unit, when students have produced a first draft of a piece of work, Ron Berger promotes the use of several critique techniques. These are covered in his book *An Ethic of Excellence* (Berger, 2003). Gallery critique is one of the techniques whereby every student is asked to display their work and initially they will be asked to walk around the classroom silently with their peers. The class is then asked for positive feedback, which piece they like and why. I have adapted this on occasion to also offer more of a constructive critique on sticky notes or directly onto the work if it is displayed on the screen. For graphic design work, text boxes can be used to add feedback; for presentations, the notes section can be used and for programming work comments can be left. By treating the classroom like an art gallery, pupils get to walk around the room and see several pieces of work of varying standard. Students also get the opportunity to offer formative feedback. Berger advises that it is important to set out some ground rules before letting students give peer feedback. Here are five simple guidelines which I use with my students based on the work of Berger (Berger, 2003) and Johnston *et al.* (Johnston *et al.*, 2012):

1   Be honest and unbiased.
2   Be kind – do not give or take offense.
3   Be specific – avoid general comments such as "I don't like it".
4   Be helpful (make sure feedback can be acted on).
5   The purpose is to grow together through the Kaizen philosophy of continual improvement.

Table 5.5 Generic marking codes

Computing Marking Codes	
Sp	Spelling
Gr	Grammar
Pu	Punctuation
CL	Capital Letter
UL	Underline with a ruler
D/T	Date/Title
^	Missing word
//	New paragraph
FS	Rephrase as a full sentence
CC	Correct / Complete
RD	Redo / Redraft
KW	Use Keywords and highlight/underline them
WHY?	Explain Why
TOC	Update your Table Of Contents
STK	Stick in loose sheets
LD	Label the diagram
EXT	Complete Extension

I would give examples of feedback which mee*t all* five criteria and pieces of feedback which do not. Having modelled this process, students understand what the expectation is and the peer feedback is useful and actionable.

If you wish to do a one-off peer assessment as opposed to a gallery critique, this should be carefully planned so that pupil pairs are of roughly similar ability. If there is too wide a gap between the pupils' current levels of understanding, a weaker pupil may not be able to access that much of their peer's work and likewise the stronger pupil may not be appropriately challenged.

I recommend that students act on feedback and complete corrections in a different colour pen. There are some criticisms on the use of different colour pens, some claim that it is unnecessary and a meaningless performance for Ofsted. I would disagree and whilst I do not claim that using different pens has a positive or negative psychological impact, a school-wide colour-coded system such as the one in Table 5.6 has several advantages:

1 Students can easily find teacher feedback as it is always in red pen.
2 When it comes to revising, students can clearly look back and see what mistakes they made and what corrections were completed as these are always in black pen.
3 Having a clear school-wide system ensures that students have a consistent experience across all their subjects.

Table 5.6 A colour code for marking and feedback

Blue Pen/Pencil	For student written work/diagrams
Black Pen	For acting on feedback
Green Pen	For peer assessment or self-assessment
Red Pen	For teacher marking and feedback

For digital work, I would advise pupils to save new versions of their work every time they receive feedback. These can simply be named "v1", "v2", "v3" or "v3.1" if the changes are minor adjustments. For programming work, this allows for better version control and maintainability of programs. For graphic design work, it allows students to showcase a portfolio of work including developmental drafts. Whilst operating systems may store their own backups, sometimes rolling back changes for a networked environment is not straightforward. Saving several versions may also be required by some exam boards to demonstrate how a product has developed over time based on testing and feedback in the development lifecycle. It is certainly a habit which I encourage developing with students from Year 7.

This chapter has explored some of the key actions, habits and routines which computing teachers should develop and perform in their classroom. The final chapter for this section will look at pedagogical content knowledge in computing.

Chapter 5 summary

1 The first lessons of any academic year should focus on building a strong classroom culture grounded in high expectations, respect and solid routines.
2 Behaviour management plans need to be unambiguous and consistently enforced.
3 Expert teachers develop classroom routines based on habits (repeated actions). These ensure that the classroom runs efficiently.
4 Differentiation techniques vary depending on the topic. The main aim of differentiation is to provide scaffolding so that students are able to access material in their zone of proximal development.
5 Questioning reveals students' thinking and current levels of understanding. Questioning should initially encourage recall; once students are able to recall knowledge we can test their higher-order thinking through increasingly complex questioning.
6 Formative assessment is an essential habit which enables teachers to elicit data about their entire class's current level of understanding. This data is analysed by the teacher to provide feedback to correct any misconceptions or to challenge students' thinking further.
7 For marking to be effective, it needs to provide actionable feedback to your students. Time should be set aside for this review process to take place and teachers are encouraged to develop checklists and marking codes to make this process more efficient.

Notes

1   Narrate the positive is another of Doug Lemov's techniques which will be explained in the following section.

2   Some schools also use Kagan Cooperative learning seating plans; these are certainly worth looking into if you have your tables set out in squares rather than rows.

3   A fully resourced series of first lesson slides are available in the eResources. The reader is encouraged to refer to these whilst reading this section of the book.

4   It may be worth asking your students at this stage how safe they think this website is and whether or not they should type their actual password in this website or similar websites.

5   A fascinating study into note taking on computers vs notebooks concluded that using a computer to take notes may impair learning because their use results in shallow processing. Students taking notes on laptops were found to perform worse on conceptual questions perhaps because computers encourage students to mindlessly transcribe verbatim rather than processing, interpreting, reframing and actively encoding the information (Mueller & Oppenheimer, 2014).

6   Classroom layout will be discussed in more detail in Chapter 9.

7   Some classrooms operate a "hands up only for questions" policy which ensures that students are not allowed to dominate or hide away.

8   A great source of MCQs is available through the Quantum Project. The project was setup to crowd-source MCQs from members of CAS. These have been vetted by Cynthia Selby and Miles Berry (Teacher trainers from the University of Southampton and University of Roehampton respectively) and are hosted for free at www.diagnosticquestions.com. At the time of writing there were over 2500 Computing MCQs.

9   Many MTPs are provided in the eResources that accompany this book. These can be used and modified for your classes.

10 Some schools run school-wide review weeks or review lessons in the last week of term. In other schools, they have introduced Dedicated Improvement and Reflection Time (DIRT).

References

Andrews, B., 1903. Habit. *The American Journal of Psychology*, XIV(2), pp. 121-49.

Bambrick-Santoyo, P., 2016. *Get Better Faster*. San Francisco: Jossey-Bass.

Baxter, M., Knight, O. & Lau, W., 2017. *The Responsive Classroom*. London: Greenwich Free School.

Berger, R., 2003. *An Ethic of Excellence: Building a Culture of Craftsmanship with Students*. Portsmouth, NH: Heinemann.

Bjork, E. L. & Bjork, R., 2011. Making things hard on yourself, but in a good way: creating desirable difficulties to enhance learning. In: M. A. Gernsbacher, R. W. Pew & L. M. Hough, eds. *Psychology and the Real World: Essays Illustrating Fundamental Contributions to Society*. New York: Worth Publishers, pp. 55-64.

CERI, 2008. *21st Century Learning: Research Innovation and Policy. Directions from Recent OECD Analyses*. [Online] Available at: http://www.oecd.org/site/educeri21st/40554299.pdf [Accessed 28 December 2016].

Dweck, C. S., 2006. *Mindset*. 1st ed. New York: Random House.

Fellows, M. R., 1991. *Computer SCIENCE and Mathematics in the Elementary Schools*. [Online] Available at: https://larc.unt.edu/ian/research/cseducation/fellows1991.pdf [Accessed 11 July 2017].

Gast, G., 2014. *Effective Questioning and Classroom Talk*. Corsham, UK: National Society for Education in Art and Design (NSEAD).

Hattie, J., 2009. *Visible Learning*. London : Routledge.

Hattie, J. A. & Donoghue, G. M., 2016. Learning strategies: a synthesis and conceptual model. *npj Science of Learning*, 10 August. Available at: https://www.nature.com/articles/npjscilearn201613 [Accessed 11 August 2017].

Hester, T., 2012. *Agape Management*. [Online] Available at: http://www.agapemanagement.org/ [Accessed 25 August 2016].

Hopkins, D., Craig, W. & Knight, O., 2015. *Curiosity and Powerful Learning*. Denver, CO: McREL International.

Johnston, R., Clark, G. & Shulver, M., 2012. *Service Operations Management: Improving Service Delivery*. 4th ed. Harlow, UK: Pearson Education Limited.

Lemov, D., 2010. *Teach Like a Champion*. San Francisco: Jossey-Bass.

Lemov, D., 2015. *Doug Lemov's Field Notes: "The Front Table": A Post from Nicole Willey's Classroom*. [Online] Available at: http://teachlikeachampion.com/blog/front-table-post-nicole-willeys-classroom-tales-positive-outlier-video/ [Accessed 4 September 2016].

Lemov, D., 2015. *Teach Like a Champion 2.0*. San Francisco: Jossey-Bass.

Linsin, M., 2011. *How to Set Up a Simple, Effective Classroom Management Plan*. [Online] Available at: https://www.smartclassroommanagement.com/2011/08/06/effective-classroom-management-plan/ [Accessed 3 August 2016].

Mueller, P. A. & Oppenheimer, D. M., 2014. The pen is mightier than the keyboard: advantages of longhand over laptop note taking. *Psychological Science,* 25(6), pp. 1-10.

Pan, G., Sen, S., Starrett, D. A., Bonk, C. J., Rodgers, M. L., Tikoo, M. & Powell, D. V. 2012. Instructor-made videos as a learner scaffolding tool. *MERLOT Journal of Online Learning and Teaching*, 8(4), pp. 298-311.

Potts, R. & Shanks, D. R., 2013. The benefit of generating errors during learning. *Journal of Experimental Psychology: General*, Volume Advance online publication, pp. 1-24.

Rogers, B., 2011. *Cracking the Challenging Class*. London: SAGE Publications Ltd & Pantechnicon.

Simmons, C. & Hawkins, C., 2015. *Teaching Computing*. 2nd ed. London: Sage Publications Ltd.

Sinek, S., 2009. *Start With Why: How Great Leaders Inspire Everyone to Take Action*. London: Penguin.

Smith, E. R. & Mackie, D. M., 2007. *Social Psychology*. 3rd ed. Hove East Sussex, UK: Psychology Press.

Tomlinson, C. A., 2001. *How to Differentiate Instruction in Mixed-Ability Classrooms*. 2nd ed. Alexandria, VA: Association for Supervision & Curriculum Development (ASCD).

Waite, J., 2017. *CAS London Master Teacher Training* [Interview] (20 March 2017).

Wiliam, D., 2011. *Embedded Formative Assessment*. Bloomington, IN: Solution Tree Press.

Wood, D., Bruner, J. S. & Ross, G., 1976. The role of tutoring in problem solving. *Journal of Child Psychology and Psychiatry*, 17, pp. 89-100.

6 Pedagogical content knowledge in computing

Chapters 4 and 5 dealt with general pedagogy and applied this to the computing classroom. This chapter looks at specific pedagogical content knowledge (PCK) in computing. Shulman defines this as:

> That special amalgam of content and pedagogy that is uniquely the province of teachers, their own special form of professional understanding ... Within the category of pedagogical content knowledge I include, for the most regularly taught topics in one's subject area, the most useful forms of representation of those ideas, the most powerful analogies, illustrations, examples, explanations, and demonstrations - in a word, the ways of representing and formulating the subject that make it comprehensible to others. Since there are no single most powerful forms of representation, the teacher must have at hand a veritable armamentarium of alternative forms of representation, some of which derive from research whereas others originate in the wisdom of practice.
>
> (Shulman, 1987, 1986)

PCK in computing brings together subject knowledge about computing content and pedagogic knowledge about instructional methods. As computing is a relatively new subject and a broad one covering diverse topics ranging from graphic design to programming, the challenge of supporting PCK with research is a significant one. Wherever possible, I have tried to reference studies of PCK in computing and where this was lacking, I've relied on my experience of teaching computing over the past decade and the collective experience of others. I will share strategies which have worked for me, and I will try to explain my rationale for my teaching methods.

I have split this chapter based on broad topics which appear in the computing national curriculum:

1   Programming
2   Algorithms
3   Computing theory
4   Data handling: spreadsheets and databases
5   Print publications
6   Web publications
7   Video and audio editing.

Programming

> This is a problem. A big problem. A problem that an interactive JavaScript lesson with badges won't solve … despite all the hype and hullaballoo from online learning startups and their marketing campaigns that now "everyone can learn to code," it's clear there are still plenty of problems with the culture and the pedagogy surrounding computer science education.
>
> (Watters, 2012)

In this opening quotation, ed-tech journalist Audrey Watters highlights one of the primary mistakes new teachers of computing make and that is the myopic focus on programming. Many online platforms and massive online open courses (MOOCs) are dedicated to learning "programming". However, the focus should really lie in teaching and learning problem solving (through programming). A significant proportion of this chapter will focus on teaching problem solving through programming.

Programming is a tool, a means to an end; it is not something which can or should be taught in isolation from problems to be solved. Jane Waite argues that the most powerful thing that we can do is to teach the process of program construction through problem solving (Waite, 2017). One of the most significant aspects of problem solving with Computational Thinking is abstraction (Kramer, 2007).

> We all know that the only mental tool by means of which a very finite piece of reasoning can cover a myriad cases is called "abstraction"; as a result the effective exploitation of his powers of abstraction must be regarded as one of the most vital activities of a competent programmer.
>
> (Dijkstra, 1972)

This is supported by the work of Waite *et al.* on abstraction, who suggest the simple framework in Table 6.1 for problem solving in programming projects.

At primary schools, Waite *et al.* (2016) suggest that these steps can be completed using labelled diagrams, concept maps or storyboards. At secondary schools, Statter and Armoni state that the second level of abstraction (the writing of algorithms) can be explained to students as "writing verbal descriptions" of the program you are about to write (Statter & Armoni, 2016). These steps are similar to those set out by Ilia Avroutine in his problem decomposition survey for secondary schools (Travi & Avroutine, 2016):

1   How many inputs are there?
2   Which of these inputs will be calculated?
3   Which operators (-+* mod div) will be needed?
4   What are the stages or steps?[1]
5   What is the output? Consider the intended audience/purpose.
6   Is anything repeated or reused?

Avroutine's problem decomposition survey is supported by the research of Cynthia Selby at the University of Southampton. Selby urges teachers to spend more time teaching and developing decomposition skills with their students before students move on to abstraction,

Table 6.1 A framework of the levels of abstraction for problem solving in programming projects (Waite et al., 2016)

Level of abstraction		Language	Description
1	Problem	English	What is needed – the requirements
2	Algorithm	CS speak	What the program should do
3	Program	Code	How it is done
4	Runtime	Results	What it does

algorithm design and the creation of their programs (Selby, 2015). Whilst arguably having the greatest impact on the final written program, the decomposition stage is sometimes neglected by novice teachers.

Teaching problem solving through a programming language is also an area where many novice teachers struggle. The choice of language, first program and subsequent follow-up programs are all non-trivial decisions. To address the first decision, ultimately the choice of language should be made based on a teacher's skillset. This should be a language that the teacher can confidently teach problem solving with and ideally, this should be a language that is recognised at GCSE and A levels. For many reasons, Python is the most popular language at secondary schools in the UK. It has a low threshold for beginners, with easy installation and readability; it is used throughout industry (NASA, Uber, Facebook, Google, IBM, CIA, Pixar, Dropbox, YouTube) and it supports object-oriented programming. Some teachers prefer C#, VB.NET or Java as these languages are better suited for A-level projects. Python is highly resourced on CAS and other learning communities and despite its flaws,[2] it is a safe choice for teaching problem solving at the secondary school level. However, the decision really depends on your skillset.

Many computer scientists will want to start with a traditional "hello world" first program and from there you could move onto a chatbot which will enable you to introduce user input to accompany the output. Very quickly the chatbot can develop to include selection using 'if' statements based on the user input. There is the temptation to build large projects from the outset, but this is likely to create a gap in the class where you will lose many whilst allowing a rare few to succeed. I would therefore advise that your first few programs should be less than 20 lines long and should focus on sequences of instructions before moving onto conditional selection and finally onto iteration.

As you begin to build more complex programs, another common trap is to only teach good habits in your chosen language. For example, some teachers will introduce data types to handle integer inputs and also include arrays (or lists) to efficiently deal with multiple values. However, both Waite and Guzdial separately argue that we should plan for misconceptions, mistakes and inefficiencies to happen and to teach these explicitly (Waite, 2017; Wolfman, 2014). If you are building a calculator which adds two numbers together, as an experienced programmer, you may instinctively declare a variable to take an integer input (or cast an input to integer if you are using Python). However, the common error that novice students will make is that they take an input (say five), add it to another input (say ten) as they would do on an electronic calculator and expect to find that the result would be 15. However, the actual result in Python would be 510 as the two inputs are taken as strings and concatenated.

Students' common misconception	Teacher pre-empting the misconception

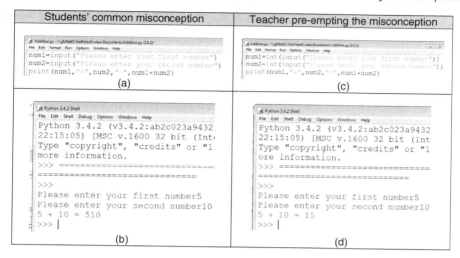

```
num1=input("Please enter your first number")
num2=input("Please enter your second number")
print(num1,"+",num2,"=",num1+num2)
```
(a)

```
num1=int(input("Please enter your first number"))
num2=int(input("Please enter your second number"))
print(num1,"+",num2,"=",num1+num2)
```
(c)

```
Python 3.4.2 (v3.4.2:ab2c023a9432
22:15:05) [MSC v.1600 32 bit (Int
Type "copyright", "credits" or "1
more information.
>>> ==============================
==============================
>>>
Please enter your first number5
Please enter your second number10
5 + 10 = 510
>>> |
```
(b)

```
Python 3.4.2 (v3.4.2:ab2c023a9432
22:15:05) [MSC v.1600 32 bit (Int
Type "copyright", "credits" or "1
ore information.
>>> ==============================
==============================
>>>
Please enter your first number5
Please enter your second number10
5 + 10 = 15
>>> |
```
(d)

Figure 6.1 Deliberately planning for logic errors and misconceptions.

The author would like to acknowledge the support of the wider Python Community and the Python Software Foundation. For full details of the Python license, please refer to: docs.python.org/3/license.html.

The expert teacher deliberately plans for logical errors like these to happen (Figure 6.1) and will use this as a teaching point to discuss data types and the difference between concatenation and addition. The alternatives to planning for misconceptions and the idiosyncrasies of programming are to either let students encounter them by chance or to teach them the solution directly so that they avoid the error altogether. The danger of these methods is that students may not encounter certain misconceptions at all – which is dissimilar from the actual realities of programming. By teaching the solution before students naturally encounter an error, you do not provide students with the opportunity to debug their program and to think like a computer scientist. Debugging is another key aspect of Computational Thinking, and if students rely on you to only produce perfect programs they may develop the habit of merely copying the "right solution". Although programming falls under computer *science*, there is not always only one correct solution, there are usually many ways to solve a problem. Many variations of these solutions should be explored and this enables students to develop their programming and problem-solving toolkit. The beauty of programming and computer science is that, "You might be able to create out of pure thought, in this world of algorithms and data structures ... something which has never existed before" (Peyton Jones, 2016).

Whilst this provides a good starting point for solving problems with programming, a question which troubles every computing teacher is "How do I help my students build fluency with their programming and problem solving?" The answer to this question ultimately lies in practice, and we will now look at different exercises and activities which can be used to improve programming fluency.

Dr Sue Sentance is a senior lecturer in computer science education at King's College London. She is an experienced teacher of computing (including both ICT and computer science at A level) and much of her current research is on PCK in computing. Sentance makes the insightful comment that as with the English language, reading is much easier than writing.

This is particularly the case for languages such as Python which is designed for readability. We should therefore ensure that students are engaged in reading programs and understanding conceptually what the program and the computer are "doing" when the program is executed (Sentance, 2017). The process of tracing was popularised by Raymond Lister at the University of Technology, Sydney. Lister defines the process of tracing as showing the values of variables as they change (Lister *et al.*, 2004). Andy McSwan, writing for PLAN C[3] builds on this definition by stating that tracing involves manually stepping through a piece of code and following the process(es) a computer goes through as it executes each line of code (McSwan, 2016). Based on Peter Donaldson's and Quintin Cutts's TRACS methodology of tracing, there are three steps in a typical tracing activity:

1   Identifying expressions (drawing a circle or box around these)
2   Drawing arrows to indicate the flow of the program
3   Working through the program to show the variables and outputs.

Sentance's modified TRACS diagram in Figure 6.2 shows what the three steps look like after one iteration of a while loop.

Tracing is further supported by Donna Teague's extensive research into strategies for teaching novice programmers (Teague, 2015). Citing the work of Piaget and Ojose and building on the work of Raymond Lister, Teague concludes that novice programmers need appropriate activities depending on their neo-Piagetian stage of cognitive development for each problem domain (programming concept) that they are being taught. These are summarised in Table 6.2.

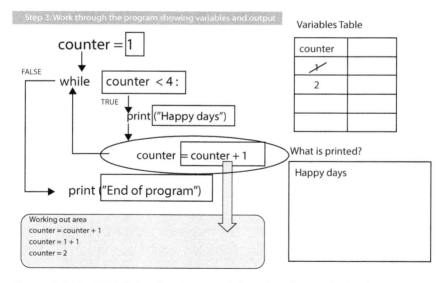

Figure 6.2 Mini TRACS tracing framework based on the work of Peter Donaldson and Quintin Cutts (Sentance, 2017).

Table 6.2 A summary of activities for developing fluency through cognitive development in programming and problem solving (based on Teague, 2015, and Lister, 2011)

Neo-Piagetian stage of development	Programming activities	Purpose of activities (pre-requisites to move on to the next stage)
Sensorimotor stage	Reading and tracing simple code with the support of the teacher	Develop a mental model of the deterministic notional machine rather than seeing the execution of code as a magical process. Develop a foundation on which abstract reasoning about programming can be built. Develop the ability to chunk knowledge to avoid cognitive overload and handle more than one abstract concept at a time.
Pre-operational stage	Exposure to reading and tracing tasks which are constituted from a minimal number of parts and which give them the freedom to work with specific values (rather than abstractions). Slow increase in the sophistication of code that is read and traced. Explaining code in plain English. Using and manipulating physical representations of objects, e.g. variables can be represented using separate pieces of paper which are physically moved as the program is executed.	Develop reasoning and explain the overall purpose of the code as opposed to simply dealing which each line of code individually. Develop mental representations of actions, operations and working with cyclic series from intermediary points. Develop ability to think about more than one abstraction at a time on familiar or real situations. Consider consequences and alternatives.
Concrete operational stage	Using diagrams to understand code. Annotating code whilst reasoning logically, consistently and systematically. Programming tasks that involve the principles of reversibility, e.g. reversing a list traversal. Programming tasks that involve the principles of conservation, e.g. alternative solutions. Programming tasks that involve transitive inference, e.g. comparing values across 3 or more different variables.	Develop the ability to reason logically, consistently and systematically. Develop fluency in ability to reason about quantities that are conserved, and processes that are reversible. Develop reasoning about hypothetical situations. Develop ability to make inferences based on incomplete data. Develop ability to systematically abstract.
Formal operational stage	Writing their own programs independently or using pair programming to solve problems. Problems will increase in difficulty as the requirements and cognitive load increases.	Develop fluency in the mental process of problem solving. Develop the ability to choose the most appropriate abstract concept to use in a specific case.

Teague and Lister believe that for each new programming construct taught, students should be explicitly taught to read and trace code before they write their own code involving the new programming constructs (Teague, 2015).[4] The most encouraging finding based on their longitudinal study of a novice programmer is that contrary to popular belief, programming is not innate and talent based but can instead be taught (Teague & Lister, 2014). Provided that teachers do not advance too quickly in terms of the types of tasks based on the stages of development, most novices can become expert programmers. The key is spending time on providing activities at an appropriate level of abstract reasoning. As students reach the formal operational stage, teachers may wish to provide programming challenges for students to practice their problem solving; great sources of such challenges include:

1   www.codeabbey.com
2   www.codingbat.com
3   www.exercism.io
4   www.tinyurl.com/OCRCodingChallenges

Whilst research indicates that novice students should primarily complete reading and tracing activities in order to learn programming, one has to confront the reality that students are excited by programming and some practical experience is necessary in order to make inferences when tracing code.

Finding the balance between the level of complexity of programs that students are required to write and the activities in Table 6.2 is one that will be developed over time with your teaching groups. Provided that the programs are not too ambitious to start with, the two types of activities should complement each other well. As programs become more complex, Margulieux *et al.* advise that teachers can break large problem-solving programming tasks into smaller tasks using subgoals (Margulieux *et al.*, 2016). *Subgoals are components of complex problem solutions that provide functional pieces of the final solution.* Initially, teachers would provide worked examples with labelled subgoals and through gradual fading, which we discussed in Chapter 4 would be removed from tasks as students develop their programming and problem-solving proficiencies. Margulieux *et al.* found that provided that students were provided with worked examples with labelled subgoals for each task, these students would develop this habit themselves and use subtasks when solving problems more independently. In an earlier study, Margulieux *et al.* found that these subgoals helped reduce cognitive load and could possibly help form mental models in novices (Margulieux *et al.*, 2012).

Eight activities to build students' programming proficiencies

1   Reading and tracing programs.
2   Annotating a program to explain how it works.
3   Completing partially completed programs.
4   Debugging programs that contain errors.
5   Adding bugs to programs for others to debug.
6   Labelling tasks with subgoals to model problem decomposition.
7   Taking an existing program and programming an alternative solution.
8   Pair programming.

Pair programming has been mentioned earlier in the book and I will try to summarise this process in the following paragraphs. The process is an agile software development technique that has been used in industry since the 1980s[5] and is widely celebrated by academics. In a meta-analysis of 18 studies with a combined total of 1,215 subjects, Hannay *et al.* found that:

> Pair programming is beneficial for achieving correctness on highly complex programming tasks. Pair programming may also have a time gain on simpler tasks. By cooperating, programmers may complete tasks and attain goals that would be difficult or impossible if they worked individually. Junior pair programmers, for example, seem able to achieve approximately the same level of correctness in about the same amount of time (duration) as senior individuals.

(Hannay *et al.*, 2009)

In pair programming, two students work together on a single computer to solve a problem collaboratively. Williams and Kessler note that pair programming can and should also be used at the analysis and design stage when students perform problem decomposition and abstraction (Williams & Kessler, 2002). Each student takes a different role: One will start as the driver; this student controls the keyboard and mouse (or pen if the students are working at the analysis and design phase). The second student assumes the role of the navigator. As per the driving metaphor, where a navigator would never touch the steering wheel or gear stick, the navigator in pair programming never touches the keyboard, mouse or pen. Their role is to observe, ask questions, clarify and where necessary correct or redirect the driver. Williams and Kessler refer to two types of defects which the navigator should look out for: tactical (syntax errors) and strategic (the direction of the driver). This latter role defines the navigator; the navigator should have the specification and big picture in mind. The big picture is the map which the navigator is mentally referring to at all times. It is essential that the driver and navigator talk to each other, which will seem unnatural for the driver initially; however, this thinking out loud, as we have discussed earlier, allows the navigator to visualise the driver's thinking as they write the code. This is supported by the theory of cognitive apprenticeship (Collins *et al.*, 1991).

Many teachers experience success when partners swap roles at timed intervals; swapping every five to eight minutes at the secondary level seems to work well. Students also appreciate the use of a timer as it means each student has a fair amount of time as the driver. In terms of ability pairings, Franklin advises pairing students by (perceived) similar ability (Franklin, 2015). To introduce the concept of pair programming, I usually show my students Code.org's introductory video, aptly titled *Pair Programming* (Code.org, 2014).

Key principles of pair programming

1   Pairs should be of similar ability.
2   The driver should sit squarely in front of the monitor.
3   The navigator should be able to read the program clearly on the screen – Change the font size or zoom if necessary.
4   Pairs should swap roles every five to eight minutes – A timer is advised.

5   Pairs should maintain constant dialogue.

6   Pairs should be rotated (perhaps on a monthly basis).

7   An expert can only be paired with a novice if the expert is willing to assume a mentoring role.

8   Pair programming should not be forced and overused; it should be used along with solo programming and the aforementioned activities in this chapter.

9   Consider friendship groups and good quality relationships in pairings.

10   For ease of swapping, consider adding a second keyboard and mouse.

(Based on Williams & Kessler, 2002; Franklin, 2015; Denner *et al.*, 2014)

Getting more girls into computing

To understand why we need to promote girls studying computing, we need to look back at the history of computing. Grace Hopper is one of the world's first recognised programmers, having learnt to program the Harvard Mark I in 1943. In 1952,[6] Grace Hopper and her team created the first compiler for a programming language, leading to the invention of common business-oriented language (COBOL). In 1958, Elsie Shutt founded one of the first software businesses in the US and the programmers were all women (NPR, 2014). In 1969, Margaret Hamilton was a programmer at the software engineering division of the MIT Instrumentation Laboratory and was recruited to manage a team of programmers to write the software for the Apollo 11 mission. It was her team's software that landed Neil Armstrong and Buzz Aldrin on the moon in 1969 (Russo, 2016). There is no doubt that there were thousands of other females working in the computing industry as programmers, yet the world of computing today is dominated by males.

Elaine Kamowitz speaking on National Public Radio found that this change in the gender balance in computing started in the 1980s. Kamowitz reviewed TV adverts from Apple, RadioShack and Commodore from 1977–84 and found that all these companies marketed their home computers explicitly towards young boys. Computing and the image of a computer geek was predominantly portrayed by young white males, and the subject and the industry has not yet managed to shake off this gender-biased image. Looking back at the number of female computer science students at university, in 1984 these numbers started falling and this number continued to plummet throughout the 1980s and 1990s. In 1984, 37 per cent of computer science undergraduates in the US were female; by 2001 this had dropped to 17 per cent (ComputerScience.org, 2015). This low uptake of computer science by females is prevalent around the world. In the UK, only 13 per cent of computer science students at university are females (Murphy, 2015). At Facebook, only 16 per cent of its technical staff are female and at Google only 18 per cent of its technical staff are female. The gender bias does not only exist in industry and at higher education – it is partly enforced at home and at school. A study by Google and Gallup found that girls are less likely than boys to report being told by parents or teachers that they would be good at computer science (39 per cent versus 56 per cent of boys) (Wang, 2016).

The cumulative effect of gender bias and stereotyping continues to have an effect in secondary schools. In 2015, GCSE and A-level computer science had one of the proportionally lowest female intakes compared to any other subject. Kemp *et al.* found that 16.1 per cent of GCSE computer science students were female and only 8.6 per cent of A-level computer science students were female (Kemp *et al.*, 2016). Yet, girls outperformed boys, achieving proportionally more A* to B grades, and proportionally fewer other grades. A level shows a similar pattern to GCSE, with girls, achieving proportionally more A* to B grades, and proportionally fewer other grades.

Clearly, there is a case for promoting computing amongst girls. There are several ways that we as teachers can do this.

- Create a more equal learning environment where females in the classroom and in the world of computing are celebrated at least as much as males.
- Design projects, for example research and graphic design projects around prominent females in computing.
- Design projects which are less game oriented and more oriented around social issues, helping others and making the world a better place.
- Consider more unplugged activities.
- Engage in competitions that encourage females to engage with computing outside of lessons such as GCHQ's Cyberfirst Girls Competition and the Technovation Challenge.
- Engage in creative computing projects such as those promoted by www.3dami.org.uk.
- Make all students aware of flawed and unconscious gender biases and stereotypes.
- Encourage a growth mindset in girls, focussing on overcoming the gender biases and stereotypes.
- Approach local companies and your social network, asking for females working in computing to come to your school to give talks to or mentor your female students.

(NCWIT.org, 2012; AAUW, 2015; ComputerScience.org, 2015;
Rheingans *et al.*, 2017)

By adopting some of these strategies, we successfully improved the number of females choosing GCSE computer science at The Greenwich Free School from 15 per cent in 2016 to 46 per cent in 2017.

Algorithms

This section will discuss effective techniques for teaching searching and sorting algorithms. Whilst these algorithms can be programmed, programming usually hides the process of its execution, particularly when conducting a search or a sort. Therefore, writing a program is not a useful starting point to visualise and understand each individual comparison of a searching or sorting algorithm pass for a novice student. A much more visual way to teach both sorting and searching algorithms is through an unplugged method, that is, not involving a computer at all. This goes contrary to what many students expect computing to be;

however, as we noted in the section on classroom culture in Chapter 5, students should develop the habit of working both with computers and unplugged as this reflects the way that most computing experts think and work.

I would ensure that students have at least been introduced to the concepts of sequence, selection and iteration before I start teaching searching and sorting algorithms. Starting with searching algorithms and a linear search, I would give each pair of students a shuffled set of A5 cards, each individually numbered zero through nine. Setting up a word-processed document and printing "two pages per sheet" and then trimming these works well. The ten unique numbers should be laid out in a linear fashion like an array. Students are then taught to pass sequentially from left to right to locate a target value. The same set of cards can then be used to teach a binary search. GCSE students who have been introduced to arrays or lists can then implement these on the computer. However, I would generally give the students partially completed code or pseudo code for them to complete.

Following this lesson, I would repeat the same process but for sorting algorithms. As binary searches can only be performed on sorted data sets, the binary search provides a natural segue to sorting algorithms. An enjoyable method of visualising these algorithms is through a series of videos made by the YouTube channel by AlgoRythmics (www.youtube.com/user/AlgoRythmics/). The award-winning channel teaches sorting algorithms through folk dances. Provided that the teacher uses the playback speed function on YouTube, these are an engaging way for students to visualise a sort. An alternative way for students to visualise algorithms is available at the website www.visualgo.net. Whilst these visualisations are enjoyable to watch, it is important that in both cases the teacher narrates what is happening with each comparison in the algorithm to facilitate understanding. Didau and Rose note that teachers should exploit the fact that verbal and visual information can be processed by our brains simultaneously (Didau & Rose, 2016). This process was proposed by psychologist Allan Paivio and is known as *dual coding*. By providing anchor images alongside a verbal commentary, we can enhance the student's understanding, recall and recognition of complex processes (Culatta, 2015).

Once the students understand these sorting algorithms through visualisation, the algorithms can then be experienced by students as they sort the cards themselves. It seems counter-intuitive that many computing principles can be taught using unplugged methods and, as fascinating research continues into technological pedagogical content knowledge (TPACK) (Giannakos *et al.*, 2015), I still find unplugged computing often the most effective way of teaching abstract principles particularly in computer science. For more examples of unplugged computing, readers should refer to the excellent website CS Unplugged: www.csunplugged.org.

Ten topics which can be taught using unplugged computing

Unplugged computing has revolutionised the way abstract computing principles are taught in both primary and secondary schools. This movement was popularised by the work of several computer scientists based in New Zealand and Australia; Tim Bell, Ian Witten and Michael Fellows. Their original set of resources which were developed in the 1990s have been developed over the years and translated into over 20 languages. These are all available under a Creative Commons license at www.csunplugged.org. More recently, Phil Bagge (based in Hampshire) has also launched a set of unplugged resources at www.code-it.co.uk, and code.org also have some examples on their YouTube channel. Based on their work, here are ten topics which can be taught using unplugged techniques:

1   Binary numbers
2   Image representation
3   Text compression
4   Image compression
5   Searching algorithms
6   Sorting algorithms
7   Packet switching using IP addresses
8   Encryption
9   Logic gates
10 Parameter passing.

Computer science is not about machines, in the same way that astronomy is not about telescopes.

(Fellows, 1991)

Computing theory

Computing theory that is quite abstract will need to be made concrete by the teacher. As mentioned in the previous section, a great way to do this is by using unplugged computing. However, there are other parts of computing theory that involve learning a large body of factual knowledge. Examples of such topics include computing legislation, hardware and types of malware. In the majority of cases, computing theory is best taught through direct instruction. The skill of an expert teacher is explaining concepts and imparting knowledge in a way that students can understand. In order to assist their understanding, students should be required to think with their newly gained knowledge. The best way to do this is to ask them to apply what they now know to solving a problem.

In some instances you will want students to research some of these topics to find case studies or up-to-date examples of technologies. In these cases, students will need to be explicitly taught how to research. Students will need to be taught how to use keywords, advanced search tools, logical operators, search operators such as 'define', 'inurl' and 'related'. Once students have entered a search query, they need to learn the skill of skimming these results, rather than clicking the top link. Students will need to be taught the difference between sponsored results and adverts along with the effect of filter bubbles. Upon accessing a webpage, students will also need to be taught how to read discerningly, evaluating the credibility of an author, distinguishing between facts and opinions and detecting bias or fake news. When students have located relevant information, they will also need to be taught how to reference and cross-reference their findings.

The final skill which is essential for secondary school students is learning how to paraphrase and derive meaning from what they are reading as opposed to simply copying and pasting. This serves two purposes: First it develops good research habits and avoids developing habits of plagiarism. Second, cognitive psychologists have found that students benefit from this process, known as 'elaboration'.

> If you're just engaging in mechanical repetition, it's true, you quickly hit the limit of what you can retain. However, if you practice elaboration, there's no known limit to how much you can learn. Elaboration is the process of giving new material meaning by expressing it in your own words and connecting it with what you already know. The more you can explain about the way your new learning relates to your prior knowledge, the stronger your grasp of the new learning will be and the more connections you create that will help you remember it later.
>
> (Brown *et al.*, 2014)

This process of research is a fundamental digital literacy skill which cannot be assumed to exist in secondary school students; it is best taught explicitly by a computing teacher.

Online safety

Formerly referred to as 'e-safety', in 2015 online safety was included in Ofsted's common inspection framework (Gov.UK, 2015). Prior to this, e-safety was primarily taught by computing teachers and occasionally by pastoral tutors during form time. However, it is now rightly recognised as a safeguarding issue due to students being at risk of bullying, radicalisation, sexual exploitation and changes in sexual behaviour due to sexting. As computing teachers, it is important that we make our students aware of these risks and also speak openly and honestly about the role of technology and peer pressure amongst secondary-school-aged children.

Some teachers may feel uncomfortable dealing with these issues and I can highly recommend a bank of videos which will also be included in the eResources. These videos are produced by the Child Exploitation and Online Protection Centre (CEOP), Orange, BBC, OnGuardOnline.Gov, Cybertipline.com and range from animations to short films. Students generally take these seriously and I usually ask my students to first reflect on what their thoughts are about the video - by informing students that there are no right or wrong answers, it promotes a mature discussion. Second, I ask them to devise some general rules or advice based on the videos. This lesson can be followed up with students producing their own online safety posters. These are then displayed around school.

Online safety cannot simply be addressed by one unit in Year 7 and Year 8, it should be revisited and case studies can be used and discussed in preparation for GCSE exams. In some cases, as a teacher of computing, your classroom monitoring software or ISP will report logs of inappropriate Internet usage. In these cases, instances should be dealt with seriously; you should follow the safeguarding procedures for your school, speaking to your school's student welfare officer and designated safeguarding lead.

Students should be asked to reflect on the real-life consequences of such an incident happening if they were employed as an adult. As computing teachers, we are there to facilitate good digital literacy skills and habits; and whilst online safety is a whole-school issue, as subject experts, we are still best placed to advise students, teachers, pastoral staff and senior leaders in the school.

Data handling: spreadsheets and databases

Both spreadsheets and databases have existed on the national curriculum for the past 20 years. However, their use has somewhat changed. Typically, students will learn how to use a spreadsheet package such as Microsoft Excel, Open Office Calc or Google Sheets and those students who have studied programming before will find writing formulae and using functions quite straightforward. The skill which students will find useful for science and the humanities will be chart creation. I have included a lesson in the eResources which guides students from creating simple pie charts, to bar charts, scatter graphs and climate graphs. A skill which is often neglected is choosing the correct chart type depending on the types of data. Students should be taught to use appropriate charts for displaying trends over time (line charts), proportions (pie charts) and correlations between two or three sets of data (scatter charts or dual axis charts).

Whilst some schools may not offer an IT qualification at GCSE level, spreadsheets are used in the majority of work places. Other spreadsheet skills worth teaching are how to use spreadsheets collaboratively through applications such as Google Sheets and also how to extract data from surveys, forms and quizzes using Google Forms. The use of Google Suite also allows you to discuss cloud computing.

Lastly, the true power of IT applications comes from using a combination of various applications. Therefore, skills such as mail merging using data from a spreadsheet and importing data from spreadsheets to databases are also worth teaching.

Relational database projects were previously the most popular form of A-level ICT project, and less complex relational databases also existed on some GCSE computing specifications. There has since been a gradual shift towards structured query language (SQL), even at GCSE level. This makes a strong argument to teach flat file databases including queries, forms and reports in Year 8 or 9 in preparation for relational database theory and SQL at GCSE level. Once again, having programmed using a high-level language such as Python in Key Stage 3, learning SQL in Key Stage 4 is relatively straightforward for most students. Students can actually refer back to the databases they made in Year 8 and 9, and (assuming you have used Microsoft Access) the queries can be viewed and edited in SQL view. CAS master teacher Darren Travi recommends an alternative approach to teaching SQL using the SQLite3 library with Python, as this better prepares students for GCSE non-exam assessments (NEAs) (Travi & Avroutine, 2016).

Print publications

There still exist many high-quality Level 2 qualifications despite the abolition of GCSE ICT. These include the Pearson BTECs and CiDA, OCR Creative iMedia and City and Guilds Technical

Awards. All of these qualifications have units which include image editing and graphic design. Whilst Adobe's Creative Cloud suite has become an industry standard, freeware alternatives such as GIMP, Paint.Net, Pixlr editor and Inkscape are perfectly usable for GCSE. There are a large range of tutorials for these applications on YouTube. One tip I would provide to teachers faced with teaching logo design is to use creative commons sources such as www.TheNounProject.com, www.commons.wikimedia.org and brushes such as www.brusheezy.com.

For extensive graphic design work, I would always advise making work which is directly related to computing, such as posters promoting online safety or celebrating women in computing. For those new to poster design, I have included some eResources which cover some basic design principles. These can be summarised as:

Eight rules for poster design:

1   Keep it simple.
2   Limit your text to one-third text and two-thirds imagery.
3   Choose an image or two that portrays your message well. Images should be able to capture the attention of a passer-by.
4   Use two contrasting font types that are readable and use only three or four font sizes.
5   Apply a simple colour scheme ensuring that there is good contrast between the colours.
6   The layout must have lots of space and must not overlap.
7   Elements should be lined up.
8   For every design brief, create several versions and keep re-drafting.

Students could also be introduced to the concept of Eye Flow (Whitbread, 2009) and once students have developed the habit of drafting and improving their work,[7] they can start to challenge design principles by breaking conventions.

Word processing deserves a brief mention. This used to be a skill which was taught extensively along with presentation software at primary schools. However, the trend of primary schools investing in tablets and apps has led to a lot of primary students missing out on essential digital literacy skills such as typing and formatting using word-processing software. It seems that these digital literacy skills have been replaced in some cases with programming using MIT Media Lab's Scratch and in rare cases, Python programming. Depending on your feeder schools and the result of your initial baseline tests, you may wish to include a unit on digital literacy whereby students start to develop these skills. If you have a small number of feeder schools and a large enough department, you could offer training for primary school teachers through your local CAS hub or directly with the feeder schools. This will serve to raise the profile of computing and improve the computing skills of teachers at your local primary schools. Often, it is simply a case of opening up a channel of communication and discussing how the primary school can help prepare students for the computing curriculum at secondary schools.

Web publications

Previously students used programs such as Adobe Dreamweaver or free software such as Microsoft Expression Web and Kompozer to build websites using a table structure and a drag and drop interface. However, as web standards have evolved, students would benefit most from gaining a solid understanding of HTML and CSS. Whilst the aforementioned software can be used, I prefer to minimise the cognitive load of a fully featured editor and instead use a basic editor such as Notepad++. This allows students to focus purely on the code being written.

CAS Master Teacher, Anthea Hoverd made an excellent set of resources entitled the *Fundamentals of HTML and CSS* which also eventually go on to incorporate elements of JavaScript and jQuery. The resources were originally aimed at teachers and can be downloaded from here: https://community.computingatschool.org.uk/resources/2394. I have also modified her resources for use with students in Year 8 and these are available in the eResources.

The ability to understand and use web languages such as HTML, CSS and JavaScript is a key skill for computing students; these are useful for both computer science and IT qualifications at Key Stage 4 and Key Stage 5. It is also worth noting that since the introduction of website templates such as Wordpress and Squarespace, the barriers to entry for a freelance web designer are now quite low provided that the freelancer is fluent in the aforementioned web languages.

Video and audio editing

There is a danger to overemphasise the computer science strand of the computing curriculum and we should be aware of the industry demand for skills in the UK creative industry. This industry is now worth £84.1 billion per year (GOV.UK, 2016). Skills in *films, music, video games, crafts and publishing are taking a lead role in driving the UK's economic recovery, according to the latest Government statistics*. I believe that all students should be exposed to computer science and programming in particular, but this should not mean that we no longer teach creative elements such as video editing and audio editing. Due to the fall in price of hardware, many students at home can download and use industry-standard tools on their home computers and many of these tools are free.

If you do not offer creative IT qualifications at Key Stage 4 or Key Stage 5, it is still worth doing some video projects. Examples of these might include

1   Advertisements
2   Music videos
3   Video campaigns
4   Stop-motion animation.

In the past, advertisements promoting healthy eating, fitness or particular products have worked quite well with students at Key Stage 3. At St Marylebone School, we ran an annual music video competition in Year 10 where students could create a music video for a range of eight songs. This was accompanied by an Academy Awards Ceremony at the end of the project. At Greenwich Free School, the community organising group Citizens UK visited the school on an annual basis to provide a stimulus for Key Stage 3 students to create a video campaign. These video campaigns raised awareness about issues such as bullying, racism and mental health. At Vijay International School Praslin, we used stop motion with a range of age groups and this did not require particularly expensive video cameras. A simple digital stills camera will be able to take thousands of photos and the key here is to use a tripod and ensure the image size is actually set to the smallest resolution (as long as it is above one megapixel). Using digital cameras at a higher resolution may result in the editing software crashing as it is dealing with hundreds of five to twelve megapixel photos. Stop-motion can also incorporate students' favourite toys, Blu Tack or play dough. Some students were particularly keen artists and they decided to individually hand draw each frame. Be warned, that even at three frames per second, a student will have to draw 20 drawings for a one-minute video!

Some of these projects were completed in a day, whereas the music videos and stop-motion animations took place over several lessons. Having taught media studies up to Key Stage 5, I would say that the best films are always those which have meticulous planning. Often students will want to rush out and film, however they should be shown plenty of exemplars just like in any other computing topic so that they understand the conventions and best practices for their genre. My general advice would be to allow students to work in a maximum group size of four and to spend at least two hours planning the storyboards, locations and scripts before students are taught some key camerawork skills and given cameras and tripods to go out and film.

For extended projects, many students chose to film in their own time so that they could use appropriate costumes, props and more exciting locations. Schools can be somewhat limiting for exciting locations! At St Marylebone School, they painted a drama studio's walls with chroma key paint, and backdrops were added successfully at the post-production stage.

Once students have gone out to film, the footage will need to be uploaded. It is best to time the collection of these *rushes* before a lunch break or at the end of the day as the uploading process can take up to 30 minutes. However, if you find that your upload takes place during lesson time, whilst the students wait for the uploading and conversion process, they can start designing the soundtrack and sourcing music and sound effects for their finished pieces. Table 6.3 provides five websites where students can legally download high-quality, free music and sound effects for use in their video productions.[8]

Table 6.3 Five websites for copyright-free music for video projects

Website	Description
www.audionautix.com	A search engine for Creative Commons–licensed music (Free for commercial use).
www.freeplaymusic.com	Free for classroom use.
www.purple-planet.com	Credit required. A paid license required if you plan on distributing or broadcasting with a third party.
www.youtube.com/audiolibrary/music	You can use it only for YouTube videos including monetised content. Attribution may be required.
www.incompetech.com/music/royalty-free/ music.html	Creative Commons By Attribution 3.0 license (Free for commercial use).

Please note that whilst all of these sites offer free music, you are required to credit the author of the music appropriately. The credit/license details are always given on the music download page and you should read these with your students before using the music in their videos. Should students wish to add their own voiceovers and edit their music, most non-linear video editing software will allow students to edit their soundtracks. However, the freeware Audacity is also useful for performing more precise editing. A more detailed breakdown of the different software options for video and audio editing is discussed in Chapter 9.

Chapter 6 summary

1   Pedagogical content knowledge (PCK) in computing like PCK in other subjects is derived from research and experience.
2   Fluency in programming is not simply developed by learning a programming language and its specific syntax. The key to fluency is building problem-solving skills with the programming language and this is developed using several strategies including reading, tracing, debugging and pair programming.
3   Gender biases and stereotypes have negatively impacted the number of girls studying computing. Girls that do choose to study computing generally outperform boys at GCSE and A levels. There are various strategies we can employ to negate these gender biases and stereotypes and thereby encourage girls to study computing.
4   Unplugged computing activities are often the most powerful method for helping students understand algorithms and other abstract concepts in computing.
5   Digital literacy remains a part of the computing curriculum and key digital literacy skills such as typing, researching, referencing and the use of office applications should be explicitly taught.
6   Video editing projects are not only fun and engaging, but the skills that are learnt are also in high demand in the UK creative industries. We cannot have a myopic focus on computer science at the expense of creative IT.

Notes

1   Samuel Hulick urges us to look more closely for gaps between the steps.
2   It's not very easy to introduce the concept of constants or objects in Python, nor is it easy to make an appealing GUI. There are workarounds; however, some teachers with prior programming experience can choose a different language that they are confident with.
3   PLAN C is a research evidence-informed project, by a community of practice-based, professional learning for computing teachers in Scotland: http://trace.dcs.gla.ac.uk/.
4   Lister notes that in reality, a student's skills will not lie in one stage of development and instead students will often exhibit a mix of the stages akin to overlapping waves for different programming constructs.

5   Williams and Kessler report pair programming taking place at universities as early as 1953 (Williams & Kessler, 2002)!

6   This jump in dates is significant. A large number of women were involved in programming and code breaking during World War II; examples of these include the Eniac programmers (www.eniacprogrammers.org) and the 7,500 women code breakers at Bletchley Park (http://www.bletchleyparkresearch.co.uk/research-notes/women-codebreakers/).

7   An inspirational book which deals with this process of drafting is Ron Berger's *An Ethic of Excellence*.

8   Schools in London also have access to an extensive library known as the LGfL Audio Network: www.audionetwork.nen.gov.uk.

References

AAUW, 2015. *Solving the Equation: The Variables for Women's Success in Engineering and Computing*. Washington, DC: AAUW.

Brown, P. C., Roediger III, H. L. & McDaniel, M. A., 2014. *How to Learn Better at Any Age*. [Online] Available at: https://www.bostonglobe.com/magazine/2014/03/09/how-learn-better-any-age/JCxes7YTWRsqEKu67V5ZNN/story.html [Accessed 16 March 2015].

Code.org, 2014. *Pair Programming*. [Online] Available at: https://www.youtube.com/watch?v=vgkahOzFH2Q [Accessed 27 January 2015].

Collins, A., Holum, A. & Seely Brown, J., 1991. Cognitive apprenticeship: making thinking visible. *American Educator: The Professional Journal of the American Federation of Teachers*, 15(Winter), pp. 38–46.

ComputerScience.org, 2015. *Women in Computer Science: Getting Involved in STEM*. [Online] Available at: http://www.computerscience.org/resources/women-in-computer-science/ [Accessed 7 April 2017].

Culatta, R., 2015. *Dual Coding Theory (Allan Paivio)*. [Online] Available at: http://www.instructionaldesign.org/theories/dual-coding.html [Accessed 5 December 2016].

Denner, J., Werner, L., Campe, S. & Ortiz, E., 2014. Pair programming: under what conditions is it advantageous for middle school students? *Journal of Research on Technology in Education*, 46(3), pp. 277–96.

Didau, D. & Rose, N., 2016. *What Every Teacher Needs to Know about Psychology*. 1st ed. Woodbridge, UK : John Catt Educational Ltd.

Dijkstra, E. W., 1972. The humble programmer. *Communications of the ACM*, 15(10), pp. 859–66.

Fellows, M. R., 1991. *Computer SCIENCE and Mathematics in the Elementary Schools*. [Online] Available at: https://larc.unt.edu/ian/research/cseducation/fellows1991.pdf [Accessed 11 July 2017].

Franklin, J. P., 2015. *Perceptions by Young People of Pair Programming When Learning Text Languages*. London: Axsied / King's College London.

Giannakos, M. N., Doukakis, S., Pappas, I. O., Adamopoulos, N. & Giannopoulou, P., 2015. Investigating teachers' confidence on technological pedagogical and content knowledge: an initial validation of TPACK scales in K-12 computing education context. *Journal of Computers in Education*, 2(1), pp. 43–59.

Gov.UK, 2015. *Common Inspection Framework: Education, Skills and Early Years from September 2015*. [Online] Available at: https://www.gov.uk/government/publications/common-inspection-framework-education-skills-and-early-years-from-september-2015 [Accessed 2 September 2015].

GOV.UK, 2016. *Creative Industries Worth Almost £10 Million an Hour to Economy*. [Online] Available at: https://www.gov.uk/government/news/creative-industries-worth-almost-10-million-an-hour-to-economy [Accessed 12 April 2017].

Hannay, J. E., Dybå, T., Arisholm, E. & Sjøberg, D. I., 2009. The effectiveness of pair programming: a meta-analysis. *Information and Software Technology*, 51(2009), pp. 1110-22.

Kemp, P. E., Wong, B. & Berry, M. G., 2016. *The Roehampton Annual Computing Education Report*. London: University of Roehampton.

Kramer, J., 2007. Is abstraction the key? *Communications of the ACM*, 50(4), pp. 36-42.

Lister, R., 2011. Concrete and other neo-Piagetian forms of reasoning in the novice programmer. *ACE '11 Proceedings of the Thirteenth Australasian Computing Education Conference*, 114, pp. 9-18.

Lister, R., Adams, E. S., Fitzgerald, S., Fone, W., Hamer, J., Lindholm, M., McCartney, R., Moström, J. E., Sanders, K., Seppälä, O. Simon, B. & Thomas, L., 2004. A multi-national study of reading and tracing skills in novice programmers. *SIGCSE Bulletin*, 36(4), pp. 119-50.

Margulieux, L. E., Catrambone, R. & Guzdial, M., 2016. Employing subgoals in computer programming education. *Computer Science Education*, 26(1), pp. 44-67.

Margulieux, L., Guzdial, M. & Catrambone, R., 2012. Subgoal-labeled instructional material improves performance and transfer in learning to develop mobile applications. *ICER '12 Proceedings of the Ninth Annual International Conference on International Computing Education Research*, pp. 71-8.

McSwan, A., 2016. *Approach - Tracing to Understand the Notional Machine*. [Online] Available at: http://trace.dcs.gla.ac.uk/tracing/ [Accessed 30 March 2017].

Murphy, M., 2015. *Fewer British Women Studying Computer Science Than in 2010*. [Online] Available at: http://www.computerworlduk.com/careers/women-studying-computer-science-in-uk-universities-is-declining-3621040/ [Accessed 7 April 2017].

NCWIT.org, 2012. *Girls in IT: The Facts*. [Online] Available at: https://www.ncwit.org/resources/girls-it-facts [Accessed 7 March 2015].

NPR, 2014. *Episode 576: When Women Stopped Coding*. [Online] Available at: http://www.npr.org/sections/money/2014/10/17/356944145/episode-576-when-women-stopped-coding [Accessed 19 December 2015].

Peyton Jones, S., 2016. *Simon Peyton Jones on Algorithmic Complexity*. [Online] Available at: https://www.youtube.com/watch?v=ixmbkpOQEDM [Accessed 23 Feb 2016].

Rheingans, P., Larkin, M., Barr, V. & Driggs-Campbell, K., 2017. *CS Programs for Women*. [Online] Available at: http://www.computerscienceonline.org/cs-programs-for-women/ [Accessed 7 April 2017].

Russo, N. P., 2016. *Margaret Hamilton, Apollo Software Engineer, Awarded Presidential Medal of Freedom*. [Online] Available at: https://www.nasa.gov/feature/margaret-hamilton-apollo-software-engineer-awarded-presidential-medal-of-freedom [Accessed 7 April 2017].

Selby, C., 2015. Relationships: computational thinking, pedagogy of programming, and Bloom's Taxonomy. *Proceedings of the WiPSCE '15 Workshop in Primary and Secondary Computing Education London, United Kingdom*, 2015, pp. 80-7.

Sentance, S., 2017. *KS3-KS5 Strategies for Teaching Programming*. [Online] Available at: https://community.computingatschool.org.uk/resources/4737 [Accessed 1 March 2017].

Sentance, S., 2017. *Mini TRACS*. London: King's College London.

Shulman, L. S., 1986. Those who understand: knowledge growth in teaching. *Educational Researcher*, 15(2), pp. 4-14.

Shulman, L. S., 1987. Knowledge and teaching: foundations of the new reform. *Harvard Educational Review*, 57(1), pp. 1-22.

Statter, D. & Armoni, M., 2016. Teaching abstract thinking in introduction to computer science for 7th graders. *WiPSCE '16 Proceedings of the 11th Workshop in Primary and Secondary Computing Education*, 11, pp. 80-3.

Teague, D., 2015. *Neo-Piagetian Theory and the Novice Programmer*. Brisbane, Queensland: Queensland University of Technology.

Teague, D. & Lister, R., 2014. Longitudinal think aloud study of a novice programmer. *ACE '14 Proceedings of the Sixteenth Australasian Computing Education Conference*, 148, pp. 41–50.

Travi, D. & Avroutine, I., 2016a. *Hands-on A-Level Computing: Transition from GCSE to A-Level Computer Science*, High Wycombe, UK: Darren Travi Events.

Travi, D. & Avroutine, I., 2016b. *Preparing to Teach GCSE Computing 9 – 1*. High Wycombe, UK: Darren Travi Events.

Waite, J., 2017. *CAS London Master Teacher Training* [Interview] (20 March 2017).

Waite, J., Curzon, P., Marsh, W. & Sentance, S., 2016. Abstraction and common classroom activities. In: *Proceedings of the 11th Workshop in Primary and Secondary Computing Education*. New York: ACM, pp. 112–13.

Wang, J., 2016. *Racial and Gender Gaps in Computer Science Learning: New Google-Gallup Research*. [Online] Available at: https://blog.google/topics/education/racial-and-gender-gaps-computer-science-learning-new-google-gallup-research/ [Accessed 7 April 2017].

Watters, A., 2012. *Top Ed-Tech Trends of 2012: Learning to Code*. [Online] Available at: https://www.insidehighered.com/blogs/hack-higher-education/top-ed-tech-trends-2012-learning-code [Accessed 4 November 2016].

Whitbread, D., 2009. *The Design Manual*. 2nd ed. Sydney: University of New South Wales Press Ltd.

Williams, L. & Kessler, R., 2002. *Pair Programming Illuminated*. Boston, MA: Pearson.

Wolfman, S., 2014. *CS Education Zoo Episode #6: Mark Guzdial*. [Online] Available at: https://www.youtube.com/watch?v=z1oTtPECHZI [Accessed 7 March 2015].

Part 3
Leadership and management

7 Personal leadership

In this world of rapid change traditional management is increasingly ineffective. What's required is leadership. As the pace of change increases so does the demand for effective leadership ... Leadership starts with leading yourself. Before you can lead others, you must lead yourself.

(Ambler, 2017)

This section of the book is based on managing yourself, managing others and leadership. I have had the good fortune of working with many successful leaders in education. In all cases, those who were effective leaders lived lives which were coherent with their vision. Having experience on a senior leadership team as an assistant head teacher in charge of teacher development, this section is based on many years of continuous professional development (CPD), research and my own experience in leading others and following the lead of others. Before we discuss leadership, we must first look introspectively at ourselves and our own lives.

Coherent leadership

We want our students to leave our classroom at the end of the year having learnt more about computing and more about how to be a better person. The only way we can do this is by modelling what good learning practices look like and what does it mean to be a respectful and professional person. In Dr Alan Watkins's compelling book *Coherence,* he brings together extensive research from the fields of psychology, medicine, sport and business to provide strategies to improve leadership in a wide range of contexts (Watkins, 2014). Results, Watkins argues, are at the tip of an iceberg and are influenced by a hierarchy of underlying factors. Our everyday decisions and actions are indisputably based on our thoughts. Digging much deeper, Watkins argues that these thoughts are influenced by our feelings and emotions and all of these are ultimately based on our physiology (see Figure 7.1).

Watkins's theories, grounded in research and used successfully with CEOs and athletes, make sense. We generally only notice the external results and manifested actions of others. Rarely do we consider the other's internal thoughts, feelings, emotions and well-being. The same is probably true with regard to how others see you. Consider working upwards from the bottom of this hierarchy and the following scenario:

It is 4pm on a Tuesday; you have taught five lessons followed by a cover lesson. You were also supervising the dining hall at lunchtime. You have just sat down at your department

Figure 7.1 The integrated performance model (adapted from Watkins, 2014).

meeting and there are more than ten agenda items, one of which is moderating the Year 11 assessments that you were marking until 11.30pm last night. Physiologically, you are probably low in energy, tired and hungry. Emotionally, you are probably experiencing negative emotions such as fear, anger and sadness. These emotions feed into your feelings, thoughts, behaviour and results over the next two hours. Compare this to the first in-service training (INSET) day in September following a summer of relaxation, regular sleep and meals which were not consumed whilst sat next to your laptop. The difference is stark and part of this chapter is about trying to maintain positive results, behaviours, thoughts, feelings and emotions throughout the year by looking after yourself and those around you.

Citing the work of psychologist Ken Wilber, Watkins discusses three stages of *coherent evolution*. These three steps can be seen as a cycle for change (see Figure 7.2).

Evolution in our own practices in the Emergence stage starts with the constant questioning of everything we do. By regularly evaluating our practice, processes and performance, we will be more aware and proactive as opposed to being overly reactive. On the micro scale, we have already looked at techniques such as Pastore's perch in Chapter 5, stepping back

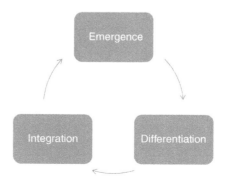

Figure 7.2 Three stages of coherent evolution (adapted from Wilber, 2001; Watkins, 2014).

and taking in the whole classroom to analyse the learning environment. However, on a macro scale, this involves metaphorically stepping back to analyse our own practice or the practice of our department or school.

In the second stage of differentiation, we attempt to define the problem(s) that exist. We can use our computational thinking skill of problem decomposition here. In much the same way that poor computer systems and software solutions are generally the result of poor analysis and design, the same is true of personal development. Once we have identified the specific problem(s) that need resolving, we can then look for solutions. These solutions may be gleaned from books, journals, mentors, colleagues and other professionals, and these may not necessarily be isolated to the field of education. The most effective leaders look at high-performing leaders from other industries and contexts and then importantly look at how best practice can be adapted and integrated into their own contexts. Integration is the most difficult stage; we cannot simply take what works somewhere else and expect it to fit exactly into our classrooms, departments or schools.

> In education, "what works?" is not the right question because everything works somewhere and nothing works everywhere, so what's interesting, what's important in education is: "Under what conditions does this work?". That is why teaching is mainly a matter of phronesis not of episteme. Teaching is all about knowing the conditions under which a particular technique is likely to work.

> (Wiliam, 2006)

Hopefully this book provides a framework for thinking, developing and improving practice rather than a fixed set of plans for you to follow. Watkins describes the three stages as an upward spiral, whereby integration is followed by re-emergence and the cycle beginning again. The education landscape is dynamic and will change as successive governments implement policy changes and the Department for Education (DFE) and exam boards change their requirements, specifications and foci. Provided we develop personally and professionally based on a model of continuous iterative improvement, the concepts and philosophies in this book will either remain directly relevant or they can be modified, providing a framework for new practices to be integrated as the world in which we operate changes.

Reflective questions for emergent leadership:

- **Personal development**: How could I develop and improve my energy levels, emotions, happiness, cognitive ability, health, fitness and wellbeing? How can I develop my relationships with students, peers, leaders and external agencies?
- **Subject knowledge**: What are my actions based on the subject knowledge audit in Chapter 1? Where and who can I go to for support on these actions? Have I been to my local CAS hub? Have I connected with others via social networks such as Twitter and the numerous computing groups on Facebook?
- **Pedagogy**: What are my actions based on lesson observations?

> - **Professional development**: What do I want to achieve and accomplish this year? What areas do I wish to develop to become a better teacher/middle leader/senior leader? What training is available on CAS locally/regionally/nationally? What are other high-performing schools, businesses or athletes doing and how can I learn from them and adapt their practices?
> - **Career development**: What do I want to achieve in three years' time? What do I want to achieve in five years' time? Who can I seek advice and mentoring from?

Coherent leadership starts with physiology and improving this will result in better emotions, cognition, maturity, values and eventually better actions, relationships and results. Teaching can be stressful and it is important to look after yourself, eat healthily, sleep sufficiently and speak only positively of yourself and others. Try not to gossip or allow negative emotions to seep in. Speaking from personal experience, lack of awareness leads to a lack of energy; this will inevitably result in emotional upset, poor thinking and in extreme cases burnout. However, the journey of *self*-development paradoxically cannot be completed alone. In much the same way that students achieve mastery through guided and independent practice, teachers can only achieve mastery in their teaching if they adopt what Anders Ericsson calls *deliberate practice*. In his research on peak performance spanning 30 years, Ericsson found that professionals in many fields achieve expert performance through the following elements of deliberate practice:

1   Practicing outside your comfort zone, trying activities beyond your current abilities – taking risks in the classroom and in your practice.
2   Identifying areas to improve on and setting well-designed goals.
3   Seeking feedback: finding a fellow teacher to be a mentor in school who will help you reflect and devise plans and strategies for achieving your goals.[1]
4   Acting on the feedback provided by your mentor.
5   Focussing on isolated elements of [classroom] practice.
6   Developing a mental model of expertise by reflecting on what it means to be an expert computing teacher and the cognitive science behind how students learn.

(Ericsson & Pool, 2016; Deans for Impact, 2016)

Ericsson and Pool note that deliberate practice is not always enjoyable and will not intuitively feel good. Wiliam goes on to suggest that,

> *Teaching is such a complex craft that one lifetime is not enough to master it, but by rigorously focusing on practice, teachers can continue to improve throughout their career. From teachers, therefore, we need a commitment—not to attending a certain number of hours of professional development per year—but a career-long commitment to the continuous improvement [of] practice, and an agreement to develop in their practice in ways that are likely to improve outcomes for their students.*

(Wiliam, 2010)

Managing your time

If Wiliam is correct, that a lifetime is not enough to master our craft then what hope do we have? I think there needs to be a balance between what is achievable in a given amount of time and how we should use our time. We should first consider Parkinson's law which states that "work expands so as to fill the time available for its completion" (Parkinson, 1955). Indeed, an experienced teacher will tell you, it is never possible to "finish", instead we should use our time wisely. In Stephen Covey's international best-sellers *7 Habits of Highly Effective People* (Covey, 2004) and *First Things First* (Covey, 1999), Covey states that tasks can be divided into one of four quadrants based on importance and urgency.

In the matrix illustrated in Figure 7.3, Covey advises readers to focus on Quadrant 2, completing tasks based on importance rather than urgency first. Whilst, inevitably some tasks are urgent, many of them are not important and urgency often gives us the illusion of

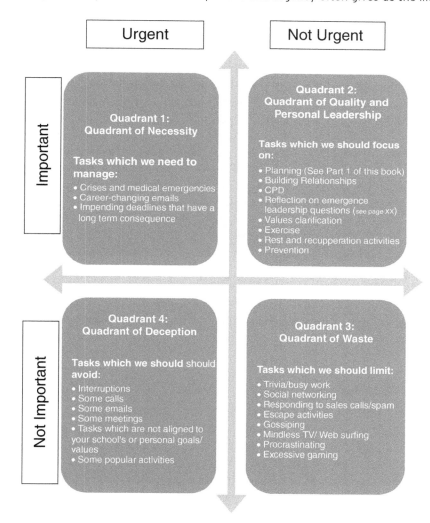

Figure 7.3 Time management matrix (adapted from Covey, 2004).

importance. Conversely, tasks which are actually important will eventually become urgent if they are neglected, putting us under pressure. As teachers with many tasks to complete and many roles to fulfil, we operate best when we are not working under stress and time pressures. In order to operate predominantly in the quadrant of quality and personal leadership, the most important activity is planning.

I would advise *planning by the week*. At the end of every week typically on a Friday or a Sunday, I will sit down with my teacher planner and plan out the week ahead. I will look at this week's and this month's deadlines which are usually communicated in my school's weekly e-mail bulletin. I will populate the planner with my lessons (which are fixed) and then add any deadlines and school events. Personal events of high importance are also added. From this point, I can very quickly identify days where I have very little time for other tasks and other days where I can perform some more Quadrant 2 activities including meetings with parents, TAs (See Chapter 3) or senior leaders. If a student requires extra help or a parent or colleague wishes to book in a meeting, I then have my planner to hand and can schedule in a date when I am not already at capacity. A novice teacher's mistake is *planning by the day*, waking up each morning and trying to plan the day ahead and then realising that they have 100 books to mark in time for the parents evening. The week is certainly the best unit of time to plan by as it allows enough foresight and lead-in time whilst still remaining relevant. Some teachers may choose to plan their time with an online calendar such as Outlook, Google Calendar or Apple Calendar. Personally, I find that having a teacher planner is much more manageable as it is less structured and allows for additional notes and prioritisation. I find that with online calendars and emails, there is a lot of noise, and events can sometimes get missed. Likewise, I would spend a lot of time checking my notifications and being pushed into Quadrant 3 (the Quadrant of Deception) by incessant reminders. The teacher planner conversely means I don't have my work emails and events attached to my personal mobile device; this makes it slightly easier to "switch off" at the end of a school day. Every person will however find their own method of working.

Ultimately, Covey (1999) argues that time management comes down to values. The picture on the front cover of his book *First Things First* shows a compass over a clock. Indeed, like Watkins, Covey states that value identification is of paramount importance. Once you understand your personal values and the values and strategic priorities of your school, time management will require less cognitive load and overtime will be almost automatic. As tasks arrive, you will be able to mentally place them into your list of priorities or ignore them where appropriate.

Values clarification

One of the activities in Covey's Quadrant 2, the Quadrant of Quality and Personal Leadership is *values clarification* (Covey, 1999). I think that this is a crucial aspect in personal leadership, because unless we define what is important to us, it is difficult to prioritise our time and efforts. Whilst Covey does not go into granular detail about how to formulate our values, he does suggest a starting point. The first step of values clarification according to Stephen Covey is defining your roles. What roles do you perform on a day-to-day basis:

1   Father
2   Husband
3   Teacher of computing
4   Head of department
5   Newly qualified teachers (NQT) mentor
6   Deliverer of CPD
7   Lunchtime supervisor.

Based on each of these roles, you should write down two or three success criteria. What does being a good father mean? What does being a good teacher look like? These must be two or three actions that you are in control of; they are actions which make you good at this role. You will have made a list of 10–20 items. We could simply put these in order of importance and say that the top ten items are our values. However, the leadership coach Marshall Goldsmith advises us to actually turn these statements into questions which can be answered with Yes, No or a number (Goldsmith, 2015). Goldsmith goes on to advise us to plot these questions on a spreadsheet like the one in Table 7.1. By questioning ourselves every day, we are engaged in the habit of living our values and reflecting on them.

Too often, schools and individuals formulate vague values and either write them in their diaries or create large vinyl wall displays with them around the school buildings, occasionally referring back to these. With Goldsmith's process, the individual is asked to put themselves in the challenging position of questioning themselves and reflecting on how they are doing on a day-by-day basis based on the things that matter to them the most. I have found this process challenging but effective over a period of time. We should use this as a positive and productive tool for living with strong values as opposed to creating feelings of guilt or regret.

 Table 7.1 Asking questions on a daily basis to clarify your values

Line Values	Mon	Tues	Weds	Thurs	Fri	Sat	Sun	Mon	Tues
Did I express gratitude and love towards Suki?	No	Yes	Yes	Yes	Yes	Yes	Yes	Yes	Yes
Did I speak to Zi more than any other teacher today?	No	Yes	Yes	No	No			No	No
Did I read to Zi?	Yes	No	No	No	No	Yes	Yes	Yes	Yes
Did I do my best to cater for SEND?	No	Yes	No	No	No			No	No
Did I disrupt learning unnecessarily?	Yes	No	Yes	Yes	No			No	No
How many minutes past 6 did I get home today?	11	10	−37	35	61			35	25
How many hours did I sleep last night?	6	7.5	6	5	9	7.5	7.5	5.5	5.5
How long did I meditate for today (mins?)	30	20	20	5	0	0	0	0	30
Did I do my best to set clear goals	Yes	Yes	Yes	Yes	Yes	Yes	Yes	Yes	Yes
Did I do my best to make progress towards achieve my goals?	Yes	Yes	Yes	Yes	Yes	Yes	Yes	Yes	Yes
Did I do my best to build positive relationships?	Yes	Yes	Yes	Yes	Yes	Yes	Yes	Yes	Yes
Did I do my best to be happy?	Yes	No	Yes	Yes	Yes	Yes	Yes	Yes	No
Did I do my best to be fully engaged?	No	No	No	Yes	Yes	No	No	Yes	Yes
Did I do my best to find meaning?	No	No	Yes	Yes	Yes	No	No	No	No
Did I spend more time procrastinating than meditating/resting?	Yes	No	No	Yes	Yes	Yes	Yes	Yes	No

> I would advise readers to revisit this exercise, starting with writing down your roles and then your success criteria at least once a year. This is because your values are likely to evolve as your role changes in school and your life circumstances change.

Covey highlights two traps: First, some people become too rigid with their time management and do not give enough time to the people they work with. He advises that you should always value relationships, particularly the relationships with people that share your values and the values of your school. I cannot re-emphasise this point; going into a new school respect and time are the two most important things you can give to everyone. This is primarily important for your students because giving students time and respect from day one will make teaching and behaviour management much less antagonistic. However, time and respect should also be afforded to those who you may not be in contact with in your daily teaching of computing such as the school receptionist and administrative team, the site managers, IT technicians and cleaners. John Brandon builds on Covey's advice, "you cannot be efficient with people ... be efficient with things and effective with people" (Brandon, 2014). Indeed, a considerable part of teaching is about building and maintaining strong relationships.

Covey's second trap is that of *urgency addiction*: Many teachers enjoy the sense of urgency and enjoy being the person that completes things in a rush, last minute or the one that saves the day. The sense of being busy and doing things quickly gives us the illusion that we're being productive and effective. However, whilst some Quadrant 1 tasks are unavoidable, there are many tasks which are only important and urgent for other people. Here is an example. Many years ago a teacher was putting on a school production, and they forgot to design the programme. They realised on the day of the show and asked if anyone in our department could help. In this case, a teacher said "Yes" without thinking first about their capacity. Think for a moment what the consequences are of you spending an hour or two on the programme for the school play. First, that means you are not able to do any of your own tasks in Quadrant 2, meaning these will likely move into Quadrant 1. Second, think about the consequences if there are no programmes. Would those attending really know that there was meant to be a programme in the first place or would they simply focus on the theatrical production in front of them? Perhaps it would also be a reminder for the person organising the play to have this organised in advance next year. Whilst we should try to help our colleagues wherever possible, sometimes we simply do not have the capacity to do so, and saying "No" does not mean you are a bad person, it just means you have more important things to do to help your students and the school. The reason why Quadrant 3 is called the Quadrant of Deception is because many people perceive all tasks that are urgent to also be important. This is often not the case.

Work-life balance

In terms of balancing our time and efforts, we must also remember that there is always more to do, but that these things cannot be done in the time that we have, unless we start to sacrifice significant amounts of our personal time and well-being time. Teacher of Toltec philosophy don Miguel Ruiz advises us not to seek perfection, but to do our best and to avoid self-judgement, self-abuse and regret (Ruiz, 1997). Some readers may be young and single without children of their own and you may feel that teaching is a noble cause which requires sacrifice. However, this sacrifice is not sustainable and sacrificing your own time can turn into a habit which is difficult to break from. One of the best pieces of advice that my head teacher Oliver Knight gave me was that "No job is worth sacrificing your health and family life for"; this built on the advice of my NQT mentor Giles Niklaus, who often reminded me that "The school year is a marathon. It's a long race, we cannot maintain a sprinter's pace throughout the whole year and sometimes it is necessary to slow down".

I want to finish this chapter by summarising Ruiz's book as it has influenced my teaching practice considerably.

A summary of *The Four Agreements* by Don Miguel Ruiz

1. Be impeccable with your word

Speak with integrity. Say only what you mean. Avoid using the word to speak against yourself or to gossip about others. Use the power of your words in the direction of truth and love.

2. Don't take anything personally

Nothing others do is because of you. What others say and do is a projection of their own reality. When you are immune to the opinions and actions of others, you won't be the victim of needless suffering.

3. Don't make assumptions

Find the courage to ask questions and to express what you really want. Communicate with others as clearly as you can to avoid misunderstandings, sadness and drama.

4. Always do your best

Your "best" is going to change from moment to moment; it will be different when you are healthy as opposed to sick. Under any circumstance, simply do your best and you will avoid self-judgment, self-abuse and regret.

Chapter 7 summary

1. Leadership starts with leading yourself.
2. We must pay attention to our physiology. This in turn impacts our emotions, feelings, thoughts and actions.
3. We must continuously question our own practice and be aware of the dynamic educational landscape.
4. Once we identify our areas for development, we can seek best practice from other teachers, schools and industries. These practices can then be adapted and integrated into our own practices.
5. High performance requires deliberate practice which involves the support of others, acting on feedback and practicing outside of our comfort zones.
6. We should focus on our relationships with people and the most important tasks based on our personal values and the strategic priorities of the school. In doing so, we should be aware of the illusion of urgency.
7. Be aware of the sustainability of your practice. Take time to rest and recuperate even if you are achieving good results.

Note

1   At The Greenwich Free School we adopted Paul Bambrick-Santoyo's model of leveraged leadership and mentoring. This works best as a school-wide initiative and senior leaders interested in adopting this should refer to (Bambrick-Santoyo, 2016).

References

Ambler, G., 2017. *Helping to Grow Your Leadership*. [Online] Available at: http://www.georgeambler.com [Accessed 9 April 2017].

Bambrick-Santoyo, P., 2016. *Get Better Faster*. San Francisco: Jossey-Bass.

Brandon, J., 2014. *Why You're Failing to Adopt the 7 Habits of Highly Effective People*. [Online] Available at: https://www.inc.com/john-brandon/7-habits-highly-effective-people-why-theyre-not-sticking.html [Accessed 9 April 2017].

Covey, S. R., 1999. *First Things First*. London: Simon & Schuster UK Ltd.

Covey, S. R., 2004. *The 7 Habits of Highly Effective People*. London: Simon & Schuster UK Ltd.

Deans for Impact, 2016. *Practice with Purpose: The Emerging Science of Teacher Expertise*, Austin, TX: Deans for Impact.

Ericsson, A. & Pool, R., 2016. *Peak: Secrets from the New Science of Expertise*. New York: Houghton Mifflin Harcourt Publishing Company.

Goldsmith, M., 2015. *Invest 2 Minutes a Day to Improve Your Leadership Skills*. [Online] Available at: https://www.inc.com/inc-live/marshall-goldsmith-tough-questions.html [Accessed 28 Jan 2015].

Parkinson, C. N., 1955. *Parkinson's Law*. [Online] Available at: http://www.economist.com/node/14116121 [Accessed 9 April 2017].

Ruiz, M., 1997. *The Four Agreements: A Practical Guide to Personal Freedom*. San Rafael,California: Amber-Allen Publishing.

Watkins, A., 2014. *Coherence: The Secret Science of Brilliant Leadership*. London: Kogan Page Limited.

Wilber, K., 2001. *A Theory of Everything: An Integral Vision for Business, Politics, Science and Spirituality*. Boston, MA: Shambhala Publications.

Wiliam, D., 2006. *Assessment for Learning – Dylan Wiliam*. [Online] Available at: http://dylanwiliam.org/Dylan_Wiliams_website/Papers_files/Cambridge%20AfL%20keynote.doc [Accessed 2017 4 April].

Wiliam, D., 2010. *Teacher Quality: How to Get More of It*. [Online] Available at: http://www.dylanwiliam.org/Dylan_Wiliams_website/Papers_files/Spectator%20talk.doc [Accessed 9 April 2017].

8 Managing and leading others

You can mandate adequacy, but you cannot mandate greatness: it has to be unleashed.

(Barber & Klein, 2016)

The best middle leaders I have worked with have also been confident classroom practitioners. They model excellence both in their classroom practice and in their professional practice. Their professional habits include being proactive, reflective, organised and positive. They have excellent relationships with those they line manage. These leaders have strong values and a clear vision for their area of responsibility which they communicate clearly with others. If we were to refer back to Covey's Time Management Matrix in the previous chapter, the effective middle leader spends most of their time in Quadrant 2, the Quadrant of Quality and Personal Leadership, and when they inevitably have to deal with tasks in Quadrant 1, they do so calmly and rationally. In doing so, they set an example for those around them to follow.

Good leaders must communicate vision clearly, creatively, and continually. However, the vision doesn't come alive until the leader models it.

(Maxwell, 2007)

I have been lucky enough to spend the past four years working closely with some excellent middle leaders, notably Jo Parkes and Corinne Flett, who were the heads of English and science respectively. Their practices inspired other middle leaders around them at The Greenwich Free School to improve their practices and rise up to the high standards that they set. In this chapter, I will reflect on some of the best practices gleaned from middle and senior leaders in education and in business. I will start by discussing how middle leaders can help develop and lead members of their team.

Developing and leading members of your team

Referring back to Dr Alan Watkins's book *Coherence*, Watkins describes how leaders should develop in themselves and their team the qualities shown in Table 8.1.

Most teachers and many leaders will be aware of their horizontal development and focus a significant proportion of their time acquiring new skills, knowledge and experience. The subject knowledge audit is a useful tool for isolating particular skills and knowledge which a teacher should focus on and teachers can gain valuable experience by visiting other high-performing teachers, classrooms and schools. Further experience can be gained from

Table 8.1 Lines of development (adapted from Watkins, 2014)

Types of development	Line of development
Horizontal development (Learning focussed)	Skills Knowledge Experience
Vertical development (Development focussed)	Physiology Emotions Cognitive Maturity Values Behaviour Networks and relationships Impact

becoming an exam board examiner or moderator or visiting technology companies. However, a common developmental blind spot even in high-performing teachers and leaders is vertical development. Watkins argues that to be a successful leader, leadership team and organisation, you must also be aware of and focus on developing other lines which involve personal and interpersonal skills such as your values, emotional intelligence, maturity and relationships.

The question is, how can we develop these attributes on our team? A word of caution: You cannot develop adults in the same way that you develop children. Indeed, being an excellent classroom teacher is distinct from being an excellent leader of a team. Whilst many excellent classroom teachers are promoted to middle management and senior management based on their classroom competencies, very rarely do these excellent teachers receive training on how to develop adults. Malcolm Knowles states that adults learn in a different way to children. Through his theory of *androgogy*, which consists of principles for adult learning and development, one of the primary differences between the way that adults learn and develop is that adults are generally more internally motivated and self-directed. This can be contrasted to pedagogy (with children) where the learning is directed by a teacher (Knowles, 1980).

If you wish to see this point in action, try to line manage and motivate teachers in your department using the same strategies that you use with your students! You will soon find that most adults do not like being directed, particularly teachers who spend most of their day in a role where they are the ones giving directions. Knowles argues that as children mature into adults, they become more independent and self-directed. Adults also become less motivated by *what* they are learning and *how* they should perform a task and instead become primarily motivated with the *why*. We have all sat in a briefing with a senior leader where we are told *what* to do and then patronisingly told *how* to do it, yet without explaining the *why*. Many adults in the room will not like being directed in this way and will leave the meeting feeling resentful, emotionally disengaged, demotivated and whilst the leader may assume they have won the battle as their audience follows the mandated actions, these adults do so reluctantly and this is not sustainable. Simon Sinek makes a compelling case for starting all developmental actions, meetings, presentations, lessons, advertisements, policy changes and so on with the *why* in his appropriately titled book, *Start With Why: How Great Leaders Inspire Everyone to Take Action* (Sinek, 2009). Sinek's theory of explaining the rationale first is based on the world of business, but it is a fascinating read and I think it would be applicable to teachers at all stages in their career. This theory has influenced the structure of my lessons,[1] line management meetings, conference talks and even this book.

When I first started at The Greenwich Free School, I was the only computing teacher, so I wrote the vision (that is presented in Chapter 1) to remind myself that all my actions as a teacher and eventually as a leader had a reason; they were there to fulfil this vision. Everything we do, from the way we speak to our students to the homework we set and the resources we develop should be based on the vision for computing. If you are already leading a department, it is a useful exercise to formulate a vision for the department. To ensure that everyone on the team is driven by this vision, the vision should be created together as a team. At the start of the year it is worth spending some time discussing the department's vision for the year ahead. This becomes the rationale (the *why*) and it should be aligned to the school's strategic aims. Once everyone understands the underlying reasons for what they are doing, they will be willing to perform to their best abilities to deliver on this vision. When a team has not agreed on a shared set of values and a vision, there will be a lack of connectedness and for each member of the team it may seem like the rationale for doing things is illogical or based on personal preference. The best leaders unite the team by allowing each member of the team to contribute towards the vision and values.

On a more personal level, leadership also involves developing each member of your team. There are at least two forums for developing teachers which exist in every school: first, line management meetings and, second, feedback meetings which follow lesson observations. In an ideal situation, you would see each member of your team teach once a week, even if it is only for ten minutes; this follows Bambrick-Santoyo's leverage leadership model for lesson observations (Bambrick-Santoyo & Peiser, 2012; Bambrick-Santoyo, 2016). However, in reality, middle leaders can be very busy and if you are in a department where your timetables are blocked against each other, you may have very few periods when you are free to observe teachers on your team. The following section gives a brief overview of effective lesson observation and feedback based on Bambrick-Santoyo's model.

Lesson observations

> *The real value of observation and feedback is not to evaluate a teacher but to develop their practice so that their pupils learn better.*
>
> (Bambrick-Santoyo & Peiser, 2012)

The case against graded summative lesson observations is supported by the previously cited report, *What Makes Great Teaching* (Coe et al., 2014) which found: "Successful teacher observations are primarily used as a formative process – framed as a development tool creating reflective and self-directed teacher learners as opposed to a high stakes evaluation or appraisal."

In observing teachers on our team, we should primarily focus on the one or two action steps or *levers* which will have the greatest impact on student outcomes. If you have access to a video camera and you have developed a trusting professional relationship with members on your team, recording lessons is helpful as it provides a bank of videos of best practice and also allows for more precise feedback as you can play back certain moments of the lesson. To start with, you could make a video camera and tripod available to your colleagues so they can film their own lessons and review them. Once this becomes a habit that teachers are comfortable with, they will be much more open to reviewing filmed lessons with you.

Seven steps for effective lesson observation and feedback

Bambrick-Santoyo advocates following a seven-step process for observation and providing effective feedback:

1   **Prepare**: Whilst you are watching the lesson, identify what action steps and areas of improvement you think the teacher should focus on.
2   **Praise**: Every lesson that you watch will have at least one thing that a teacher is doing effectively. This specific praise in some cases will be tied to a previous action step. It is worth asking the teacher why this identified strength in practice was effective.
3   **Probe**: Ask a series of open-ended questions about the area you think they should improve on.[2]
4   **Action step**: Explicitly state a single, actionable and observable step that will have a high impact on the teacher's practice and the student's learning.
5   **Plan ahead**: Co-plan a lesson to integrate this new action step into.
6   **Practice**: Rehearse the action step through role play.
7   **Follow-up**: Schedule when you can see this action step in a lesson.

(Bambrick-Santoyo, 2016)

Of the seven steps, step six is often the most difficult step. Many teachers are not used to rehearsing and role playing. However this type of practice is well supported by both Kolb's theories on experiential learning (Kolb, 1984) and Knowles's theories on androgogy which both state that adults learn from and through experiences. The practice is also supported by the work of Grossman *et al.* who found that practice needs to be *decomposed* into smaller elements for teachers to focus on and that this practice can be performed using *approximations* or simulations of the actual learning environment (Grossman *et al.*, 2009). Merely explaining an action step and then discussing this action step is not enough; teachers need this to be modelled and they need to rehearse their action step in a practical way. The process of teaching children contains significant elements of performance. This further strengthens the argument and rationale for rehearsal; most expert performers including footballers, dancers, musicians and actors will practice by rehearsing before they perform and teaching is no different. The key to helping teachers who are initially reluctant to role play and rehearse is for you to model the action step yourself in the empty classroom and then ask them to try.

Having reviewed Bambrick-Santoyo's model, readers may have noticed that these seven steps fit into Watkins's three stages of coherent evolution in Chapter 7. Essentially we are 1. *emerging* by watching our colleague; 2. *differentiating* by identifying an issue which needs resolving and planning an action step; and 3. *integrating* by planning how we can implement the action step in their current practice.

Line management meetings

Positive development of our team members should happen constantly, not just during line management meetings and departmental meetings. We should be offering feedback, support and advice to our colleagues in our department on a daily basis. A department office or central space greatly facilitates these kinds of developmental conversations, celebrations of success and sharing of best practice.

However, line management meetings are also an essential part of developing individuals on your team. It is a private forum for discussion and allows the individual to reflect honestly on their current developmental needs as a teacher. Dorothy Billington's article on highly effective adult learning programs provides a solid framework for the effective development and growth of the teachers that we manage.

Conditions for effective line management

1   A safe, supportive environment where individual needs are honoured and achievements are acknowledged and respected.
2   An environment that fosters intellectual freedom and encourages experimentation and creativity.
3   An environment where those that you line manage are treated as peers.
4   An environment where learning and development are self-directed, whilst plans of action are planned collaboratively with the line manager.
5   The development has an appropriate level of intellectual challenge and pacing.
6   The development is based on active involvement as opposed to passively absorbing material.
7   A forum for regular feedback to discuss what is going well and what their needs are; this feedback is listened to and acted on.

Based on Billington's Seven Characteristics of Highly Effective Adult Learning Programs (Billington, 1996)

A great amount of research into management and leadership supports the idea that the development of adults should be self-directed. In referring back to one of these researchers, Knowles notes that whilst "adults have a deep psychological need to be generally self-directing, there are occasions where adults are dependent" (Knowles, 1980). These occasions may be where change is necessarily directive, for example when you need an underperforming member of your team to recognise an area of development. This team member may or may not be aware of this area for development and they will need guidance as to *why* this is a development priority. However, once you have identified an area for development, the remainder of the planning process needs to be collaborative, so that your colleague feels a sense of ownership in the process. The best line managers take on the role of facilitators (Brookfield, 1986). You will need to judge how much guidance your colleague needs; perhaps they are uncertain about which classrooms to visit to observe best practice or what resources they need. As your relationship develops, you will be able to make more accurate judgements and I would follow Ruiz's advice from Chapter 7, namely do not make assumptions; it is best to ask questions to seek to understand their needs and the level of support that they require.

Training for computing teachers and leaders

Training in computing is particularly important as our subject is always changing. New modules are released for programming languages, and applications are constantly upgraded and in some cases discontinued. Fortunately, the UK has a great support network through CAS (https://community.computingatschool.org.uk/). Many of the resources on CAS are free and CAS also offers affordable training through its own sponsored events. Whilst Chapter 9 will discuss the management of a departmental budget in more detail, my advice would be to support members of your department with as much CPD as possible. The annual CAS conference in Birmingham and the numerous regional CAS conferences are all worth travelling to. If you are an experienced teacher and have devised useful techniques or resources for teaching a topic, it is worth submitting a workshop at one of these conferences or at your local CAS hub. If you feel that you can share best practice with the CAS community more regularly and wish to develop as a teacher and leader in computing, you could also consider becoming a CAS master teacher.

Other very affordable computing-specific training programs include courses at local universities, the British Computer Society (BCS) Certificate in Computer Science Teaching and Raspberry Pi Foundation's Picademy. STEM learning (www.stem.org.uk) have also started offering computing CPD with ENTHUSE awards covering the cost of the CPD (in some cases up to £900). There are also various massive open online courses (MOOCs), many of which are free. A collection of free computer science MOOCs are available here: www.class-central.com/subject/cs and www.futurelearn.com/courses. Finally there are many TeachMeets organised on Twitter and teachmeet.pbworks.com, and whilst many of these are focussed on general pedagogy, there are computing-specific ones advertised on both networks.

The greatest barrier to attending training events is the prohibitive cover costs and school policies which limit each teacher to one CPD course a year. However, I have found that senior leaders are generally more understanding when it comes to computing, and if you can make a strong case for it improving the outcomes for the students, as opposed to it being a CPD that you are attending to tick the CPD box, then senior leaders are usually more accommodating. This is particularly the case when you are willing to cover the absence internally in your department. Many of the CAS regional and national events take place at the weekend or during school holidays, and I have found that if I mention to members of my department that I'll be attending one of these events, they also feel more inclined to attend. In some cases these conferences even run a crèche which is useful for teachers with families.

Department meetings

Department meetings can be a useful forum for communicating the departmental priorities for the week or month ahead and performing vital activities such as joint planning, marking and moderation. Most schools will have department meetings on a weekly basis and for these to be effective, I would follow the following ten guidelines:

1   Plan the agenda carefully. Do not have more than seven agenda items.
2   Standing items on the agenda should include actions from last meeting, the week ahead – what lessons we are all teaching and any other business (AOB).

3   Publish the agenda at least 24 hours in advance.

4   Start and finish on time.

5   Delegate one person to take minutes: Ensure actions have owners to maintain accountability and that the actions are recapped at the end of the meeting.

6   Most meetings should last between 30–60 minutes. If they are necessarily longer than this, inform staff in advance. You may also wish to provide refreshments and offer a break in the middle of the meeting.

7   Do not fill time for the sake of it or feel that a meeting is sacrosanct. If workload is high and there are few pressing agenda items, department meetings can and should be cut short or cancelled.

8   If it is possible to timetable a meeting in a mutual free period, the ideal time for a department meeting is the morning when energy levels, cognitive functioning and alertness are higher.

9   AOB's should be submitted in advance or at the start of the meeting so that you can manage time accordingly.

10   Whilst discussing issues, try at all times to focus on solutions rather than debate.

Decision making and everyday operations

Elizabeth Hidson started mentoring me in my first year as a trainee teacher at St Marylebone School. As a head of department (HOD) and mentor, she always spoke openly about her decisions and everyone understood her rationale. She taught me that communication was the key to building a strong team. Elizabeth was also a member of the senior leadership team and this team was effective in limiting our levels of stress by ensuring that unpredictability was minimised and lead-in times were always reasonable. Most events and departmental assessment and reporting deadlines were already scheduled a year in advance, thus ensuring our capacity was never stretched for prolonged periods of time. Rarely did we have anything to complain about, and as I gained more experience and moved towards a HOD role, I always reflected on the high standards that Elizabeth had set. I hoped that one day I would be able to run a department as effectively as she did.

One of the decisions that a HOD will have to make is how to best deploy their team. With regard to staffing and deployment, Elizabeth made a point to never give new teachers any classes with significant behaviour issues. Teachers need to learn how to address challenging behaviour; however, this is difficult when you are learning how to teach and there are several students exhibiting challenging behaviour. The HOD should protect the least experienced members of their staff and help them develop and grow by gradually increasing the level of the challenge provided by both the classes and the curriculum. In order to ensure the best outcomes for the students, Elizabeth often deployed herself or another experienced member of staff for the most challenging classes. I occasionally see HODs avoiding these challenging classes and giving themselves "easier" classes to teach. This rarely works out well; members of your team will become resentful and the attainment gap between these challenging classes and their peers will increase. In some cases, you may decide that in the middle of an academic year, you will either support a teacher struggling with the behaviour of a challenging class by team teaching with them or changing the staffing completely. Where computing classes are taught in forms, it is not unusual for a strong head of year (HOY) to intervene by separating students who conflict regularly by moving them into different forms.

At the other end of the spectrum, teachers with little experience teaching a specific exam specification should ideally be given Year 10 or Year 12 classes rather than a Year 11 or Year 13 classes (in their final year of a GCSE or A-level qualification). This is to ensure that your most experienced and strongest members of your team can focus on delivering good outcomes for these externally examined classes. In larger schools (>800 pupils), there may be scope to discuss with your head teacher the creation of a second-in-command (2IC) role or a Key Stage responsibility. This strategy can be used when you are preparing an experienced and high-performing member of staff for the HOD role, and in some schools this strategy is also used to retain exceptional teachers. Where a 2IC role or Key Stage responsibility is not feasible, for example in smaller schools, it is recommended that the HOD teaches at least one class in every year group to monitor the progress of the year group and understand the needs of the current cohort. There have been some schools who have experimented with deploying teachers to individual year groups so that they become experts in (say) the Year 8 curriculum. However, I find this system somewhat flawed. If this member of staff underperforms, the entire cohort will be affected. Likewise, it is difficult to empathise fully and support members of your team unless you have experience of teaching the current cohort.

There are many other operational decisions which may overwhelm a new HOD. I recommend having regular conversations with other middle leaders, co-planning with them and perhaps seeking a more experienced mentor. Corinne Flett and Jo Parkes were instrumental with helping me become a better HOD when I first arrived at The Greenwich Free School. It is almost assumed that lead teachers in a new school with one-person departments can "step up" and become HODs as the school grows. However, the role of HOD is complex and the types of tasks will vary from school to school. For example, in some schools the HOD will be required to collate all of their department's data to do their own data analysis, whereas in other schools, a data manager may collate all the data and produce a condensed spreadsheet filtering all the data into the required subgroups for data analysis to take place.

I have found that the key to making good day-to-day operational decisions is to spend the early mornings looking at the day ahead and spend at least two additional hours a week reflecting on the current situation and thereby planning the following week, month and term. Part of this planning may need to be done in a quiet space away from distractions and part of this planning may need to be done collectively with your department. A good HOD provides structures, systems and processes for their team to succeed. All teachers in your team will come to work primarily to teach good lessons and get the best outcomes for their students; anything that you can do to facilitate this will motivate your team. If you become disorganised and appear to make irrational decisions such as announcing deadlines with little lead-in time (anything less than seven days), then your team will be forced to work in Quadrant 1 of Stephen Covey's Time Management Matrix (discussed in Chapter 7). Working in this quadrant is not sustainable. If teachers do not feel in control of their workload and this is ever increasing in unpredictable ways, their levels of stress will also increase leading eventually to burnout. If you can provide a positive working environment with appropriate levels of challenge and support, then you are more likely to create and maintain a sustainable and high-performing team.

Whilst many leaders strive to work in what Mihály Csíkszentmihályi calls the state of *Flow*, defined as an immersive, enjoyable and seemingly timeless state (Csikszentmihalyi, 2014), these same leaders may try to create an environment for Flow to occur for their team members. Dr Evan Sinar explains that being in the state of Flow also consumes energy and it is important for your team to rest and recuperate (Sinar, 2017). Flow cannot be a permanent state. In studying the effects of recovery with Flow, Debus *et al.* found that people who started a day feeling recovered would experience a curvilinear U-shaped pattern of Flow, where they would experience high levels of Flow during the morning leading to a gradual decrease in alertness and cognitive functioning around noon. This would be followed by a rise in productivity. This is believed to be due to the effect of the body's circadian clock (Debus *et al.*, 2014). Debus also found that poorly recovered people experienced a gradual decrease in Flow experiences over the course of the working day. The implications for leaders are clear. Good leaders are aware of the capacity and likely circadian rhythms of individuals on their team and they plan accordingly. Emailing your team at 11pm and expecting a response does not provide time for your team members to truly rest, which will impact their performance the following day. If we want our team members to be high performing for sustained periods of time, we must ensure that our team is well rested.

Chapter 8 summary

1   Development should not be limited to skills, knowledge and experience. You should proactively seek to develop physiology, emotions, cognitive ability, maturity, values, behaviour and relationships in yourself and the members of your team.
2   Lesson observations should focus on formative development as much as possible and feedback should include a maximum of two specific actions in order to improve the teacher's practice and the students' learning.
3   Adults are more self-directed than children and are increasingly motivated by the *why* or the rationale behind leadership decisions.
4   Line managers should see their role as facilitators. Line management meetings should encourage your teachers to take responsibility for their own development.
5   Subject training is a vital development tool for teachers in your department. Much of this development is available at low cost.
6   In order to lead a department, you need to lead by example whilst valuing the input from all of the members of your team.
7   A good head of department plans meticulously and communicates the rationale for decisions clearly to create and maintain a productive working environment.

Notes

1   As we teach secondary school students, these students are already moving away from childhood whereby (according to Knowles) they accept learning based on society and school's demands. Having taught students from Key Stage 1 to Key Stage 5, I think Knowles' assertion is true. As students mature they begin to question the relevance of

what they are learning a lot more, whereas students in earlier key stages happily accept the lesson topics without too much explanation for the rationale of the lesson.

2   This step is much more nuanced and going into granular detail about how to perform this step is outside the scope of this book. I do not wish to merely replicate Bambrick-Santoyo's excellent work, and I would advise all middle leaders to read both of his books (listed in the bibliography) for a more precise breakdown of each of these steps and a more thorough overview of his theories on teacher development.

References

Bambrick-Santoyo, P., 2016. *Get Better Faster.* San Francisco: Jossey-Bass.

Bambrick-Santoyo, P. & Peiser, B., 2012. *Leverage Leadership: A Practical Guide to Building Exceptional Schools.* San Francisco: Jossey-Bass.

Barber, M. & Klein, J., 2016. *Unleashing Greatness: Nine Plays to Spark Innovation in Education,* Cologny/Geneva: World Economic Forum.

Billington, D. D., 1996. *Seven Characteristics of Highly Effective Adult Learning Programs.* [Online] Available at: http://education.jhu.edu/PD/newhorizons/lifelonglearning/workp lace/articles/characteristics/ [Accessed 10 April 2017].

Brookfield, S. D., 1986. *Understanding and Facilitating Adult Learning.* Buckingham: Open University Press.

Coe, R., Aloisi, C., Higgins, S. & Major, L. E., 2014. *What Makes Great Teaching,* Durham: The Sutton Trust.

Csikszentmihalyi, M., 2014. *Applications of Flow in Human Development and Education: the Collected Works of Mihaly Csikszentmihalyi.* Dordrecht: Springer.

Debus, M. E., Sonnentag, S., Deutsch, W. & Nussbeck, F. W., 2014. Making flow happen: The effects of being recovered on work-related flow between and within days. *Journal of Applied Psychology,* 99(4), pp. 713-22.

Grossman, P. et al., 2009. Teaching practice: a cross professional perspective. *Teachers College Record,* 111(9), pp. 2055-100.

Knowles, M. S., 1980. *The Modern Practice of Adult Education: From Pedagogy to Androgogy.* New York: Cambridge, The Adult Education Company.

Kolb, D. A., 1984. *Experiential Learning: Experience as the Source of Learning and Development (Vol. 1).* Englewood Cliffs, NJ: Prentice-Hall.

Maxwell, J. C., 2007. 21 *Irrefutable Laws of Leadership.* 2nd ed. Nashville, Tennessee: Thomas Nelson Inc.

Sinar, E., 2017. *Is There a Flow State of Leadership?* [Online] Available at: http://www.ddiworld. com/challenging-thinking/is-there-a-flow-state-of-leadership [Accessed 16 April 2017].

Sinek, S., 2009. *Start with Why: How Great Leaders Inspire Everyone to Take Action.* London: Penguin.

Watkins, A., 2014. *Coherence: The Secret Science of Brilliant Leadership.* London: Kogan Page Limited.

9 Cultivating an environment for growth

The previous chapter discussed our most valuable resource, the people we work with. In any successful organisation, leaders must manage not only the human resources but also the capital resources. In a school, our capital resources can be seen as the classrooms that we teach in, the hardware and software we use, our educational resources used for teaching and our department's budget. As a head of department, it is your job to ensure that these are managed carefully so that students can learn and teachers can teach in an environment that promotes growth. It makes sense to begin this chapter by looking at the physical classroom environment and this may affect student outcomes.

Classroom environment

> The way we set up our classroom gives our students a clear message about the culture of the classroom, the kind of work they will do and the expectations we have for them.
>
> (Sibberson & Szymusiak, 2010)

The classroom environment should be consistent across the department and this should be based on sound research as opposed to solely on aesthetics and personal preference. This environment should be a physically and emotionally safe place that facilitates and encourages engagement, involvement, curiosity and focussed attention from all students (Leamnson, 2000). Citing a plethora of scientific research into the impact of classroom environment on student achievement, Cheryan *et al.* and Barett *et al.* remark on several factors that we should consider when devising a policy for a consistent computing classroom environment (Table 9.1).

Whilst the reports both site minimal structural requirements, as a head of department, these are not usually under your control unless you are being consulted on a new building or renovation. However, these findings should inform your expectations for teachers in your department. The findings based on classroom displays are the most fascinating and in some cases quite controversial and as such I have elaborated on these in the next section.

Table 9.1 A summary of research on classroom design to maximise student outcomes (based on Cheryan *et al.*, 2014; Barrett *et al.*, 2015)

Key finding	Implication for teachers
Classrooms should be exposed to natural light.	Teachers should keep glazing clear although external shading should be installed on windows which are south facing (in the UK) as these are oriented towards the sun's path.
Excessive external noise negatively impacts learning.	Doors and windows facing noisy environments should be closed and you should consider the implication of seating students near noisy ventilation units.
The optimal temperature of the classroom is between 20 and 23 degrees.	The temperature should be controlled thermostatically. Air conditioning should be used sparingly as this sometimes masks poor air quality. In the summer months the windows can be opened in the cooler mornings and closed in the afternoon.
CO_2, which is constantly being produced by humans and computers, can cause drowsiness and inattention.	Air should be circulated actively within a one-hour lesson – Windows should be opened to allow for ventilation.
Plants can be beneficial to learners' outcomes.	Plants provide a link to nature which is beneficial to learning. Plants also help clean the air of toxins produced by electronic equipment such as computers, projectors and printers. Based on NASAs clean air study, plants such as ferns, snake plants, peace lilies, dracaena and spider plants can help clean the air in your classroom (Wolverton *et al.*, 1989).
Objects and décor can have an impact on classroom culture and student achievement.	See following section on Objects and décor.
Classrooms should allow for individualisation.	Computer chairs should be ergonomic and adjustable in height and angle. Classrooms should include some pupil-created work. Distinctive displays outside the classrooms or at junctions can create orienting landmarks.
Classrooms should have an appropriate level of stimulation.	20-50% of the wall space should be clear. Assess the unchangeable colour elements in a classroom and add colour to increase stimulation in a dull classroom or reduce the amount of colour if it is already too bright. See also the following section on Classroom display.

Classroom display

The main purpose of a classroom display should be to inform students and minimise cognitive load. Whilst teachers have the best intentions when they create displays, in too many classrooms, students' work is printed on A4 sheets making it too small to read. This work is often stapled to display boards and never referred to for the entire year. In other classrooms, student work is so dense that it is difficult to isolate and identify individual pieces of best practice.

Seven principles for effective classroom displays

Based on the separate works of Hubenthal and O'Brien (2009), Joe Kirby (2014) and Carey Jewitt (2008), I have compiled the following seven principles for effective classroom displays:

1   Consider the type and size of displays to ensure that they are readable from where the students are sat.

2   Teachers should explicitly make connections between the displays and the topics being taught, referring to them throughout lessons.

3   Displays should be usable on a day-to-day basis.

4   Displays should be simple with a low signal–noise ratio.

5   Displays should relay the curriculum and disciplinary rules of the school.

6   Displays should include student exemplars and provide a framework of what is to be learnt and what is valued, thereby shaping learners actions, behaviours, qualities and expectations.

7   Imagery should be used to represent abstract concepts, objects, phenomena and to make relationships between different topics visible.

(Jewitt, 2008) (Hubenthal & O'Brien, 2009) (Kirby, 2014)

Jewitt's detailed literature review also asks us to consider the use of screens to show items too small to be seen, for example the microscopic gates that make up a CPU or the pits and lands of a CD which are used in the inverted encoding of binary data. Screens can also be used to create artificial environments, put lifeless artefacts into motion, give a sense of scale and space, augment reality and personalise information. It is possible to deliver content to the screen economically using a Raspberry Pi computer.

A final suggestion from Jewitt's report is to consider how the teacher and the school can design learning environments to disrupt the traditional one-way transmission of information and ideas and turn this into more of a dialogue with and between students. Jewitt questions how we can transform the use of portable technology such as mobile phones, tablets, cameras, smart watches and games consoles from non-legitimate uses in school to productive ways of supporting learning. We have to consider the multimodal ways in which students consume information and look at ways of adapting these for dissemination and the generation of knowledge in education and creativity. One way you could do this is through the use of free revision courses on platforms such as Memrise. There are many revision courses on Memrise tailored to specific exam boards and the platform is grounded on sound theories of cognitive science; the material is multimodal, spaced, interleaved and repeated. It is used extensively across departments at The Greenwich Free School, and we have found that the students enjoy the sense of competition that the public score boards offer.

Supporting Barrett *et al.*'s theories on appropriate levels of simulation, it is worth considering a study by Anna Fisher and her colleagues at Carnegie Mellon University which found that:

[Young] children were more distracted by the visual environment, spent more time off task, and demonstrated smaller learning gains when the walls were highly decorated than when the decorations were removed.

(Fisher *et al.*, 2014)

Whilst this study was conducted with primary school students, this is not to say that attention allocation theory does not apply to learning outcomes in secondary school students. Fisher *et al.* clarify that they are not advocating sterilising the learning environments of young children by removing all decorations, artwork or educational displays. In support of a balanced approach to classroom display, consider these findings from Maslow and Mintz who found that "ugly" rooms produced feelings of discontent, fatigue and a desire to escape (Maslow & Mintz, 1956). Clearly, if our environment sets the expectation for how we should behave, then an orderly, clean and tidy classroom with displays which meet the criteria outlined earlier will have a positive impact on student outcomes.

Objects and décor

In the same study on classroom design to maximise student outcomes, Cheryan *et al.* found the following:

Stereotypically masculine objects in the classroom undermine many female students' career aspirations ... and anticipated success in computer science ... Undergraduate women who were randomly assigned to view a computer-science classroom with objects that were perceived by students as highly associated with computer-science environments (e.g., Star Trek and Star Wars items, video games) expressed less interest on average in pursuing computer science than women in a computer-science classroom with non-stereotypical objects (e.g., art and nature pictures, plants) (Cheryan *et al.*, 2011).

This is a fascinating finding considering the section in Chapter 6 entitled "Getting more girls to study computing". Based on Cheryan's findings, the University of Washington Computer Science and Engineering Department renovated their computer lab to take into account the scientific findings on stereotypes and belonging, decorating the lab with large framed photos of landscapes. Some may find this slightly controversial; if we remove *all* the stereotypically masculine computer science objects, would this have the adverse effect of making the subject less appealing to males? Cheryan *et al.* found that this was not the case and that male interest and their anticipation of success were not similarly affected by the environmental changes.

The positive impact of the University of Washington's diversity and inclusion policies can be seen in their statistics: 30 per cent of their computer science undergraduate degrees are earned by women – this is double the US average and also compares favourably to the UK's latest figure of 13 per cent. Of those studying computer science and engineering at Ph.D. level at the University of Washington, 25 per cent of these students are women.

Classroom layout

The layout of the classroom needs to be designed to ensure that the teacher can move quickly and easily to facilitate student learning. In his book *Tools for Teaching*, Jones discusses at length the power of proximity (Jones, 2007). Put simply, *students* are more likely to go off task when they are furthest away from the teacher and when they know that the teacher is not looking. By carefully designing the layout of our tables, we should be able to improve teacher circulation in the room (Table 9.2). Ideally, it should take you less than five seconds to move from any space in the classroom to a student when they need assistance or encouragement. If it takes longer, then the classroom layout is inefficient and you should consider redesigning the layout of the room.

Table 9.2 Three typical layouts of computer labs (adapted from Thompson, 2011)

Layout	Rows	Inverted U-Shape	Clusters
Diagram			
Advantages	• If monitor are low enough, students can see the teacher clearly • Worksheets can be handed out quickly along the rows	• Tables can be placed in the middle for discrete planning and theoretical work • Teacher can see each student's screen • The teacher can circulate freely and easily assist students	• Could offer the potential to be a more collaborative and constructivist working space • Teacher circulation is fairly free
Disadvantages	• Very little room for tables without the distraction of computers and screens • Teacher cannot see any of the student screens • Teacher movement can be restricted by continuous rows	• Students may be asked to turn around several times in the lesson to watch a teacher demonstrating a technique • Requires a large room	• Some students cannot see the teacher as their view is obscured by their screen or desktop • Teacher cannot see many of the student screens • Little space for students to place exercise books and worksheets

The computing classroom is a unique environment which has not been researched extensively. Whilst many teachers write about the benefits and drawbacks of different layouts for computers, few consider the fact that computing will involve a significant amount of time (perhaps up to 40 per cent) at desks. As we have discussed in earlier chapters, many of the abstract concepts of computing are best explored on pen and paper, and in many cases, a computer is just a distraction. Maria Parkes has been teaching computing since 2004 at St Marylebone School. When I first started teaching, I remember doing some team teaching with her. One thing that struck me at the time of teaching ICT was that she would start every lesson at desks in the middle of the room. At first I found this frustrating; as a novice teacher I never understood why she didn't just let the students log in and start their work. Many years later, the penny dropped. I taught in a few rooms without central desks and found the experience very challenging. Students rushed ahead to complete practical tasks without a thorough understanding of what was required of them. It was difficult to model to students who all had screens in front of them and who were all eager to "get on with it". Students had also developed a bad habit due to their classroom layout which was not valuing the design phase of any task. When asked to sketch a layout before completing their work on the computers, students did so reluctantly and often rushed their design work so they could log in and create their digital artefacts. Students that rushed this process did not produce as high a quality of work as those that planned meticulously; this was true in graphic design, spreadsheets, programming and even presentations. Having spent many years in industry designing multimedia educational resources, Maria Parkes clearly understood the value of design and her excellent student outcomes were a testament to her attention to detail at the design stage. The instilling of good design habits was greatly facilitated by her classroom design.

All of the rooms at St Marylebone School have an inverted U shape with computers on the perimeter of the room facing inwards and there are tables in the middle for students to complete written work. As you can see in Figure 9.1, I kept this design when I became the head of computing at The Greenwich Free School.

The primary benefit of this is that when students are at the computers you can see all their screens and when students are working in the middle at tables, it is easy to circulate through the aisles. Jones recommends that students should never be more than two seats from an aisle, thus making it easy for the teacher to check every student's work. One disadvantage of the inverted U shape for the computers is that students have to turn around to see you or the board when you need to do some modelling. However, students can be taught to develop the habit of turning off their screens and facing the front based on a teacher countdown from three to one or another auditory signal that is likely to cut through the low-level noise of a classroom. For many years, I used a calming wind chime to get students' attention to the front. However, for consistency across a small department, I reverted back to the countdown. For demonstrations using applications which rely on the menu bar, I would generally revert to using classroom management software to broadcast my screen so that students can clearly see the menu items being used.

The other common alternative that I have seen in schools is rows. Having rows instead of an inverted U-shaped layout for computers means that whilst you can generally see students' faces at all times, you cannot see what they are doing and it is difficult to navigate a continuous row of computers unless there are gaps allowing you to move in-between the rows.

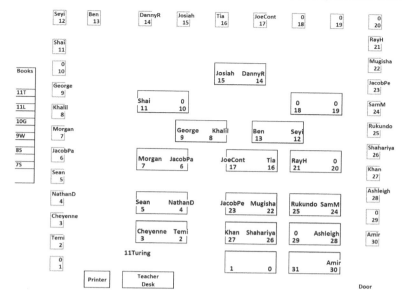

Figure 9.1 A typical classroom design, with an inverted U-shape on the outside and tables in the middle.

Alfred Thompson who has been teaching computer science in American high schools since 1995 writes about the problem with rows of computers in a blog post entitled *The Perfect Educational Computer Lab*:

> [S]ure, you can set up monitoring software and keep an eye out this way but I find that less appealing because it means you can look at their screens or their body language but generally not both. It also means that while you are talking and not able to look at a monitor they can be doing anything.

(Thompson, 2011)

In a rare research paper on the topic of computer room layouts and their effect on pedagogy, Gabriella Pretto examined rows, clusters, U shapes and other layouts and noted the following:

1   Students must be able to see the teacher's actions (facial expressions and gesticulations); this should not be obscured by the computer monitor.
2   The teacher should also avoid turning off the lights to enhance what is seen on the projector, as this obscures the teacher's actions.
3   Students should not be constantly requested to turn around. Teachers could consider using classroom management software to complete some modelling.
4   Pedagogical considerations should be a priority when designing a computer lab and a computing teacher should be consulted on the lab design.
5   The height of CPUs and monitors in a cluster layout can make discussion difficult.
6   Classrooms designed using clusters are usually designed for the purpose of collaboration, however teachers will need training on collaborative working practices to exploit the benefits of this layout.

(Pretto, 2011)

Pretto concludes that classroom layout actually imposes a certain style of pedagogy on the teacher. If you have the choice, I would choose an inverted U shape. If you do not have a choice, you will need to make modifications to how the desktop cases themselves are positioned and be wary of monitors obscuring the view of students and vice versa. The following further suggestions are based on two sources: a conference paper by Mike May and the Centre for Research on Learning and Teaching (CRLT) at the University of Michigan. I have also added my own comments:

1   Whilst working at computers, students still need room to be able to take notes and work with their exercise books. The depth of the computer benching and spacing between computers need to allow for this.
2   Wherever possible, tables should also be provided in the middle of the room.
3   To improve sight lines and reduce noise, consider mounting the desktop cases under the tables.
4   The tables should have enough space to allow the teacher to move behind students and point at certain areas on the screen. There needs to be sufficient spacing behind student chairs to facilitate movement.
5   There needs to be a storage space for consumables such as toner cartridges, exercise books, example storage media, paper and so on. This is best stored in overhead cupboards mounted on the walls to avoid reducing the amount of floor space.
6   To reduce damage and the loss of equipment, cables at the back of a desktop should be cable tied.

(May, 1999; University of Michigan, 2016)

Laptop management

Some schools may deem that desktops are not suitable for their classrooms. This may be because the school is at capacity and all classrooms need to be generic; it may be because there is insufficient infrastructure, that is, mains outlets and Ethernet sockets for desktops. At the time of writing, I would consider laptops a last resort for the following reasons:

1   Laptops are more expensive compared to their desktop equivalents.
2   If students do not shut down the laptops, the batteries will run out in one to three hours. These batteries will also degrade through over-charging whilst plugged into the laptop trolley's charging ports.
3   Not shutting down laptops can also cause IP address conflicts.
4   Shutting down laptops may mean students waiting up to ten minutes for a machine to boot up and receive necessary updates.
5   Laptop trolleys need at least one member of staff to manage the cabling, charging, maintenance and booking of them.
6   The battery life on a laptop is approximately three years, less than this if laptops are left to constantly charge. If you have 100 laptops in a school and batteries are £30 each, you could be paying out £3,000 for batteries every one to three years.

7   Laptops, due to their portability, are easily damaged.

8   Laptops rely on school Wi-Fi which can be unreliable compared to an Ethernet connection.

If for the aforementioned reasons, desktop devices are not an option for you, I would consider the following:

1   Only ever moving the trolleys around the school and into classrooms, never moving the laptops individually from classroom to classroom without a case.

2   Training a team of student technicians to help with laptop trolley maintenance.

3   When students are working on laptops and you need their attention, asking them to close their screens to 45° rather than fully, to prevent them from going into standby or hibernate modes.

4   Having your technicians manage your Wi-Fi settings and IP address allocation carefully using a DHCP server.

5   Asking parents to sign a damage waiver and/or take out comprehensive insurance.

6   Explicitly teaching students how to carry the laptops – not by the screen.

7   Considering a Chromebook solution (see following paragraph).

Streetly Academy is one school in the UK which has opted for a 1:1 Chromebook programme which was successfully rolled out by Andrew Caffrey. Chromebooks are slightly different to laptops in that they are much cheaper, have a very quick boot-up time and they can be set up on G Suite for Education which includes a Google Drive account giving each student unlimited storage. These devices also have a 12-hour battery life, that is, they will rarely need charging during a school day. However, they do require Internet access at all times. Whilst programming can be completed online using free tools such as Trinket, you will need to research whether a cloud-based solution can be used to deliver all your qualifications. Should you require further information regarding a 1:1 Chromebook roll out, feel free to contact Andrew Caffrey at a.caffrey@ thestreetlyacademy.co.uk or on Twitter @MrCaffrey.

Teaching resources

My personal recommendation is to keep all resources stored centrally. This includes physical resources such as stationary, toner cartridges and exercise books along with digital resources such as worksheets, presentations, lesson plans and curriculum maps. For the latter, most technicians and outsourced IT service providers will usually set up a shared central drive. This drive should allow access from home and you should be able to either upload files from home or synchronise your drive when you return to school. Some departments have realised that a managed IT solution can be somewhat bloated and slow and found that the free G Suite for Education offers unlimited storage provided you have an Internet connection.[1]

If you are a head of a large department, you may delegate a unit, year group or an entire Key Stage's curriculum planning to a different member of staff depending on their experience and expertise. Whilst this division of labour ensures that you share the workload and one member of staff becomes the expert for these units, it is important that these are planned at least a day in advance. This 24-hour lead-in time enables other members of the department to modify the resources and differentiate them where necessary. Every teacher will have their own teaching style and their group is likely to be at a different stage to other teaching groups. Every class is also likely to have their own set of misconceptions that have developed in the previous lesson(s). It is therefore recommended that whilst there may be a master resource, this will always need adjusting for each of your classes. Rarely is it possible to use a resource unmodified. This is also true of resources which may have been bought or downloaded from sites such as the CAS community and the Times Educational Supplement (TES).

Over time you will probably realise that the best lessons are usually the ones you design and resource yourself; however, we all recognise the reality that we have a finite amount of time and sometimes our colleagues or other teachers on the CAS network will have created a good lesson already for any given topic on the national curriculum. Most schools' schemes of work (SOW) are a mixture of self-created resources and modified versions of others' resources.

An A to Z guide to the best resources for teaching computing

When Simon Peyton Jones read an early draft of the book, he commented that new teachers may feel lost as there are thousands of free online resources and commercial resources and it may be difficult to know which resources to choose for a given topic. Simon helpfully suggested that it would be useful to have a short annotated bibliography of teaching resources. This is provided in Table 9.3 and is also available as an eResource.

Reading books

Many schools have a computing section in their school library, other schools have a department bookcase in the corridor for students to access a range of books, and others have a bookshelf in their classroom or department office. Despite being perceived as a predominantly digital subject, there are many wonderful computing books which will greatly facilitate learning and develop a culture of curiosity in your students. In Table 9.4 I have listed 15 books which I think every computing department should have available for their students to borrow.[2]

Table 9.3 An A to Z guide to online computing resources

Topic	URL	Description
3D animation	www.3dami.org.uk	A great starting point to learn more about 3D animation using Blender. Run by Tom Haines and Peter Kemp, 3DAmi also runs free holiday workshops for students.
A-Level	en.wikibooks.org/wiki/A-level_Computing	Peter Kemp has been leading on this free wikibook project since 2006. Through crowdsourcing, Peter has completed several online wikibooks with the help of students and teachers from all over the UK.
Algorithms	csfieldguide.org.nz	A great site developed by Tim Bell covering a wide range of computer science principles with informative videos as well as detailed written content.
Algorithms	www.visualgo.net	Various algorithms and data structures visualised with animations and pseudocode.
Algorithms	www.cs.usfca.edu/~galles/visualization/Algorithms.html	Another excellent website for visualising a large range of algorithms.
Assembly	peterhigginson.co.uk/lmc	Peter Higginson's Little Man Computer (LMC) is a great way to teach about the CPU instruction cycle, assembly and RAM. Peter has since improved this program to create an ARM-like RISC simulator here: peterhigginson.co.uk/RISC/
Binary numbers	games.penjee.com/binary-bonanza	A fun way for students to test their binary to denary conversion.
Colour	color.adobe.com/	A great tool to explore different colour schemes based on colour theory. The tool provides RGB and Hex codes, making it ideal for graphic design and web design.
Computational thinking	challenge.bebras.uk	Chris Roffey is the author of the coding club Python books and is also the organiser of an international computational thinking competition. Previous challenges are hosted on the Bebras website, allowing students to practice their computational thinking. Chris has also developed a new set of complex challenges here: tcsocc.weebly.com .
Computer science	computerscienceuk.com	Sam Wickins has created a fully resourced computer science curriculum ready to deliver. There are some free resources. However, I think that the annual subscription is excellent value for money. There are video tutorials included as well as slides and all the resources are mapped to exam boards.
Computer science	code.org	A US-based charity has developed a comprehensive website seeking to expand access to computer science. Their Hour of Code resources are an excellent introduction for students new to computer science.
CPU	community.computingatschool.org.uk/resources/95	Romayne Sorhaindo's Flash animation of the CPU instruction cycle can be used to help explain the Fetch, Decode and Execute stages in the classroom.
Creative Commons icons	www.TheNounProject.com	A great starting point for logo design projects.
Creative Commons Images	www.commons.wikimedia.org	Whilst Google has its own search engine with Creative Commons filtering, this goes straight to the source and has detailed licensing information.

Continued

Table 9.3 Continued

Creative Commons music and sounds	www.audionautix.com www.freeplaymusic.com www.purple-planet.com www.youtube.com/audiolibrary/music www.incompetech.com/music/royalty-free/music.html	Various websites hosting creative commons music and sounds which can be used on video projects. See page 136 for more details.
Curriculum	www.computingatschool.org.uk	Most readers will be familiar with CAS. However, if you have not signed up and teach in a UK school or at a British international school, sign up today – it's free! CAS is a wonderful network of teachers, researchers and professionals. The site remains the number-one place to go to for news, discussion, events and resources.
Flowcharts	www.flowgorithm.org	This free program not only allows students to draw flowcharts, it also allows students to convert these to actual programs in a variety of languages.
Flowcharts	www.draw.io	Simple and effective website app for creating flowcharts
Hexadecimal Colours	www.hexinvaders.com	A fun way for students to understand how Hexadecimal Colour codes work
International baccalaureate	ib.compscihub.net	Chris Coetzee has created a comprehensive website on the IB computer science curriculum which is becoming more popular in the UK.
Keyboard skills	www.keyhero.com	A brilliant way to track each of your classes' typing speeds
Keyboard skills	www.bbc.co.uk/guides/z3c6tfr	A great way for younger students to develop their typing skills
Logic	logic.ly/demo	A simple yet effective logic simulator
Logic	www.neuroproductions.be/logic-lab	An audio visual tool for students to see and hear the effect of various inputs, gates and flip flops
MOOCs	www.class-central.com/subject/cs www.futurelearn.com/courses	Hundreds of free MOOCs are listed on these two sites.
Multiple-choice Questions	www.DiagnosticQuestions.com	Multiple-choice Questions, crowdsourced and approved by Cynthia Selby and Miles Berry
Networks	www.youtube.com/watch?v=xGjGQ24cXAY	Gary Sims explains how the Internet and VPNs work. A great way for students to visualise this content as most VPNs are blocked in schools.
P-levels	www.gfscomputing.net/p-levels.html	Some students with complex special educational needs and disabilities (SEND); for students who cannot access the Key Stage 3 content of secondary schooling, some of these exercises and games are appropriate ways of developing interaction and fine motor skills.
Programming	trinket.io	Run and write Python, HTML or Blocks directly in the web browser. No installation required. Great for setting homework, embedding on VLEs and for students who may not be able to install software at home.
Programming challenges	www.codeabbey.com www.codingbat.com www.exercism.io	Various interactive sites for completing programming challenges in a variety of languages

Topic	URL	Description
Python programming	www.pythontutor.com/visualize.html#mode=edit	Programs involving iteration are particularly difficult for novice students to understand; the python tutor tool allows you to step through a program, essentially allowing students to trace their program interactively.
Python programming	pythonschool.net usingpython.com	Two sites which can be used for students to independently learn and practice Python techniques
Raspberry Pi	www.raspberrypi.org	For all things to do with the Raspberry Pi computer
Revision	mrocallaghanedu.wordpress.com/category/revision	Stephen O'Callaghan is a reflective computing teacher who blogs regularly and has created a wealth of resources on his site. His resources to aid students with their revisions are brilliant.
Software deployment	ninite.com	Package and deploy a large range of free software with this streamlined website.
Sorting algorithms	www.youtube.com/user/AlgoRythmics	Sorting algorithms visualised in the form of traditional folk dances!
SQL	sqlzoo.net	An interactive set of exercises which teach students the basics of SQL; scripts can be run in a web browser.
TeachMeet	teachmeet.pbworks.com	Find a local TeachMeet here.
Tracing	trace.dcs.gla.ac.uk/category/approach/tracing	An excellent set of tracing resources, developed by PLAN C in Scotland.
Unplugged computing	csunplugged.org	Many abstract topics can be taught using unplugged methods. This is the most comprehensive site.

Table 9.4 Recommended books to support and enrich curious students

Title	Author	Category
The Power of Computational Thinking: Games, Magic and Puzzles to Help You Become a Computational Thinker	Paul Curzon and Peter W. McOwan	Computational thinking
Computational Fairy Tales	Jeremy Kubica	Computational thinking
Hello Ruby: Adventures in Coding	Linda Liukas	Computational thinking
Aha! Insight or Aha! Gotcha	Martin Gardner	Problem solving
Computing with Quantum Cats: From Colossus to Qubits	John Gribbin	Computer science theory
Brown Dogs and Barbers: What's Computer Science All About?	Karl Beecher	Computer science theory
Code: The Hidden Language of Computer Hardware and Software	Charles Petzold	Computer science theory
How Computers Work: The Evolution of Technology	Ron White	Computer science theory
Python Basics Level 1	Chris Roffey	Python programming
Invent Your Own Computer Games with Python E-book: inventwithpython.com	Al Sweigart	Python programming
Adventures in Raspberry Pi	Carrie Anne Philbin	Raspberry Pi and programming
The Pragmatic Programmer	Andrew Hunt and David Thomas	Programming
The Maker's Guide to the Zombie Apocalypse: Defend Your Base With Simple Circuits, Arduino, and Raspberry Pi	Simon Monk	Maker, physical computing and electronics
The Vignelli Canon e-book: www.vignelli.com/canon.pdf	Massimo Vignelli	Graphic design
Thinking With Type	Ellen Lupton	Typography

Hardware and software (open sourced, portable apps, cloud based)

Choosing the correct hardware and software for your school is vital to ensuring the longevity of your computer systems. The initial considerations are the operating system, the amount of RAM and the graphics cards. The latter is an important decision if you require the computer to do any 3D rendering or video encoding. When specifying a new computer system, if you choose Microsoft Windows, you should ensure that you explicitly specify a 64-bit operating system. Doing so will ensure you can upgrade your RAM and also install a range of software which is only compatible with 64-bit operating systems. I have encountered schools where a 32-bit operating system has been installed and as such, they have been faced with a costly bill to migrate their system to a 64-bit operating system in order to run certain software. The amount of RAM will be based on the minimum system requirements of your most intensive programs, these generally being image-editing, video-editing and 3D-animation software.

With regard to software, I have listed different software options for the most popular platforms, Windows PC and Apple Mac, in Table 9.5. Proprietary commercial software is shown in *italics*.

In today's education landscape, we have to accept that industry tools may not be realistic for many schools' modest budgets. Given that software companies are moving away from one-off purchase prices and site licenses, introducing costly annual subscriptions in their place, in

Table 9.5 Recommended software for teaching computing

Type of Application	Windows PC	Apple Mac
Office	*Microsoft Office* Apache Open Office G Suite	
Internet browser	Chrome, Firefox	
Raster image editing	*Adobe Photoshop* Paint.Net, GIMP, Krita	*Adobe Photoshop* GIMP, Krita,
Vector image editing	*Adobe Illustrator* Inkscape	
Video editing	*Adobe Premiere, Sony Vegas Pro* HitFilm Express, DaVinci Resolve	*Adobe Premiere, Final Cut Pro X* iMovie
Audio editing	Audacity	
Video conversion	Handbrake	Handbrake
HTML editor	Notepad++, Kompozer, Microsoft Expression	Coda
Python IDE	IDLE Eclipse with Pydev Pycharm Community (requires Java)	
3-D	Blender Sketchup-Make	
Screen recorder	Open broadcaster software	
Other	Foxit reader – PDF reader Google Earth Calibre – e-book management VLC Media Player Java Scratch *Netsupport – classroom management* *4Matrix – whole school data analysis* Sonic Pi-Live coding music Kinoni Epoccam-Mobile document camera (visualiser)	
Cloud-based	Pixlr express: Photo editorDraw.io: FlowchartsFlowgorithm: Flowcharts	

many cases open-source software has become the de-facto standard for many schools. Given the improvements to open-source software over the past decade and the extensive online communities of support, there is no reason why open-source software cannot be primarily relied upon. Despite this, most schools do still opt for Microsoft Office as their standard office application suite. Some schools have moved towards Google Chromebooks and therefore G Suite for education; however, the implementation of G Suite would depend on your school's Wi-Fi connectivity and whether or not the majority of your students at home have access to a reliable home Internet connection (as opposed to one that is provided through their mobile devices).

Regarding video editing software, provided that you have a 64-bit operating system, HitFilm Express is a free alternative to Adobe Premiere and will certainly offer similar results up until Key Stage 5. For those using Apple Macs, iMovie has many in-built filters, effects and titles which also make it an ideal editor for Key Stages 3 and 4. At Key Stage 5, some students may wish to use a non-linear editor with colour and grading tools and as such, DaVinci Resolve can be used. DaVinci Resolve is a free piece of software which has been used in industry by colourists working on *Dawn of Planet of the Apes* and *X-Men* Films (Fruia, 2014).

For vector images, many schools use the free software Inkscape and there are hundreds of tutorials on both the official site inkscape.org/en/learn/ and on: design.tutsplus.com. Likewise,

GIMP and Paint.Net are both usable alternatives for Adobe Photoshop; GIMP supports brushes which can be useful when creating logos and graphics for websites. Students who are familiar with Adobe Photoshop may also consider the cloud-based Pixlr editor at www.pixlr.com.

Teachers coming from industry or with programming experience may want to get students started with a fully-featured integrated development environment (IDE) such as Eclipse when teaching programming. However, most experienced teachers agree that students should start with a very basic IDE such as IDLE for Python. This helps students learn a programming language's syntax without relying on auto-completion. However, at Key Stages 4 and 5, teachers and students appreciate the debugging, auto-completion and auto-indentation tools that IDEs such as Eclipse and PyCharm offer. These IDEs also better prepare students for their transition from school to higher education, apprenticeships or industry.

Most of the other software titles have been discussed throughout the book. However, it is worth mentioning classroom management software again. In my opinion the open-source alternatives such as iTALC are not sufficient. Given that computing teachers will be spending a significant amount of time modelling skills and also pushing content or monitoring students' productivity, I would strongly recommend a commercial title such as LanSchool, NetSupport, Impero or Ranger. At the time of writing, NetSupport offered the most competitive pricing and the education market usually offers good discounting at technology conferences such as the Bett Show. One final point for teachers in small community schools without the support of an IT technician, I sympathise and can empathise with you as I have been in your position! I would highly recommend Ninite as a way of packaging and deploying open-source software if you are working independently without IT support: https://ninite.com/.

Managing your department budget

According to the Institute for Fiscal Studies and the Leeds Schools Forum, a combination of factors including increases to National Insurance and pension contributions and cuts to per-pupil funding (in real terms) means that the funds that schools can allocate to departmental budgets will continue to decrease over the next few years (Adams, 2015) (Belfield & Sibieta, 2017). The main implication for this is that heads of departments and senior leaders will have to ensure their financial planning is meticulous and that a cost–benefit analysis is performed on all purchases to ensure expenditure has a positive impact on student outcomes.

As an experienced head of computing, I would generally prioritise CPD above all other expenditure and it is useful to forecast expenditure on a monthly basis for the year. A simple spreadsheet like the one in Figure 9.2 should suffice. This is also included as an eResource.

There are various ways that departments can raise funds, for example running training courses for other computing teachers, accepting students on PGCE placements or running affordable digital literacy classes for the local community. Some teachers also sell their resources. This will depend on the school's policy. When the computing national curriculum was in its infancy, thousands of resources were uploaded to the CAS community at community.computingatschool.org.uk/resources. However, over time some teachers have learnt that their resources, which they have spent considerable time creating can also have a commercial value and these teachers sell their resources.

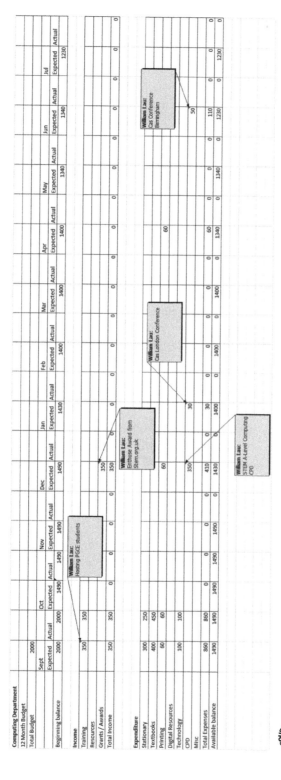

Figure 9.2 Example budget spreadsheet available in the eResources.

In most cases, finance officers will want you to obtain three quotes to prove you have sourced the cheapest supplier. It is worth developing a relationship with suppliers, particularly OEM as they usually offer discounts for buying directly and in large quantities. An example of this would be buying headphones or specialist software. Likewise, local businesses and universities may have a corporate social responsibility (CSR) officer who may be willing to donate equipment such as old desktops for your students to dismantle and re-assemble. It is not uncommon for businesses to sponsor your department and a good place to start is writing to the parents of your students.

Chapter 9 summary

1   The classroom environment can greatly influence student outcomes and this environment should be carefully curated by the teacher to ensure all students have the best conditions for learning.

2   Classroom displays should be considered as a pedagogical tool. The displays should facilitate learning rather than serving a decorative purpose.

3   Classroom layouts in computing classrooms need to be carefully designed to facilitate teaching, behaviour and learning. Teachers with large enough rooms should consider having separate tables in the middle of the room for planning and theory work, and computers located on the perimeter of the room with monitors facing inwards for easy monitoring and support.

4   Physical and digital resources should be stored centrally. All lesson resources should be modified by the class teacher to ensure that these are tailored to the needs of the individuals in the class.

5   The head of computing should be consulted on all large orders of hardware to ensure that they are compatible with the school's software.

6   Open-source software can be used in most cases to secure strong student outcomes, with the only exception being classroom management software which should be bought from a commercial vendor.

7   Heads of computing should plan and manage their departmental budget. The general advice for computing, a subject which is constantly changing, is to prioritise CPD above all other purchases.

Notes

1   You can also set a partition of your drive to show your Google Drive, so you can potentially have access even when there is no Internet connection.

2   Some of the books are made available by the authors as free e-books. The URLs indicate the sources of these free e-book versions.

References

Adams, R., 2015. *State Schools Must Save over £1bn a Year to Balance Budgets in Next Parliament.* [Online] Available at: https://www.theguardian.com/education/2015/feb/16/state-schools-balance-budgets-parliament-funding-teaching [Accessed 9 April 2017].

Barrett, P., Davies, F., Zhang, Y. & Barrett, L., 2015. The impact of classroom design on pupils' learning: final results of a holistic, multi-level analysis. *Building and Environment*, 89(2015), pp. 118–33.

Barrett, P., Zhang, Y., Davies, F. & Barrett, L., 2015. *Clever Classrooms: Summary Report of the HEAD Project*. Salford, UK: University of Salford.

Belfield, C. & Sibieta, L., 2017. *The Short- and Long-Run Impact of the National Funding Formula for Schools in England*. [Online] Available at: https://www.ifs.org.uk/publi cations/9075[Accessed 9 April 2017].

Cheryan, S., Meltzoff, A. N. & Kim, S., 2011. Classrooms matter: the design of virtual classrooms influences gender disparities in computer science classes. *Computers and Education*, 57(2), pp. 1825–35.

Cheryan, S., Ziegler, S. A., Plaut, V. C. & Meltzoff, A. N., 2014. Designing classrooms to maximize student achievement. *Policy Insights from the Behavioral and Brain Sciences 1*, 1(1), pp. 4–12.

Fisher, A. V., Godwin, K. E. & Seltman, H., 2014. Visual environment, attention allocation, and learning in young children: when too much of a good thing may be bad. *Psychological Science*, 25(7), pp. 1362–70.

Fruia, J., 2014. *What Summer Films Were Graded with DaVinci Resolve?* [Online] Available at: http://hdslrshooter.com/summer-films-graded-davinci-resolve/[Accessed 15 April 2017].

Hubenthal, M. & O'Brien, T., 2009. *Revisiting Your Classroom's Walls: The Pedagogical Power of Posters*. [Online] Available at: https://www.iris.edu/hq/files/programs/education_and_ outreach/poster_pilot/Poster_Guide_v2a.pdf [Accessed 10 April 2017].

Jewitt, C., 2008. *The Visual in Learning and Creativity: A Review of the Literature*. Newcastle upon Tyne, UK: Creative Partnerships.

Jones, F., 2007. *Tools for Teaching: Discipline, Instruction, Motivation*. 2nd ed. Santa Cruz, CA: Fredric H. Jones & Associates, Inc.

Kirby, J., 2014. *From Transience to Endurance: What Makes School Display Effective?* [Online] Available at: https://pragmaticreform.wordpress.com/2014/02/08/display/ [Accessed 10 February 2014].

Leamnson, R., 2000. Learning as biological brain change. *Change*, November/December, pp. 34–40.

Maslow, A. H. & Mintz, N. L., 1956. Effects of esthetic surroundings: I. initial effects of three esthetic conditions upon perceiving "energy" and "well-being" in faces. *The Journal of Psychology*, 41(2), pp. 247–54.

May, M., 1999. Designing a computer classroom. *Proceedings of 12th International Conference on Technology in Collegiate Mathematics*, 12, pp. 14–18.

Pretto, G., 2011. Pedagogy and learning spaces in IT. *Proceedings Ascilite 2011 Hobart*, 2011, pp. 1021–31.

Sibberson, F. & Szymusiak, K., 2010. *What Is an Anchor Chart?*. [Online] Available at: http://www.scholastic.ca/education/litplace_earlyyears/pdfs/tip_archives/teachingguides5.pdf [Accessed 10 April 2017].

Thompson, A., 2011. *The Perfect Educational Computer Lab*. [Online] Available at: https://blogs.msdn.microsoft.com/alfredth/2011/11/30/the-perfect-educational-computer-lab/ [Accessed 15 April 2017].

University of Michigan, 2016. *Computer Classroom Design*. [Online] Available at: http://www.crlt.umich.edu/learningspaceguidelines/computerclassroom[Accessed 15 April 2017].

Wolverton, B., Johnson, A. & Bounds, K., 1989. *Interior Landscape Plants for Indoor Air Pollution Abatement*. [Online] Available at: https://ntrs.nasa.gov/archive/nasa/casi.ntrs.nasa.gov/19930073077.pdf [Accessed 10 April 2017].

10 Where next?

I hope that this book has been useful and that it has influenced your practice in a positive way. I also hope that this book has taken you on a journey and that along the way this has challenged your existing beliefs and assumptions about teaching computing. I realise that there may be parts of the book that you disagree with and that is perfectly fine. I think context is an important factor in implementing change, and my aim was to present my rationale for teaching and share what has worked in the various contexts that I have taught in and accompany this with the work of other teachers, leaders and researchers. Hopefully, by sharing my rationale throughout this book, you will be able to understand my reasoning and this will help you integrate some of these strategies into your current practice, making contextual modifications where necessary.

As one of the first books to address the teaching of computing in secondary schools, I hope this book will generate some dialogue amongst the global community of computing teachers both online and in person. And as we continue to share our stories and best practices, we will continue to improve the outcomes for our students.

Should you have any further questions regarding any of the material covered in this book, please feel free to email me at: william.lau@computingatschool.org.uk or on Twitter @MrLauLearning.

References

AAUW, 2015. *Solving the Equation: The Variables for Women's Success in Engineering and Computing*, Washington, DC: AAUW.

Adams, R., 2015. *State Schools Must Save Over £1bn a Year to Balance Budgets in Next Parliament.* [Online] Available at: https://www.theguardian.com/education/2015/feb/16/state-schools-balance-budgets-parliament-funding-teaching [Accessed 9 April 2017].

Ambler, G., 2017. *Helping to Grow Your Leadership.* [Online] Available at: http://www.georgeambler.com[Accessed 9 April 2017].

Anderson, R. O., 2011. Brain, mind and the organization of knowledge for effective recall and application. *LEARNing Landscapes*, 5(1), pp. 45–61.

Andrews, B., 1903. Habit. *The American Journal of Psychology*, XIV(2), pp. 121–49.

AQA, 2016. *AS and A-Level Computer Science Specifications.* Manchester: AQA.

Atherton, J. S., 2013. *Learning and Teaching.* [Online] Available at: http://www.learningandteaching.info/teaching/advance_organisers.htm[Accessed 18 February 2016].

Atkinson, R. C. & Shiffrin, R., 1968. Human memory: a proposed system and its control processes. In: K. Spence & J. Spence, eds. *The Psychology of Learning and Motivation.* New York: Academic Press, pp. 89–195.

Atkinson, R. L., Atkinson, R. C. & Smith, E. E. B. D. J., 1993. *Introduction to Psychology.* 11th ed. Fort Worth, TX: Harcourt Brace Jovanovich.

Ausubel, D. P., 1968. *Educational Psychology. A Cognitive View.* New York: Holt, Rinehart and Winston.

Baddeley, A. D., 2000. The episodic buffer: a new component of working memory? *Trends in Cognitive Science*, 4(11), pp. 417–23.

Baddeley, A. D. & Hitch, G., 1974. Working memory. *The Psychology of Learning and Motivation: Advances in Research and Theory*, 8, pp. 47–9.

Bagge, P., 2014. *Computer Science Terminology for Primary Teachers.* [Online] Available at: http://code-it.co.uk/csvocab [Accessed 27 November 2014].

Bahrick, H. P. & Phelps, E., 1987. Retention of Spanish vocabulary over 8 years. *Journal of Experimental Psychology: Learning, Memory, and Cognition*, 13, pp. 344–49.

Bambrick-Santoyo, P., 2016. *Get Better Faster.* San Francisco: Jossey-Bass.

Bambrick-Santoyo, P. & Peiser, B., 2012. *Leverage Leadership: A Practical Guide to Building Exceptional Schools.* San Francisco: Jossey-Bass.

Bangert-Downs, R. L., Kulik, J. A. & Kulik, C.-L. C., 1991. Effects of frequent classroom testing. *The Journal of Educational Research*, 85(2), pp. 89–99.

Barber, M. & Klein, J., 2016. *Unleashing Greatness: Nine Plays to Spark Innovation in Education.* Cologny/Geneva: World Economic Forum.

Barrett, P., Davies, F., Zhang, Y. & Barrett, L., 2015. The impact of classroom design on pupils' learning: final results of a holistic, multi-level analysis. *Building and Environment*, 89(2015), pp. 118–33.

Barrett, P., Zhang, Y., Davies, F. & Barrett, L., 2015. *Clever Classrooms: Summary Report of the HEAD Project*. Salford, UK: University of Salford.

Baxter, M., Knight, O. & Lau, W., 2016. *GFS Teaching Handbook*. London: Greenwich Free School.

Baxter, M., Knight, O. & Lau, W., 2017. *The Responsive Classroom*. London: Greenwich Free School.

BBC, 2016. *Github Coding Study Suggests Gender Bias*. [Online] Available at: http://www.bbc.co.uk/news/technology-35559439[Accessed 25 January 2017].

Belfield, C. & Sibieta, L., 2017. *The Short- and Long-Run Impact of the National Funding Formula for Schools in England*. [Online] Available at: https://www.ifs.org.uk/publica tions/9075 [Accessed 9 April 2017].

Berger, R., 2003. *An Ethic of Excellence: Building a Culture of Craftsmanship with Students*. Portsmouth, NH: Heinemann.

Billington, D. D., 1996. *Seven Characteristics of Highly Effective Adult Learning Programs*. [Online] Available at: http://education.jhu.edu/PD/newhorizons/lifelonglearning/work place/articles/characteristics/ [Accessed 10 April 2017].

Bjork, E. L. & Bjork, R., 2011. Making things hard on yourself, but in a good way: creating desirable difficulties to enhance learning. In: M. A. Gernsbacher, R. W. Pew & L. M. Hough, eds. *Psychology and the Real World: Essays Illustrating Fundamental Contributions to Society*. New York: Worth Publishers, pp. 55–64.

Bjork, R., 2014. *Applying Cognitive Psychology to Enhance Educational Practice*. [Online] Available at: http://bjorklab.psych.ucla.edu/research.html[Accessed 18 February 2014].

Boulding, K., 1971. The diminishing returns of science. *New Scientist and Science Journal*, 25 March, 49(744), pp. 682–85.

Brandon, J., 2014. *Why You're Failing to Adopt the 7 Habits of Highly Effective People*. [Online] Available at: https://www.inc.com/john-brandon/7-habits-highly-effective-people-why-theyre-not-sticking.html [Accessed 9 April 2017].

Brookfield, S. D., 1986. *Understanding and Facilitating Adult Learning*. Buckingham, UK: Open University Press.

Brown, P. C., Roediger III H. L., & McDaniel, M. A., 2014a. *How to Learn Better at Any Age*. [Online] Available at: https://www.bostonglobe.com/magazine/2014/03/09/how-learn-better-any-age/JCxes7YTWRsqEKu67V5ZNN/story.html [Accessed 16 March 2015].

Brown, P. C., Roediger, H. L. & McDaniel, M. A., 2014b. *Make it Stick: The Science of Successful Learning*. Cambridge, MA: Belknap Press of Hardward University Press.

Bruner, J., 1960. *The Process of Education*. Cambridge, MA: Harvard University Press.

Brynjolfsson, E. & McAfee, A., 2014. *The Second Machine Age - Work, Progress, and Prosperity in a Time of Brilliant Technologies*. 1st ed. New York: W. W. Norton.

Carless, D. & Chan, K. K. H., 2016. Managing dialogic use of exemplars. *Assessment and Evaluation in Higher Education*, 20 July, pp. 1–12.

Carless, D. & Kennedy, K. H, C., 2016. Managing dialogic use of examplars. *Assessment & Evaluation in Higher Education*, pp. 1–12.

Carpenter, S. K., Cepeda, N. J., Rohrer, D., Kang, S. H. K. & Pashler, H., 2012. Using spacing to enhance diverse forms of learning: review of recent research and implications for instruction. *Educational Psychology Review*, 24(3), pp. 369–78.

CAS TV, 2016. *Simon Peyton Jones on Algorithmic Complexity*. [Online] Available at: https://www.youtube.com/watch?v=ixmbkp0QEDM [Accessed 23 Feb 2016].

Cepeda, N. J. , Rohrer, D. & Pashler, H., 2006. Distributed practice in verbal recall tasks: a review and quantitative synthesis. *Psychological Bulletin*, 132(3), pp. 354–80.

CERI, 2008. *21st Century Learning: Research Innovation and Policy. Directions from Recent OECD analyses*. [Online] Available at: http://www.oecd.org/site/educeri21st/40554299.pdf [Accessed 28 December 2016].

Cheryan, S., Meltzoff, A. N. & Kim, S., 2011. Classrooms matter: the design of virtual classrooms influences gender disparities in computer science classes. *Computers and Education*, 57(2), pp. 1825–35.

Cheryan, S., Ziegler, S. A., Plaut, V. C. & Meltzoff, A. N., 2014. Designing classrooms to maximize student achievement. *Policy Insights from the Behavioral and Brain Sciences 1*, 1(1), pp. 4–12.

Clarkson, M., 2012. *GCSE Computing the Unofficial Teacher's Guide.* [Online] Available at: http://www.ocr.org.uk/Images/139051-the-unofficial-teacher-s-guide-for-gcse-computing.pdf [Accessed 30 August 2015].

Code.org, 2014. *Pair Programming.* [Online] Available at: https://www.youtube.com/watch?v=vgkahOzFH2Q [Accessed 27 January 2015].

Code.org, 2014. *Unplugged Computational Thinking.* [Online] Available at: http://code.org/curriculum/course3/1/Teacher.pdf [Accessed 27 November 2014].

Coe, R., Aloisi, C., Higgins, S. & Major, L. E., 2014. *What Makes Great Teaching,* Durham, UK: The Sutton Trust.

Collins, A., Holum, A. & Seely Brown, J., 1991. Cognitive apprenticeship: making thinking visible. *American Educator: The Professional Journal of the American Federation of Teachers*, 15(Winter), pp. 38–46.

ComputerScience.org, 2015. *Women in Computer Science: Getting Involved in STEM.* [Online] Available at: http://www.computerscience.org/resources/women-in-computer-science/ [Accessed 7 April 2017].

Covey, S. R., 1999. *First Things First.* London: Simon & Schuster UK Ltd.

Covey, S. R., 2004. *The 7 Habits of Highly Effective People.* London: Simon & Schuster UK Ltd.

Csikszentmihalyi, M., 2014. *Applications of Flow in Human Development and Education: The Collected Works of Mihaly Csikszentmihalyi.* Dordrecht: Springer.

CSTA, 2011. *Operational Definition of Computational Thinking for K-12 Education.* [Online] Available at: https://csta.acm.org/Curriculum/sub/CurrFiles/CompThinkingFlyer.pdf [Accessed 2014 18 June].

Culatta, R., 2015. *Dual Coding Theory (Allan Paivio).* [Online] Available at: http://www.instructionaldesign.org/theories/dual-coding.html [Accessed 5 December 2016].

Datapolitan, 2014. *The Missing Pedagogy in Computer Science.* [Online] Available at: https://blog.datapolitan.com/2014/09/02/the-missing-pedagogy-in-computer-science/[Accessed 4 April 2016].

Deans for Impact, 2015. *The Science of Learning.* Austin, TX: Deans for Impact.

Deans for Impact, 2016. *Practice with Purpose: The Emerging Science of Teacher Expertise.* Austin, TX: Deans for Impact.

Debus, M. E., Sonnentag, S., Deutsch, W. & Nussbeck, F. W., 2014. Making flow happen: the effects of being recovered on work-related flow between and within days. *Journal of Applied Psychology*, 99(4), pp. 713–22.

Denner, J., Werner, L., Campe, S. & Ortiz, E., 2014. Pair programming: under what conditions is it advantageous for middle school students? *Journal of Research on Technology in Education*, 46(3), pp. 277–96.

Department for Education, 2013. *National Curriculum in England: Computing Programmes of Study.* [Online] Available at: https://www.gov.uk/government/publications/national-curriculum-in-england-computing-programmes-of-study [Accessed 26 July 2016].

Didau, D. & Rose, N., 2016. *What Every Teacher Needs to Know about Psychology.* 1st ed. Woodbridge: John Catt Educational Ltd.

Dijkstra, E. W., 1972. The humble programmer. *Communications of the ACM*, 15(10), pp. 859–66.

Dorling, M. & Woodman, A., 2015. *Skills and Knowledge Audit Tool.* [Online] Available at: http://tools.quickstartcomputing.org/secondary/audit-tool/[Accessed 1 April 2017].

Dunlosky, J., Rawson, K. A., Marsh, E. J., Nathan, M. J. & Willingham, D. T., 2013. Improving students' learning with effective learning techniques. *Psychological Science in the Public Interest*, 14(1), pp. 4–58.

Dweck, C. S., 2006. *Mindset.* 1st ed. New York: Random House.

Ebbinghaus, H., 1885. *Memory: A Contribution to Experimental Psychology* (Henry A. Ruger & Clara E. Bussenius, trans. 1913). New York: Teachers College, Columbia University.

Ericsson, A. & Pool, R., 2016. *Peak: Secrets from the New Science of Expertise.* New York: Houghton Mifflin Harcourt Publishing Company.

Fellows, M. R., 1991. *Computer SCIENCE and Mathematics in the Elementary Schools.* [Online] Available at: https://larc.unt.edu/ian/research/cseducation/fellows1991.pdf [Accessed 11 July 2017].

Fisher, A. V., Godwin, K. E. & Seltman, H., 2014. Visual environment, attention allocation, and learning in young children: when too much of a good thing may be bad. *Psychological Science*, 25(7), pp. 1362–70.

Franklin, J. P., 2015. *Perceptions by Young People of Pair Programming When Learning Text Languages.* London: Axsied / King's College London.

Fruia, J., 2014. *What Summer Films Were Graded With DaVinci Resolve?* [Online] Available at: http://hdslrshooter.com/summer-films-graded-davinci-resolve/[Accessed 15 April 2017].

Gast, G., 2014. *Effective Questioning and Classroom Talk.* Corsham, UK: National Society for Education in Art and Design (NSEAD).

Giannakos, M. N., Doukakis, S., Pappas, I. O., Adamopoulos, N. & Giannopoulo, P., 2015. Investigating teachers' confidence on technological pedagogical and content knowledge: an initial validation of TPACK scales in K-12 computing education context. *Journal of Computers in Education*, 2(1), pp. 43–59.

Gibbons, P., 2002. *Scaffolding Language, Scaffolding Learning.* Portsmouth, NH: Heinemann.

Goldsmith, M., 2015. *Invest 2 Minutes a Day to Improve Your Leadership Skills.* [Online] Available at: https://www.inc.com/inc-live/marshall-goldsmith-tough-questions.html[Accessed 28 Jan 2015].

Gordon Training Ltd, 2016. *Learning a New Skill Is Easier Said Than Done.* [Online] Available at: http://www.gordontraining.com/free-workplace-articles/learning-a-new-skill-is-easier-said-than-done/[Accessed 23 December 2016].

Gov.UK, 2015. *Common Inspection Framework: Education, Skills and Early Years from September 2015.* [Online] Available at: https://www.gov.uk/government/publications/common-inspection-framework-education-skills-and-early-years-from-september-2015 [Accessed 2 September 2015].

GOV.UK, 2016. *Creative Industries Worth Almost £10 Million an Hour to Economy.* [Online] Available at: https://www.gov.uk/government/news/creative-industries-worth-almost-10-million-an-hour-to-economy [Accessed 12 April 2017].

Green, J., 2016. *Question Level Analysis in Science.* [Online] Available at: http://thescienceteacher.co.uk/question-level-analysis/ [Accessed 29 December 2016].

Grossman, P., Compton, C., Igra, D., Ronfeldt, M., Shahan, E. & Williamson, P.W., 2009. Teaching practice: a cross professional perspective. *Teachers College Record*, 111(9), pp. 2055–100.

Guzdial, M., 2015. *Media Computation Teachers.* [Online] Available at: http://coweb.cc.gatech.edu/mediaComp-teach [Accessed 21 September 2015].

Hannay, J. E., Dybå, T., Arisholm, E. & Sjøberg, D. I., 2009. The effectiveness of pair programming: a meta-analysis. *Information and Software Technology*, 51(2009), pp. 1110–22.

Harpaz, Y., 2005. Teaching and learning in a community of thinking. *Journal of Curriculum and Supervision*, 20(2), pp. 136–57.

Hattie, J., 2009. *Visible Learning.* London: Routledge.

Hattie, J. A. & Donoghue, G. M., 2016. Learning strategies: a synthesis and conceptual model. *npj Science of Learning*, 10 August. Available at: https://www.nature.com/articles/npjscilearn201613 [Accessed 11 August 2017].

Hester, T., 2012. *Agape Management.* [Online] Available at: http://www.agapemanagement.org/ [Accessed 25 August 2016].

Hopkins, D., Craig, W. & Knight, O., 2015. *Curiosity and Powerful Learning.* Denver, CO: McREL International.

Hubenthal, M. & O'Brien, T., 2009. *Revisiting Your Classroom's Walls: The Pedagogical Power of Posters*. [Online] Available at: https://www.iris.edu/hq/files/programs/education_and_outreach/poster_pilot/Poster_Guide_v2a.pdf[Accessed 10 April 2017].

Hulick, S., 2017. *Product People, Mind the Gap!* [Online] Available at: https://ux.useronboard.com/product-people-mind-the-gap-da363018cc57 [Accessed 7 March 2017].

Hunter, M., 1982. *Mastery Teaching*. El Segundo, CA: TIP Publications.

Jewitt, C., 2008. *The Visual in Learning and Creativity: A Review of the Literature*. Newcastle upon Tyne, UK: Creative Partnerships.

Johnston, R., Clark, G. & Shulver, M., 2012. *Service Operations Management: Improving Service Delivery*. 4th ed. Harlow, UK: Pearson Education Limited.

Jones, F., 2007. *Tools for Teaching: Discipline, Instruction, Motivation*. 2nd ed. Santa Cruz, CA: Fredric H. Jones & Associates, Inc.

Kemp, P., 2014. *Computing in the National Curriculum - A Guide for Secondary Teachers*. 1st ed. s.l.:Computing at School.

Kemp, P. E., Wong, B. & Berry, M. G., 2016. *The Roehampton Annual Computing Education Report*. London: University of Roehampton.

Kingsbury, G. G., Wiliam, D. & Wise, S. L., 2011. *Connecting the Dots: Formative, Interim and Summative Assessment*. College Park, MD, Northwest Evaluation Association (NWEA).

Kirby, J., 2014. *From Transience to Endurance: What Makes School Display Effective?* [Online] Available at: https://pragmaticreform.wordpress.com/2014/02/08/display/ [Accessed 10 February 2014].

Kirschner, P. A. & De Bruyckere, P., 2017. The myths of the digital native and the multitasker. *Teaching and Teacher Education*, 67, pp. 135–142.

Knight, O. & Benson, D., 2014. *Creating Outstanding Classrooms*. London: Routledge.

Knowles, M. S., 1980. *The Modern Practice of Adult Education: From Pedagogy to Androgogy*. New York: Cambridge, The Adult Education Company.

Kolb, D. A., 1984. *Experiential Learning: Experience as the Source of Learning and Development (Vol. 1)*. Englewood Cliffs, NJ: Prentice-Hall.

Kolb, D. A. & Lewis, L. H., 1986. Facilitating experiential learning: observations and reflections. *New Directions for Adult and Continuing Education*, 1986(30), pp. 99–107.

Kramer, J., 2007. Is abstraction the key? *Communications of the ACM*, 50(4), pp. 36–42.

Leamnson, R., 2000. Learning as biological brain change. *Change*, November/December, pp. 34–40.

Learn That Foundation, 2005. *Wrong Answer*. [Online] Available at: https://www.learnthat.org/pages/view/wrong-answer.html [Accessed October 29 2016].

Lemov, D., 2010. *Teach Like a Champion*. San Francisco: Jossey-Bass.

Lemov, D., 2015. *Doug Lemov's Field Notes: "The Front Table": A Post from Nicole Willey's Classroom*. [Online] Available at: http://teachlikeachampion.com/blog/front-table-post-nicole-willeys-classroom-tales-positive-outlier-video/ [Accessed 4 September 2016].

Lemov, D., 2015. *Teach Like a Champion 2.0*. San Francisco: Jossey-Bass.

Lewis, M. & Wray, D., 2000. *Literacy in the Secondary School*. London: David Fulton Publishers Ltd.

Linsin, M., 2011. *How To Set Up A Simple, Effective Classroom Management Plan*. [Online] Available at: http://www.smartclassroommanagement.com/2011/08/06/effective-classroom-management-plan/ [Accessed 10 April 2016].

Linsin, M., 2011. *How to Set Up a Simple, Effective Classroom Management Plan*. [Online] Available at: https://www.smartclassroommanagement.com/2011/08/06/effective-classroom-management-plan/ [Accessed 3 August 2016].

Lister, R., 2011. Concrete and other neo-Piagetian forms of reasoning in the novice programmer. *ACE '11 Proceedings of the Thirteenth Australasian Computing Education Conference*, 114, pp. 9–18.

Lister, R., 2016. Toward a developmental epistemology of computer programming. *WiPSCE '16 Proceedings of the 11th Workshop in Primary and Secondary Computing Education*, 11, pp. 5-16.

Lloyd, S., 2015. *Subject Audit for Computing Teachers*. [Online] Available at: http://community. computingatschool.org.uk/resources/3250 [Accessed 27 July 2016].

Margulieux, L. E., Catrambone, R. & Guzdial, M., 2016. Employing subgoals in computer programming education. *Computer Science Education*, 26(1), pp. 44-67.

Margulieux, L., Guzdial, M. & Catrambone, R., 2012. Subgoal-labeled instructional material improves performance and transfer in learning to develop mobile applications. *ICER '12 Proceedings of the Ninth Annual International Conference on International Computing Education Research*, pp. 71-8.

Maslow, A. H. & Mintz, N. L., 1956. Effects of esthetic surroundings: I. initial effects of three esthetic conditions upon perceiving "energy" and "well-being" in faces. *The Journal of Psychology*, 41(2), pp. 247-54.

Maxwell, J. C., 2007. *21 Irrefutable Laws of Leadership*. 2nd ed. Nashville, Tennessee: Thomas Nelson Inc.

May, M., 1999. Designing a computer classroom. *Proceedings of 12th International Conference on Technology in Collegiate Mathematics*, 12, pp. 14-18.

McSwan, A., 2016. *Approach - Tracing to Understand the Notional Machine*. [Online] Available at: http://trace.dcs.gla.ac.uk/tracing/ [Accessed 30 March 2017].

Miller, G. A., 1956. The magical number seven, plus or minus two: some limits on our capacity for processing information. *The Psychological Review*, 63(2), pp. 81-97.

Moss, C. M. & Brookhart, S. M., 2012. *Learning Targets: Helping Students Aim for Understanding in Today's Lesson*. Alexandria, VA: ASCD.

Mueller, P. A. & Oppenheimer, D. M., 2014. The pen is mightier than the keyboard: advantages of longhand over laptop note taking. *Psychological Science*, 25(6), pp. 1-10.

Murphy, M., 2015. *Fewer British Women Studying Computer Science Than in 2010*. [Online] Available at: http://www.computerworlduk.com/careers/women-studying-computer-sci ence-in-uk-universities-is-declining-3621040/ [Accessed 7 April 2017].

NASA, 2008. *The 5E Instructional Model*. [Online] Available at: https://web.archive.org/ web/20080923034649/http://www.nasa.gov/audience/foreducators/nasaeclips/ 5eteachingmodels/index.html [Accessed 27 April 2016].

NCWIT.org, 2012. *Girls in IT: The Facts*. [Online] Available at: https://www.ncwit.org/resources/ girls-it-facts [Accessed 7 March 2015].

NPR, 2014. *Episode 576: When Women Stopped Coding*. [Online] Available at: http://www.npr. org/sections/money/2014/10/17/356944145/episode-576-when-women-stopped-coding [Accessed 19 December 2015].

Nuthall, G., 2007. *The Hidden Lives of Learners*. Wellington: NZCER Press.

OCR, 2016. *A Level Computer Science Specification H446*. Cambridge: OCR.

Ofqual, 2011. *GCSE, GCE, Principal Learning and Project Code of Practice*, Coventry: Ofqual.

Paas, F. G. W. C. & Van Merriënboer, J. J. G., 1994. Variability of worked examples and transfer of geometrical problem solving skills: a cognitive load approach. *Journal of Educational Psychology*, 86(1), pp. 122-33.

Pan, G., Sen, S., Starrett, D. A., Bonk, C. J., Rodgers, M. L., Tikoo, M. & Powell, D. V., 2012. Instructor-made videos as a learner scaffolding tool. *MERLOT Journal of Online Learning and Teaching*, 8(4), pp. 298-311.

Papert, S., 1980. *Mindstorms*. New York: Basic Books, Inc.

Parkinson, C. N., 1955. *Parkinson's Law*. [Online] Available at: http://www.economist.com/ node/14116121 [Accessed 9 April 2017].

Pearson, 2017. *BTEC Nationals: Information Technology*. [Online] Available at: http:// qualifications.pearson.com/en/qualifications/btec-nationals/information-technology- 2016.html#tab-1 [Accessed 17 April 2017].

Pearson, P. D. & Gallagher, M. C., 1983. The instruction of reading comprehension. *Contemporary Educational Psychology*, 8(3), pp. 317-44.

Perkins, D. & Blythe, T., 1994. Putting understanding up front. *Educational Leadership*, 51(5), pp. 4-7.

Perkins, D. N., 2009. *Making Learning Whole*. San Francisco: Jossey-Bass.

Peyton Jones, S., 2011. *Computing at School, International Comparisons*. Cambridge: Microsoft Research.

Peyton Jones, S., 2015. *The Dream of a Lifetime, Shaping How Our Children Learn Computing*. Cambridge: Microsoft Research and Computing at School.

Peyton Jones, S., 2016. *Simon Peyton Jones on Algorithmic Complexity*. [Online] Available at: https://www.youtube.com/watch?v=ixmbkpOQEDM [Accessed 23 Feb 2016].

PGBailey, 2011. *Unconscious Incompetence*. [Online] Available at: https://www.flickr.com/photos/pgbailey/6429568067 [Accessed 23 December 2016].

Potts, R. & Shanks, D. R., 2013. The benefit of generating errors during learning. *Journal of Experimental Psychology: General*. Volume Advance online publication, pp. 1-24.

Pretto, G., 2011. Pedagogy and learning spaces in IT. *Proceedings Ascilite 2011 Hobart*, 2011, pp. 1021-1031.

Radford, J., Bosanquet, P., Webster, R. & Blatchford, P., 2015. Scaffolding learning for independence: clarifying teacher and teaching assistant roles for children with special educational needs. *Learning and Instruction*, 36(2015), pp. 1-10.

Renkl, A. & Atkinson, R. K., 2003. Structuring the transition from example study to problem solving in cognitive skill acquisition: a cognitive load perspective. *Educational Psychologist*, 38(1), pp. 15-22.

Reuell, P., 2013. *Understanding Student Weaknesses*. [Online] Available at: http://news.harvard.edu/gazette/story/2013/04/understanding-student-weaknesses/ [Accessed 3 August 2015].

Rheingans, P., Larkin, M., Barr, V. & Driggs-Campbell, K., 2017. *CS Programs for Women*. [Online] Available at: http://www.computerscienceonline.org/cs-programs-for-women/ [Accessed 7 April 2017].

Robertson, D. S., 1998. *The New Renaissance: Computers and the Next Level of Civilization*. New York: Oxford University Press.

Rogers, B., 2011. *Cracking the Challenging Class*. London: SAGE Publications Ltd & Pantechnicon.

Rosenshine, B., 2012. Principles of instruction: research-based strategies that all teachers should know. *American Educator*, Spring, pp. 12-39.

Ruiz, M., 1997. *The Four Agreements: A Practical Guide to Personal Freedom*. San Rafael, CA: Amber-Allen Publishing.

Russo, N. P., 2016. *Margaret Hamilton, Apollo Software Engineer, Awarded Presidential Medal of Freedom*. [Online] Available at: https://www.nasa.gov/feature/margaret-hamilton-apollo-software-engineer-awarded-presidential-medal-of-freedom [Accessed 7 April 2017].

Sadler, D. R., 1989. Formative assessment and the design of instructional systems. *Instructional Science*, 18, pp. 119-44.

Sadler, D. R., 2002. Ah! … So that's 'quality'. In: P. L. Schwartz & G. Webb, eds. *Assessment: Case Studies, Experience and Practice from Higher Education*. London: Kogan Page, pp. 130-6.

Selby, C., 2015. Relationships: computational thinking, pedagogy of programming, and Bloom's Taxonomy. *Proceedings of the WiPSCE '15 Workshop in Primary and Secondary Computing Education London, United Kingdom*, 2015, pp. 80-7.

Selby, C. C. & Wollard, J., 2014. *Refining an Understanding of Computational Thinking*. Southampton, UK: University of Southampton.

Sentance, S., 2017. *KS3-KS5 Strategies for Teaching Programming*. [Online] Available at: https://community.computingatschool.org.uk/resources/4737 [Accessed 1 March 2017].

Sentance, S., 2017. *Mini TRACS*. London: King's College London.

Sentance, S., Waite, J., Bragg, T. & Rickus, N., 2017. *Secondary Master Teacher Subject Knowledge Audit*, London: CAS London CRC.

Shulman, L. S., 1986. Those who understand: knowledge growth in teaching. *Educational Researcher*, 15(2), pp. 4–14.

Shulman, L. S., 1987. Knowledge and teaching: foundations of the new reform. *Harvard Educational Review*, 57(1), pp. 1–22.

Sibberson, F. & Szymusiak, K., 2010. *What Is an Anchor Chart?* [Online] Available at: http://www.scholastic.ca/education/litplace_earlyyears/pdfs/tip_archives/teachingguides5.pdf [Accessed 10 April 2017].

Simmons, C. & Hawkins, C., 2015. *Teaching Computing*. 2nd ed. London: Sage Publications Ltd.

Sinar, E., 2017. *Is There a Flow State of Leadership?* [Online] Available at: http://www.ddiworld.com/challenging-thinking/is-there-a-flow-state-of-leadership [Accessed 16 April 2017].

Sinek, S., 2009. *Start with Why: How Great Leaders Inspire Everyone to Take Action*. London: Penguin.

Smith, A., 2001. *Accelerated Learning in the Classroom*. 5th ed. Stafford, UK: Network Educational Press Ltd.

Smith, E. R. & Mackie, D. M., 2007. *Social Psychology*. 3rd ed. Hove, East Sussex: Psychology Press.

Statter, D. & Armoni, M., 2016. Teaching abstract thinking in introduction to computer science for 7th graders. *WiPSCE '16 Proceedings of the 11th Workshop in Primary and Secondary Computing Education*, 11, pp. 80–3.

Sweller, J., 2016. Story of a research program. *Education Review*, 10 February, 23, pp. 1–19.

Syed, M., 2015. *Black Box Thinking: The Surprising Truth about Success*. London: John Murray Publishers.

Teague, D., 2015. *Neo-Piagetian Theory and the Novice Programmer*. Brisbane: Queensland University of Technology.

Teague, D. & Lister, R., 2014. Longitudinal think aloud study of a novice programmer. *ACE '14 Proceedings of the Sixteenth Australasian Computing Education Conference*, 148, pp. 41–50.

The Learning Machine (TLM), 2016. *Computing Qualifications*. [Online] Available at: https://theingots.org/community/Computing_qualification_info_units [Accessed 27 July 2016].

The Royal Society, 2012. *Shut Down or Restart? The Way Forward for Computing in UK Schools*. London: The Royal Society.

Thomas, A. K. & McDaniel, M. A., 2007. Metacomprehension for educationally relevant materials: dramatic effects of encoding-retrieval interactions. *Psychonomic Bulletin and Review*, 14(2), pp. 212–18.

Thompson, A., 2011. *The Perfect Educational Computer Lab*. [Online] Available at: https://blogs.msdn.microsoft.com/alfredth/2011/11/30/the-perfect-educational-computer-lab/ [Accessed 15 April 2017].

To, J. & Carless, D., 2016. Making productive use of exemplars: peer discussion and teacher guidance for positive transfer of strategies. *Journal of Further and Higher Education*, 40(6), pp. 746–64.

Tomlinson, C. A., 2001. *How to Differentiate Instruction in Mixed-Ability Classrooms*. 2nd ed. Alexandria, VA: Association for Supervision & Curriculum Development (ASCD).

Travi, D. & Avroutine, I., 2016. *Hands-on A-Level Computing: Transition from GCSE to A Level Computer Science*. High Wycombe, UK: Darren Travi Events.

Travi, D. & Avroutine, I., 2016. *Preparing to Teach GCSE Computing 9–1*. High Wycombe, UK, Darren Travi Events.

University of Michigan, 2016. *Computer Classroom Design*. [Online] Available at: http://www.crlt.umich.edu/learningspaceguidelines/computerclassroom [Accessed 15 April 2017].

Waite, J., 2017. *CAS London Master Teacher Training* [Interview] (20 March 2017).

Waite, J., Curzon, P., Marsh, W. & Sentance, S., 2016. Abstraction and common classroom activities. In: *Proceedings of the 11th Workshop in Primary and Secondary Computing Education*. New York: ACM, pp. 112–13.

Wang, J., 2016. *Racial and Gender Gaps in Computer Science Learning: New Google-Gallup Research*. [Online] Available at: https://blog.google/topics/education/racial-and-gender-gaps-computer-science-learning-new-google-gallup-research/ [Accessed 7 April 2017].

Watkins, A., 2014. *Coherence: The Secret Science of Brilliant Leadership*. London: Kogan Page Limited.

Watters, A., 2012. *Top Ed-Tech Trends of 2012: Learning to Code*. [Online] Available at: https://www.insidehighered.com/blogs/hack-higher-education/top-ed-tech-trends-2012-learning-code [Accessed 4 November 2016].

Webb, M., Davis, N., Bell, T., Katz, Y. J., Reynolds, N., Chambers, D. P. & Systo, M. M., 2016. Computer science in K-12 school curricula of the 21st century: why, what and when? *Education and Information Technologies*, 28 April, pp. 1–24.

Whitbread, D., 2009. *The Design Manual*. 2nd ed. Sydney: University of New South Wales Press Ltd.

White, D., 2016. *Computer Science Pedagogy*. [Online] Available at: http://ispython.com/computer-science-pedagogy/ [Accessed 27 March 2016].

Whitehead, A. N., 1922. *The Rhythm of Education*. London: Training College Association.

Wilber, K., 2001. *A Theory of Everything: An Integral Vision for Business, Politics, Science and Spirituality*. Boston, MA: Shambhala Publications.

Wiliam, D., 2006. *Assessment for Learning - Dylan Wiliam*. [Online] Available at: http://dylanwiliam.org/Dylan_Wiliams_website/Papers_files/Cambridge%20AfL%20keynote.doc [Accessed 2017 4 April].

Wiliam, D., 2010. *Teacher Quality: How to Get More of It*. [Online] Available at: http://www.dylanwiliam.org/Dylan_Wiliams_website/Papers_files/Spectator%20talk.doc [Accessed 9 April 2017].

Wiliam, D., 2011. *Embedded Formative Assessment*. Bloomington, IN: Solution Tree Press.

Wilkinson, I. & Anderson, R., 2007. Teaching for learning: a summary. In: *The Hidden Lives of Learners*. Wellington: New Zealand Council for Educational Research, pp. 153–63.

Williams, L. & Kessler, R., 2002. *Pair Programming Illuminated*. Boston, MA: Pearson.

Willingham, D., 2013. *Better Studying = Less Studying. Wait, What?* [Online] Available at: http://www.danielwillingham.com/daniel-willingham-science-and-education-blog/better-studying-less-studying-wait-what [Accessed 31 July 2016].

Willingham, D. T., 2008. What will improve a student's memory. *American Educator*, Issue Winter, pp. 17–26.

Willingham, D. T., 2009. *Why Don't Students Like School*. San Francisco: Jossey-Bass.

Wing, J. M., 2006. Computational thinking. *Communications of the ACM*, 49(3), pp. 33–5.

Wing, J. M., 2008. *Computational Thinking: Two and a Half Years Later*. [Online] Available at: http://www.cs.cmu.edu/~CompThink/seminars/wing/index.html [Accessed 21 March 2016].

Wolfman, S., 2014. *CS Education Zoo Episode #6: Mark Guzdial*. [Online] Available at: https://www.youtube.com/watch?v=z1oTtPECHZI [Accessed 1 August 2015].

Wolverton, B., Johnson, A. & Bounds, K., 1989. *Interior Landscape Plants for Indoor Air Pollution Abatement*. [Online] Available at: https://ntrs.nasa.gov/archive/nasa/casi.ntrs.nasa.gov/19930073077.pdf [Accessed 10 April 2017].

Wood, D., Bruner, J. S. & Ross, G., 1976. The role of tutoring in problem solving. *Journal of Child Psychology and Psychiatry*, 17, pp. 89–100.

Zagami, J., 2013. *Computational Thinking*. Brisbane: EduTechPress.

Index

Taylor & Francis eBooks

Helping you to choose the right eBooks for your Library

Add Routledge titles to your library's digital collection today. Taylor and Francis ebooks contains over 50,000 titles in the Humanities, Social Sciences, Behavioural Sciences, Built Environment and Law.

Choose from a range of subject packages or create your own!

Benefits for you

» Free MARC records
» COUNTER-compliant usage statistics
» Flexible purchase and pricing options
» All titles DRM-free.

Benefits for your user

» Off-site, anytime access via Athens or referring URL
» Print or copy pages or chapters
» Full content search
» Bookmark, highlight and annotate text
» Access to thousands of pages of quality research at the click of a button.

REQUEST YOUR FREE INSTITUTIONAL TRIAL TODAY

Free Trials Available
We offer free trials to qualifying academic, corporate and government customers.

eCollections – Choose from over 30 subject eCollections, including:

Archaeology	Language Learning
Architecture	Law
Asian Studies	Literature
Business & Management	Media & Communication
Classical Studies	Middle East Studies
Construction	Music
Creative & Media Arts	Philosophy
Criminology & Criminal Justice	Planning
Economics	Politics
Education	Psychology & Mental Health
Energy	Religion
Engineering	Security
English Language & Linguistics	Social Work
Environment & Sustainability	Sociology
Geography	Sport
Health Studies	Theatre & Performance
History	Tourism, Hospitality & Events

For more information, pricing enquiries or to order a free trial, please contact your local sales team:
www.tandfebooks.com/page/sales